ENGLISH INDUSTRIES

OF THE

MIDDLE AGES

Oxford University Press

London   Edinburgh   Glasgow   Copenhagen
New York Toronto   Melbourne   Cape Town
Bombay   Calcutta   Madras   Shanghai
Humphrey Milford Publisher to the UNIVERSITY

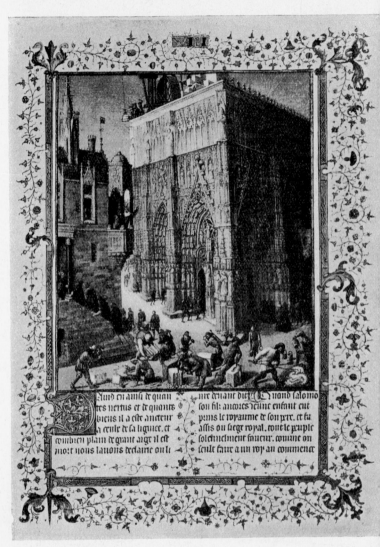

MASONS AT WORK ON A CHURCH, c. 1470

ENGLISH INDUSTRIES

OF THE

MIDDLE AGES

BY

L. F. SALZMAN, M.A., F.S.A.

AUTHOR OF 'MEDIÆVAL BYWAYS', 'HENRY II', 'ORIGINAL SOURCES
OF ENGLISH HISTORY', ETC.

New Edition

Enlarged and Illustrated

OXFORD

AT THE CLARENDON PRESS

1923

1475₹

Printed in England

It is not unfitting that a book about the early Industry of England should be associated with one who, in my eyes, stands for all that is best in modern business life. I therefore dedicate it

to

my good friend

WILLY NICHOLSON

PREFACE

To the first edition of this book, published in 1913, I gave the sub-title—' An Introduction to the Industrial History of Mediaeval England.' Although I have now added a great deal of fresh material and made my account of the various industries in many ways more complete, that sub-title still indicates at once the aim and limitations of my work. It makes no pretence to be a complete history of the early industrial life of England, but at the same time it does claim to be an introduction to the study of that subject. It is my hope, and indeed my belief, that from it the general reader, equipped with interest in the history of his country rather than with technical knowledge, will obtain something more than a bare outline of industrial conditions in pre-Elizabethan days. The student who is anxious to go more deeply into the subjects here treated may use this book as a road map and the footnotes as finger-posts to guide him to the heights of completer knowledge.

From the nature of my subject it was inevitable that the book should be full of technicalities, figures, and statistics, but it has been my endeavour to render the technicalities intelligible and to prevent the significance of the statistics being obscured by an excess of detail. The scheme which I have adopted is to treat the leading mediaeval industries one by one, showing as far as possible their chief centres, their chronological development, the conditions and the methods of working. With the disposal of the finished products through inter-mediaries, merchants, or shopkeepers, I have not concerned myself, deeming such matters rather to belong to the realms of trade and commerce than of industry; and for this same reason, and also because it has been dealt with by other writers, I have not dealt with the great source of England's wealth—wool. Agriculture, also, I have excluded from my definition of industry. The subjects treated in the several sections are thoroughly representative, if not completely exhaus-tive, of English industrial life, and a general survey of the subject is contained in my last chapter, where I have outlined as broadly as possible the general principles that governed the Control of Industry—the typical regulations made by, or for, the craftsmen in the interest of the employer, the workman, or the consumer. This last section might, of course, easily have been extended to cover more pages than this whole volume, but it is questionable whether multiplicity of detail tends to ease of assimilation. A single typical instance of a prevalent custom or regulation is as significant as a list of a dozen local variations, and far easier to remember. A rule is more easily remembered by one example than by a score, and with such a wealth of material as exists the risk of obscurity is greater from amplification than from concentration. The temptation, therefore, to expand the chapter by the addition of much that was interesting rather than essential has been carefully resisted.

As to defining what is meant by the mediaeval period, it is not easy to lay down any hard and fast rule, for the change from old methods or conditions to new, which practically constitutes the division between the mediaeval and the modern periods, occurred at a different date in each industry. The crucial point in gunfounding was the invention of solid casting in the time of Henry VIII; in the cloth industry it was the introduction of the 'new draperies' by Protestant refugees in the reign of Elizabeth; for iron mining it was the adoption of pit coal for smelting in the seventeenth century; for coal mining, the application of steam power to solve the problems of drainage at great depths early in the eighteenth century. Yet, taking one thing with another, the sixteenth century may be considered to be the period of transition. The rise of the capitalist and the monopolist, the social revolution of the Reformation, with the abolition of the monastic houses and the beginnings of the Poor-Law system, constituted a new era for the working classes, even when unaccompanied by any startling change in methods or mechanical media. Moreover, from the middle of the sixteenth century documents and records relating to industrial matters become more numerous and more accessible, and this is therefore the usual starting-point for those who write upon these subjects. For these reasons my accounts of the various selected industries will be found to end at such dates within the sixteenth century as have seemed convenient, though I have not slavishly refrained from taking out of the seventeenth century occasional details applicable to the earlier period.

As to the sources from which my information is taken : I believe that every statement will be found to be buttressed by at least one reference, and I may add that the reference is invariably to the actual source from which I obtained my information. Of printed sources, much the most valuable have been the series of articles on local industries printed in the *Victoria County Histories*, those on mining and kindred subjects by Mr. C. H. Vellacott being of exceptional importance. In very few cases have I found any published history of any industry dealing at all fully with the early period : the one conspicuous exception was Mr. G. Randall Lewis's book on *The Stannaries*, second to which may be put Mr. Galloway's *Annals of Coal Mining* ; to these may be added the section on the woollen industry in Mr. Lipson's excellent *Economic History*, which has appeared since my first edition was published. The various volumes of municipal records published by, or with the consent of, the public-spirited authorities of some of our ancient boroughs, notably those of Norwich, Bristol, Coventry, and Leicester, have been of great value to me, as have Mr. Riley's *Memorials of London* and his editions of the *Liber Albus* and *Liber Custumarum*. To such other printed works as I have drawn upon, acknowledgement is made in the footnotes ; but so far as possible I have made use of unpublished manuscript material at the British Museum and still more at the Record Office. Needless to say, I collected far more material than it was possible to use, and I can only hope that my selection has been wise, as it certainly was careful, and that I have not overlooked or omitted any evidence of essential importance.

For the illustrations also I am responsible. They have been taken almost entirely from mediaeval sources, and in many instances will be found interesting from an artistic as well as from a technical standpoint. For permission to reproduce them I am indebted to the courtesy of many publishers and owners of manuscripts.

L. F. S.

Cambridge
1923

CONTENTS

LIST OF ILLUSTRATIONS

PAGE

PAGE

I

MINING—COAL

COAL is so intimately connected with all that is essentially modern—machinery, steam, and the black pall that overhangs our great towns and manufacturing districts—that it comes almost as a surprise to find it in use in Britain at the beginning of the Christian era. Yet excavation has proved beyond all doubt that coal was used by the Romans, ashes and stores of the unburnt mineral being found all along the Wall, at Lanchester and Ebchester in Durham,[1] at Wroxeter[2] in Shropshire, and elsewhere. For the most part it appears to have been used for working iron, but it was possibly also used for heating hypocausts, and there seems good reason to believe that it formed the fuel of the sacred fire in the temple of Minerva at Bath, as Solinus, writing about the end of the third century, comments on the ' stony balls ' which were left as ashes by this sacred fire.[3] That such coal as was used by the Romans was obtained from outcrops, where the seams came to the surface, is more than probable. There appears to be no certain evidence of any regular mining for coal at this period.

With the departure of the Romans from Britain coal went out of use, and no trace of its employment can be found prior to the Norman Conquest, or indeed for more than a century after that date. It was not until quite the end of the twelfth century that coal was

[1] Galloway, *Annals of Coal Mining*, 5.
[2] See Wright's *Uriconium*.
[3] Petrie and Sharp, *Mon. Hist.*, i. x.

B

rediscovered, and the history of its use in England may be said for all practical purposes to begin with the reign of Henry III (1216). In the ' Boldon Book ' [1] survey of the see of Durham, compiled in 1183, there are several references to smiths who were bound to make ploughshares and to ' find the coal ' therefor, but unfortunately the Latin word *invenire* bears the same double meaning as its English equivalent ' to find ', and may imply either discovery or simple provision. In view of the fact that the word used for coal (*carbonem*) in this passage is unqualified, and that *carbo*, as also the English ' cole ', practically always implies charcoal,[2] it would be unsafe to conclude that mineral coal is here referred to. The latter is almost invariably given a distinguishing adjective, appearing as earth coal, subterranean coal, stone coal, quarry coal, &c., but far most frequently as ' sea coal '. The origin of this term may perhaps be indicated by a passage in a sixteenth-century account of the salt works in the county of Durham : [3] ' As the tide comes in it bringeth a small wash sea coal which is employed to the making of salt and the fuel of the poor fisher towns adjoining.' It is most probable that the first coal used was that thus washed up by the sea and such as could be quarried from the face of the cliffs where the seams were exposed by the action of the waves. The term was next applied,

---

[1] Printed by the Surtees Society and, more recently, in *V. C. H Durham*.

[2] Even ' coal-pit' was occasionally used of the place in which charcoal was burnt ; e. g. in 1577 we find leave given to colliers to ' dyge delfe and make cole pyttes in the soile of the said woodes (in Cornwall) to burn and make coles of the said woode '. Anct. Deeds, A. 13269.

[3] *V. C. H. Durham*, ii. 293.

for convenience, to similar coal obtained inland, and as an export trade grew up it acquired the secondary significance of sea-borne coal. Yet another formula that was occasionally used for coal was ' burning stone '; thus in 1313 we find land at Keresforth held by payment of a rent which included ' a cartload of burning stones (*lapidum ardentium*) at Christmas ',[1] and a few years earlier, at Wakefield, Richard del Dene of Heton is recorded to have dug and sold ' stone for burning '.[2]

No references to purchases of sea coal occur in the Pipe Rolls of Henry II, nor, so far as I am aware, in those of Richard I and John, and although, at the end of the twelfth century, Alexander Neckam in his treatise, *De Naturis Rerum*,[3] places the section ' *De Carbone* ' at the beginning of his discourse on minerals, it is evident that he is referring to charcoal, and the fact that he does not make any allusion to mineral coal rather suggests that it was unknown to him. Coal was apparently worked in Scotland about 1200,[4] and it would seem that about a quarter of a century later it was being imported into London, as a mention of Sea Coal Lane, just outside the walls of the city, near Ludgate, occurs in 1228.[5] As property in this lane belonged to William ' de Plessetis ', it is probable that the coal was brought from Plessey, near Blyth, in which neighbourhood the monks of Newminster were given the right to take coal along the shore about 1236.[6] The monks also obtained leave from Nicholas de Aketon about the same time to take sea coals in his wood of

[1] *V. C. H. Yorks.*, ii. 339.
[2] *Wakefield Court Rolls* (Yorks. Rec. Soc.), i. 268.
[3] *Op. cit.* (Rolls Ser.), 160. [4] Galloway, *op. cit.*, 18.
[5] Riley, *Mems. of London*, p. xvi. [6] Galloway, *op. cit.*, 30.

Middlewood for use at their forge of Stretton, near Alnwick. It may be remarked that at this time, and for the greater part of the next three centuries, the use of coal was restricted to iron-working and lime-burning, the absence of chimneys rendering it unsuitable for fuel in ordinary living rooms. So particularly was it associated with lime-burning that we find Sea Coal Lane also known as Lime-burners Lane, and references in building accounts to purchases of sea coal for the burning of lime are innumerable.

It is in 1243 that we get our first dated reference to an actual coal working. In that year Ralf, son of Roger Ulger, was recorded to have been drowned ' in a delf of sea coals ' (*in fossato carbonum maris*).[1] The use of the word *fossatum* is interesting, as clearly indicating an ' open cast working ', that is to say, a comparatively shallow trench carried along the seam where it comes close to the surface, a step intermediate between the mere quarrying of outcrop and the sinking of regular pits. An indication of the spread of coal mining is to be found in one of the articles of inquiry for the Forest Assize of 1244, which relates to ' sea coal found within the forest, and whether any one has taken money for the digging of the same '.[2] It is probable that special reference was intended to the Forest of Dean, coal being worked about this time at Blakeney, Stainton, and Abinghall; from the last-named place a penny on every horse-load of coal was paid to the Constable of St. Briavels, as warden of the Forest.[3] By 1255 the issues of the Forest of Dean included payments

[1] Assize R., 223, m. 4.   [2] Mat. Paris, *Chron.* (Rolls Ser.), vi. 96.
[3] *V. C. H. Glouc.*, ii. 218.

for digging sea coals, and customs on all sea coal brought
down the Severn.[1] Some of this latter may have been
quarried in Shropshire, as about 1260 Walter de Clifford
licensed Sir John de Halson to dig for coals in the forest

PROSPECTING AND DIGGING FOR MINERALS
16th cent.

of Clee,[2] and there are other indications of the early
exploitation of the Shropshire coal-field. The Midland
field of Derbyshire and Notts was also working, coal
being got in Duffield Frith in 1257,[3] the year in which

[1] Pat., 40 Hen. III, m. 21.   [2] V. C. H. Shrops., i. 449.
[3] V. C. H. Derby, ii. 349.

Queen Eleanor was driven from Nottingham Castle by
the unpleasant fumes of the sea coal used in the busy
town below,[1] a singularly early instance of the smoke
nuisance which we are apt to consider a modern evil.
Half a century later, in 1307, the growing use of coal
by lime-burners in London became so great a nuisance
that its use was rigorously prohibited, but whether
successfully may be questioned.[2]

By the end of the thirteenth century it would seem
that practically all the English coal-fields were being
worked to some extent. In Northumberland so numerous were the diggings round Newcastle that it was
dangerous to approach the town in the dark, and the
monks of Tynemouth also were making good use of
their mineral wealth ;[3] in Yorkshire coal was being
got near Pontefract in 1241,[4] and at Shippen at least as
early as 1263.[5] Twelve years later Richard le Nayler
paid 6*d.* for licence to dig coal for his smithy at Hipper-
holme,[6] and in 1278 a man was fined for digging coal
in the highway at Ackton.[7] In Warwickshire the coal
was worked at Chilvers Coton in 1275.[8] The small
Somerset field near Stratton-on-Fosse and the Staffordshire coal measures may be possible exceptions, but in
the latter county coal was dug at Bradley in 1315 and
at Amblecote during the reign of Edward III.[9] The

[1] *Ann. Mon.* (Rolls Ser.), iii. 105.

[2] Pat., 35 Edw. I, m. 5d. Complaints had been made and com-
missions of inquiry appointed in 1285 (Pat., 13 Edw. I, m. 18d) and
1288 (Pat., 16 Edw. I, m. 12).

[3] Galloway, *op. cit.*, 23.   [4] *V. C. H. Yorks.*, ii. 338.

[5] Colman, *Hist. of Barwick in Elmet*, 205.

[6] *Wakefield Court Rolls*, i. 96.   [7] *V. C. H. Yorks*, ii. 338.

[8] Mins. Accts., bdle. 1040, no. 18.

[9] *Journ. Brit. Arch. Ass.*, xxix. 174.

diggings were still for the most part open-cast works, but pits were beginning to come in. These ' bell pits ', of which numbers remained until recently in the neighbourhood of Leeds,[1] at Oldham in Lancashire,[2] and elsewhere, were narrow shafts sunk down to the coal and then enlarged at the bottom, and widened as far as was safe—and sometimes farther, if we may judge from the case of Piers le Graver, who was killed by the collapse of the pit in which he was working by himself at Silkstone in 1290,[3] or from a number of instances in Derbyshire in which miners were killed by the fall of their pits.[4] When as much coal as could safely be removed had been obtained, the pit was abandoned and a fresh pit sunk as near to it as possible. As a rule the old pit had to be filled up,[5] and at Nuneaton we find this very properly enforced by the bailiff in 1343,[6] and at later dates. Open coal-delfs were a source of considerable danger to men and animals, especially when water had accumulated in them, and a number of cattle were drowned at Morley in Derbyshire in 1372,[7] while it was probably in an abandoned working at Wingerworth that a beggar woman, Maud Webster, was killed in 1313 by a mass of soil falling on her as she was picking up coal.[8] From the pits the coal was raised in corves, or large baskets, and as early as 1291 we hear of a man being killed at Denby in a ' colpyt ' by one of these loaded corves falling upon his head.[9]

[1] *Proc. Soc. of Ant.*, xx. 262.   [2] *V. C. H. Lancs.*, ii. 359.
[3] *V. C. H. Yorks.*, ii. 338.   [4] *V. C. H. Derby*, ii. 350.
[5] E. g. Aug. Off. Misc. Chs., xiii. 106.
[6] Add. Ch., 49516.
[7] *V. C. H. Derby*, ii. 351.   [8] *Ibid.*
[9] *Ibid.*, 350.

A case of some interest is recorded in Derbyshire in 1322, when Emma, daughter of William Culhare, while drawing water from the ' colepyt ' at Morley was killed by ' le Damp ', i. e. choke damp.[1] This is one of the very few early references to choke damp, or ' stithe ', as it was often called, and the case is also interesting because, as water from a coal-pit could hardly be good for either drinking or washing purposes, she must have been engaged in draining the pit, and this suggests a pit of rather exceptional dimensions. A more certain indication of a considerable depth having been attained is given forty years later in the case of another pit at Morley Park, said to have been drowned, or flooded, ' for lack of a gutter '.[2] This may only refer to a surface drain, but there is abundant proof that regular drainage by water-gates, soughs, or adits had already come into use, and that coal-mining had reached the ' pit and adit ' stage. In this system of working, the water, always the most troublesome enemy of the miner, was drawn off by a subterranean drain leading from the bottom of the pit. It need hardly be pointed out that the system was only practicable on fairly high ground, where the bottom of the pit was above the level of free drainage : in such a case a horizontal gallery, or adit, could be driven from a suitable point on the face of the hill slightly below the bottom of the pit to strike the latter, and a wooden sough,[3] or drain, of which the

[1] *V. C. H. Derby*, 351. Cf. a reference to ' le dampe ' in 1316 ; *Hist. MSS. Com. Rep., Middleton MSS.*, 88 ; this *Report* contains a great deal of value for the early history of coal mining.

[2] *V. C. H. Derby*, ii. 350.

[3] A ' sowe ' is mentioned at Cossall in 1316. *Hist. MSS. Com. Rep. Middleton MSS.*, 88.

PUMP, with component parts. 16th cent.

sections were known in Warwickshire as ' dearns ', could be laid to carry the water from the pit to a convenient point of discharge. In 1354 the monks of Durham, when obtaining a lease of coal-mines in Ferry, had leave to place pits and water-gates where suitable,[1] and ten years later a lease of a mine at Gateshead stipulated for provision of timber for the pits and water-gate.[2] During the next century a certain number of pits were sunk in lower ground, or to a greater depth, below the level of free drainage, and in 1486 we find the monks of Finchale, active exploiters of the northern coal measures, erecting a pump worked by horse power at Moorhouse,[3] but it is not until the second half of the sixteenth century, nearly at the end of the mediaeval period, that we find such pumps, ' gins,' or baling engines, and similar machines in common use.

Piecing together information afforded by scattered entries, we can obtain some idea of the working of a coal-pit about the end of the fifteenth century. After the overseer, or a body of miners, had inspected the ground and chosen a likely place, a space was marked out, and a small sum distributed among the workers as earnest money. The pit was then sunk at such charge as might be agreed upon : at Heworth in 1376 the charge was six shillings the fathom,[4] at Griff in 1603 six shillings the ell.[5] A small ' reward ' was paid when the vein of coal was struck, the pit was then cleaned up and timbered, and a water-gate or adit driven to afford drainage and ventilation. Over the mouth of the pit was erected

---

[1] Galloway, *op. cit.*, 53.　　　　　[2] *Ibid.*, 46.

[3] *Finchale Priory* (Surt. Soc.), p. cccxci.

[4] *V. C. H. Durham*, ii. 322.　　　[5] *V. C. H. War.*, ii. 221.

SHAFTS, with windlasses, miners, and barrow men
16th cent.

a thatched ' hovel ' with wattled sides to keep the wind and rain from the pit, and in this was a windlass for raising the corves. The workmen consisted of hewers, who cut the coal, and bearers who carried it to the bottom of the pit and filled the corves : they were under the control of the ' viewer ', whose duty it was ' to see under the ground that the work was orderly wrought ', and the ' overman ', who had ' to see such work as come up at every pit to be for the coal-owner's profit '.[1] Their wages do not appear to have been much, if at all, above those of the ordinary labourer or unskilled artisan. Owing no doubt to the comparatively late rise of the industry and the simplicity of the work, no refining or skilled manipulation being required as in the case of metallic ores, the coal-miners never acquired the privileged position of the ' free miners ' of Dean, Derby-shire, Cumberland, and Cornwall.[2] The work was not attractive, and the supply of labour seems occasionally to have run dry. So much was this the case after the Black Death in 1349 and the second epidemic of 1366 that the lessees of the great mines at Whickham and Gateshead had to resort to forced labour, and obtained leave to impress workmen.[3] Much later, about 1580, the Winlaton pits were hampered by lack of workmen ; and the owners, having sent into Scotland for more

[1] In 1366 in the manor of Bolsover, £4 11s. was paid in wages to ' a man looking after the coals and mine at Shutehoode, and keeping tally against the colliers and diggers of the same coals and stones.' Foreign R., 42 Edw. III, m. 13.

[2] Except that the coal-miners in the Forest of Dean, thanks to their intimate association with the iron-miners there, shared in the latter's privileges.

[3] *V. C. H. Durham*, ii. 322

hands with little success, had to hire women and even then were short-handed, to say nothing of being troubled with incompetent men who for their negligence and false work had to be ' laid in the stocks ', and even ' expulsed oute of their worke '.[1]

The question of mineral rights as regards coal is complicated by the variety of local customs. In some cases, as at Bolsover,[2] the manorial tenants had the right to dig sea coal in the waste and forest land for their own use ; but it was probably usual to charge a fee for licence to dig, and this was clearly the practice at Wakefield.[3] So far as copyhold lands were concerned, the lord of the manor, or his farmer, appears as a rule to have had the power to dig without paying the tenant compensation. This was certainly being done at Houghton, in Yorkshire, and in the adjacent manor of Kipax, in 1578, and the undoubted injury to the copyholders was held to be counterbalanced by the advantage to the neighbourhood of a cheap supply of coal.[4] The uncertainty of the law and the conflicting claims of ground landlords, tenants, and prospectors led to a plentiful crop of legal actions. For the most part these were actions for trespass in digging coal without leave, occasionally complicated by counter appeals.[5] In the first half of the sixteenth century, for instance, Nicholas Strelley, being

---

[1] Exch. Dep. by Com., 29 Eliz., East. 4.

[2] *V. C. H. Derby*, ii. 352.

[3] ' Fines for digging coals in the lord's waste,' in fifteenth century. Galloway, *op. cit.*, 76 ; ' Licences to dig in sixteenth century,' *ibid.*, 113.

[4] Exch. Dep. by Com., 21 Eliz., Hil. 8.

[5] See, e. g., *V. C. H. War.*, ii. 219 ; *V. C. H. Derby*, ii. 350 ; De Banco R., 275, m. 163 d.

impleaded for trespass by Sir John Willoughby, set forth
that he had a pit in Strelley from which he obtained
much coal, to the advantage of the neighbourhood and
of ' the schyres of Leicestre and Lincoln, being very
baren and scarce contres of all maner of fuell ', and no
doubt, though he omitted to say so, to his own advantage;
now, owing to the deepness of the mine and the amount
of water, the old pit could only be worked if a sough or
drain were constructed at an unreasonable expense ;
he had therefore dug a fresh pit on the borders of Strelley
close to Sir John's manor of Wollaton, purposing to use
an old sough running through Sir John's ground.
Sir John had promptly blocked the sough with a ' counter-
mure ' and brought actions for trespass, and Nicholas
Strelley, much aggrieved, invoked the aid of the Star
Chamber.[1] The same court was also invoked a few years
later by William Bolles, who complained that by the
procurement of Sir William Hussey certain persons came
to Newthorpe Mere in Gresley and ' most cruelly and
maliciously cutt in peaces brake and caste downe dyvers
frames of tymbre made upon and in one pitte made and
sonken to gett cooles, and cutt in peaces dyvers greate
ropes loomes and tooles apperteyninge to the said
woorke at the said pitte ', the offenders being unidenti-
fied as the outrage took place ' in the night tyme when
every good trew and faithful subjecte ought to take their
reste '.[2]

Presuming an undisputed title, the owner of coal
measures could exploit them in a variety of ways.
He might work them himself ; the outlay would be

[1] Star Chamber Proc., Hen. VIII, file 22, no. 94.
[2] *Ibid.*, Edw. VI, file 6, no. 99.

small, provided extensive drainage operations were not required, for wages, as we have said, were low, and the equipment of the mine, consisting of a few picks, iron bars or wedges, wooden shovels shod with iron, and baskets, buckets, and ropes, inexpensive, and there was a steady sale for the coal, though the price of coal varied so greatly and was so much affected by cost of carriage that it is not possible to give even an approx- imate average value for the mediaeval period ; the question being fur- ther complicated by the extraordinary variety of measures employed. Coal is quoted in terms of the 'hundredweight',

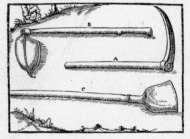

TOOLS. 16th cent.

the 'quarter' (valued at Colchester in 1296 at 6*d*.),[1] the 'seam' (or horse-load), the 'load', which may be either horse or wain load, the 'scope', which appears to be equivalent to the 'corf' or basket, the 'roke' or 'rowe', the 'rod' or 'perch' (a measure apparently peculiar to Warwickshire),[2] the 'butress' and the 'three-quarters' (of a buttress), and most commonly in the Tyne district by the 'fother', 'chalder,' or 'chaldron' and 'ten', and also by the 'keel' or barge load. Where the owner did not work the coals himself he could either issue annual licences to dig coal or lease the mines for a term of years.[3] The earliest leases give a vague general permission to

[1] *Rot. Parl.*, i. 228, 229.   [2] See *V. C. H. War.*, ii. 219.

[3] The rent was sometimes paid, partly or wholly, in kind ; as at Shippen in 1262 (Colman, *Hist. of Barwick-in-Elmet*, 205).

dig coal wherever found within the lands in question, but it soon became usual to limit the output either by fixing the maximum amount to be taken in one day, or more usually in early leases by restricting the number of workmen to be employed. In 1326 Hugh of Scheynton granted to Adam Peyeson land at Benthall with all quarries of sea coal, employing four labourers to dig the same, and as many as he chose to carry the coals to the Severn.[1] Slightly before this date we find that payment was made at Belper according to the number of picks employed, the royalty on one pick in 1315 being over £4.[2] In 1380 the prior of Beauvale in leasing a mine of sea coal at Newthorpe to Robert Pascayl and seven other partners,[3] stipulated that they should have only two men in the pit, a viewer (*servaunt de south la terre*), and three men above ground.[4] The lessees of a pit at Trillesden in 1447 were ' to work and win coal every day overable [i. e. working day] with three picks and ilk pick to win every day 60 scopes ',[5] and at Nuneaton, in 1553, the lessees were not to employ more than six workmen at the time.[6] In this latter case there was a further stipulation that the pits when exhausted should be filled up with ' yearthe and slecke ', while at Trillesden the pit was to be worked workmanlike and the miners were to ' save the field standing ', pointing to a fairly elaborate system of galleries and pillars liable

---

[1] *V. C. H. Shrops.*, ii. 454.   [2] *V. C. H. Derby*, ii. 350.

[3] Such partnerships were not uncommon ; e. g. in 1351 W. de Allesworth demanded 2s. 10½d. from Geoffrey Hardyng, as the seventh part of 20s. paid to Geoffrey and his partners for coal got at Nuneaton.—Add. Ch. 49532.

[4] Aug. Off. Misc. Chs., ii. 211.

[5] Galloway, *op. cit.*, 70.   [6] Add. Ch. 48948.

to subsidence if not properly planned.[1] But the most important lease was that of five mines in Whickham, made in 1356 by Bishop Hatfield of Durham to Sir Thomas Gray and the Rector of Whickham for the enormous rent of 500 marks (£333 6s. 8d.).[2] In this case the lessees were limited to one keel (about twenty tons) daily from each mine ; but on the other hand the bishop agreed never to take their workmen away, and not to open any fresh pits in the district, and not to sell the coal from his existing pits at Gateshead to ships. A century later Sir William Eure leased some of the most important Durham coal mines, his daily output being restricted to 340 corves at Raly, 300 at Toftes, 600 at Hartkeld, and 20 at any other mines, with the right of making up from one mine any deficiency in another, and also of making up any deficiency caused by delays due to ' styth ' or choke-damp, which appears to have been so troublesome in the hot season as to cause a complete suspension of work. Under this lease Sir William obtained at Raly in one week of 1460 some 1,800 corves, each of $2\frac{1}{2}$ bushels, making rather over 140 chalders, paying 5d. a day to each of the three hewers, the three barrowmen, who brought the coal to the foot of the shaft, and the four drawers who raised and banked it.[3]

In the Whickham lease of 1356 it will be noticed that the bishop undertook not to allow coals from his own

[1] Galloway (*op. cit.*, 113–14) gives a late sixteenth-century case in Wakefield, where the ' heads, pillars, and other works . . . for bearing up the ground ' being cut away, the ground suddenly fell in.

[2] Galloway, *op. cit.*, 45.

[3] *V. C. H. Durham*, ii. 324.

pits to be exported by sea.[1] The sea-borne trade in coals from Newcastle and the Tyne was obtaining considerable dimensions; ten years later, in 1366, a large purchase of coal was made at Winlaton for the king's works at Windsor. The sheriff of Northumberland accounted for £165 5s. 2d. expended on the purchase and carriage to London of 576 chalder of coals, reckoning by the 'great hundred' of six score, so that there were actually shipped 676 chalder, but of this 86 chalder had to be written off, partly through some being jettisoned during a sudden storm at sea, and partly because the London chalder was much bigger than that used in Northumberland, the difference amounting to about 5 per cent.[2] The chalder, or chaldron, seems to have been originally about eighteen to twenty hundredweight, and from early times twenty of these made the load of a keel, or coal barge, but in order to evade the export duty of 2d. on every keel, or at least to compensate for it, it became the practice to build keels of twenty-two or twenty-three chalder burden. This was forbidden in 1385,[3] but the prohibition being evaded, an Act was passed in 1421[4] by which the actual capacity of each keel had to be marked upon it. This in turn was evaded by a rapid increase in the size of the chalder, until by the time of Elizabeth it had doubled its original weight and the 'ten' (chalder) was the equivalent of the keel of twenty tons.[5] Returning to the fourteenth century,

---

[1] In 1383 the bishop complained that the men of Newcastle prevented ships loading coals on his side of the Tyne and levied dues on each chalder taken out, so that he had lost the profits of his pits.—*Cal. Charter Rolls*, v. 290.

[2] Foreign R., 42 Edw. III, m. E.   [3] Pat., 8 Rich. II.

[4] *Rot. Parl.*, iv. 148.   [5] Galloway, *op. cit.*, 70, 87.

the customs accounts of the port of Newcastle [1] show
that between Michaelmas 1377 and Michaelmas 1378 as
much as 7,338 chalder of coal, valued at 2s. the chalder,
was exported to foreign countries. For the most part
this went to the Low Countries—Sluys, Bremerhaven,
Flushing, and Dunkirk being amongst the ports mentioned, though in a number of cases ships of ' Lum-
bardye ' occur, the average quantity taken by each
vessel being a little less than fifty chalder. Of the home
trade for this period no record is obtainable, and it is
not until the time of Elizabeth that we can compare
the exports to home and foreign ports. For the seven
years 1591–7, the amount sent abroad was 95,558 chalder,
rising from 10,000 in 1591 to 18,000 in 1593, and then
falling gradually back to 10,000, while the home trade
amounted to 418,200 chalder, increasing steadily from
45,700 up to over 70,000 per annum.[2] The supremacy
of Newcastle is shown by a comparison of the amounts
of coal exported to foreign countries from the chief
English ports in 1592.[3] Newcastle comes first with
12,635 chalder, then Bristol with 580, Wales with 464,
and Liverpool with 448.

The expansion of the home trade noticed in the
returns for 1591–7 is borne out by an abundance of
corroborative evidence, and may be largely attributed
to the great increase at this period in the use of chimneys.
Practically the chimney was a Tudor innovation so far
as the smaller houses were concerned, and ' the multitude
of chimneys lately erected ' was one of the changes most
remarked upon by Harrison's old friends at the time that

[1] Customs Accts., 106, no. 1.
[2] *Ibid.*, 111, no. 40.   [3] *Ibid.*, 171, no. 26.

he wrote his *Description of England*, published in 1577. Mineral coal was still unpopular for household use in 1554 when the Venetian envoy, Soranzo, wrote an account of England, in which he says : ' In the north towards Scotland they find a certain sort of earth, almost mineral, which burns like charcoal and is extensively used by blacksmiths, and but for a bad odour which it leaves it would be yet more employed, as it gives great heat and costs but little.' [1] Even late in Elizabeth's reign the more old-fashioned and dainty ladies would not go into a room where sea coal was burnt or eat meat cooked with that fuel ; but that by that time it was in fairly common use in less fastidious circles is evident from the speech which Shakespeare puts into Dame Quickly's mouth : ' Thou didst swear to me upon a parcel-gilt goblet, sitting in my Dolphin chamber, at the round table, by a sea-coal fire, upon Wednesday in Whitsun week.' [2] The reign of Elizabeth, therefore, when the great increase in the demand for house coal, coupled with a rise in the price, resulted in a rapid expansion of the industry in all parts of the country, marks the end of the mediaeval period of coal mining and the initiation of a new epoch with which we are not concerned.

[1] *S. P. Venice.*
[2] *King Henry IV*, pt. II, act II, scene i.

II

MINING—IRON

IRON has been worked in Britain from the earliest
historical times, and flint implements have been found
at Stainton-in-Furness and at Battle in Sussex in
positions suggesting that ironworks may have existed
in those places at the end of the Stone Age.[1] Julius
Caesar relates that iron was produced along the coast
of Britain, but only in small quantities, its rarity
causing it to be considered as a precious metal, so that
iron bars were current among the natives as money.[2]
The coming of the Romans soon changed this. They
were not slow to see the value of the island's mineral
wealth and to turn it to account. Ironworks sprang up
all over the country : at Maresfield in Sussex they were
apparently in full swing by the time of Vespasian (died
A. D. 69), and in the neighbourhood of Battle fifty years
later. Even more important were the workings in the
West, on the banks of the Wye and in the Forest of
Dean. Near Coleford have been found remains of Roman
mines with shallow shafts and adits, while round Whitchurch, Goodrich, and Redbrook are enormous deposits
of ' cinders ', or slag, dating from the same period.[3]
Ariconium, near Ross, was a city of smiths and forge-
men ; and Bath (Aquae Sulis) is often said to have had
a ' collegium fabricensium ', or gild of smiths, as one
of its members, Julius Vitalis, armourer of the 20th

[1] Kendall, *Iron Ores*, 15 ; *V. C. H. Sussex*, ii. 241.
[2] A hoard of iron currency-bars, averaging 22 ounces in weight,
was found in 1919 near Winchester. *The Antiquaries Journal*,
. 321–7.   [3] *Journ. of Brit. Arch. Ass.*, xxix. 121–9.

Legion, dying after nine years' service, was given a public funeral here by his gild ; but it seems more probable that the seat of the gild was at Chester, and that Julius had come to Bath for his health.[1]

It is a most remarkable fact that although abundant circumstantial evidence of the Roman exploitation of British iron exists in the shape of coins and other relics found upon the site of the works, there is practically no trace of any such working during the Saxon period until shortly before the Conquest. The furnaces must have been still in blast when the Saxons landed ; they were a warlike race, possessing a full appreciation of iron and something of the Scandinavian admiration for smithcraft, yet there is hardly a trace of their having worked iron in this country. Few, if any, objects definitely assignable to this period have been found upon the site of iron works, and documentary evidence is almost non-existent. There is a charter of Oswy, King of Kent, given in 689, by which he grants to the abbey of St. Peter of Canterbury land at Liminge ' in which there is known to be iron-ore ' ; [2] and there is the legend that about A. D. 700 Alcester, in Warwickshire, was the centre of busy ironworks, peopled with smiths, who, for their hardness of heart in refusing to listen to St. Egwin and endeavouring to drown his voice by beating on their anvils, were swallowed up by the earth ; [3]

---

[1] *V. C. H. Somers.*, i. 275. There was also a ' collegium fabrorum ' at Chichester (Regnum). *Suss. Arch. Coll.*, vii. 61–3.

[2] Kemble, *Cod. Dipl.*, no. 30.

[3] *Chron. Evesham* (Rolls Ser.), 26. The legend was probably invented as an explanation of the remains of the (Roman) town found below the ground here, but the tradition of the smiths had, no doubt, some foundation.

but the rest is silence, until we come to the time of
Edward the Confessor. The Domesday Survey shows
that in the time of the Confessor, Gloucester rendered as
part of its farm 36 ' dicres ' of iron, probably in the form
of horseshoes, and 100 rods suitable for making bolts
for the king's ships,[1] while from Pucklechurch in the
same country came yearly 90 ' blooms ' of iron.[2] The
same Survey mentions that there were six smiths in
Hereford, each of whom had yearly to make for the
king 120 horseshoes ; at Hessle, in the West Riding—
one of the few Yorkshire manors which had increased
in value between 1066 and 1086—it records six iron-
workers, and it also refers to iron mines on the borders
of Cheshire, in Sussex, and elsewhere.

During the twelfth century the industry appears to
have expanded. In the North, at Egremont, we read
of the grant of an iron mine to the monks of St. Bees,[3]
and at Denby a similar grant was made about 1180 by
William FitzOsbert to the Cistercians of Byland,[4]
whose mining activities had already, ten years earlier,
brought them into collision with their brethren of the
neighbouring Abbey of Rievaulx.[5] Still earlier, in 1161,
Robert de Busli had given the monks of Kirkstead a site
in Kimberworth for four forges—two for smelting and
two for working iron—with the right to dig ore and to
take dead wood for fuel. In the next generation they
agreed to modify their rights, so that they would not
dig in arable land unless it was lying fallow, they would

[1] Dom. Bk., i. 162. The ' dicre ' is a measure of ten, presumably
of ten bars of standard size or weight.   [2] *Ibid.*

[3] *V. C. H. Cumberland,* ii. 340.

[4] *Facsimiles of Charters in B. M.,* no. 64.

[5] *V. C. H. Yorks.,* ii. 342.

fill up their trenches and would not cut down timber trees.[1] In Derbyshire, towards the end of the century, Sir Walter de Abbetoft gave to the monks of Louth Park wood at Birley in Brampton and two smithies, namely one bloomery and one forge, with the right to take beech and elm for fuel.[2] But it was in the south-west that the greatest development took place. During the whole of this century the Forest of Dean was the centre of the iron industry, and played the part that Birmingham has played in more recent times. All through the reign of Henry II the accounts of the sheriffs of Gloucester [3] tell of a constant output of iron, both rough and manufactured, iron bars, nails, pickaxes, and hammers sent to Woodstock, Winchester, and Brill, where the king was carrying out extensive building operations, horseshoes supplied to the army, arrows and other warlike materials dispatched to France, spades, pickaxes, and other miners' tools provided for the Irish expedition of 1172, iron bought for the Crusade which Henry projected but did not live to perform, and 50,000 horseshoes made for the actual Crusade of Richard I. Throughout the thirteenth century the Forest of Dean retained its practical monopoly of the English iron trade, so far at least as the southern counties were concerned, and during the whole of that time members of the family of Malemort were employed at a forge near the castle of St. Briavels turning out enormous stores of bolts for cross-bows and other war material.[4] But a rival was now growing up in the Weald of Sussex and Kent. As

[1] *V. C. H. Yorks.*, 343.   [2] *V. C. H. Derby*, ii. 356.
[3] Pipe Rolls, quoted in *V. C. H. Gloucs.*, ii. 216.
[4] *V. C. H. Gloucs.*, ii. 217.

early as 1254 the sheriff of Sussex had been called upon
to provide 30,000 horseshoes and 60,000 nails, presumably of local manufacture,[1] and in 1275 Master Henry of
Lewes, who had been the king's chief smith for the past
twenty years,[2] purchased 406 iron rods (*kiville*) ' in the
Weald ' for £16 17s. 11d.,[3] while a year or two later he
obtained another 75 rods from the same source and
paid £4 3s. 4d. ' to a certain smith in the Weald for
100 iron rods.' [4]

The Wealden works had the advantage, a great
advantage in the case of so heavy a material as iron,
of nearness to London, and soon obtained a footing in
the London markets with the imported Spanish iron
at the expense of Gloucestershire, which at the beginning
of the reign of Henry III had been sending its iron to
Westminster and into Sussex.[5] It must not be imagined
that the northern counties were neglecting their mineral
wealth all this time ; they were on the contrary very
active, and were exploiting their iron with vigour and
success. On the lands of Peter de Brus in Cleveland in
1271 there were five small forges each valued at 10s.,
and two larger worth £4 each : [6] these sums may not
sound very imposing, but it must be borne in mind that
the best land in that district was then worth only 1s. an
acre. Twenty years later the forges belonging to Furness
Abbey yielded a profit of £6 13s. 4d., as compared with
a profit on flocks and herds of only £3 11s. 3d., and it is
probable that the Abbey had at least forty forges then

---

[1] *V. C. H. Sussex*, ii. 241.
[2] See Exch. K. R. Accts., 467, 7.
[3] *Ibid.*, 467, 7 (7).   [4] *Ibid.*
[5] *Roy. and Hist. Letters* (Rolls Ser.), i. 278.
[6] *Furness Coucher* (Chetham Soc.), pt. III, Introd.

working on their lands.[1] The great quantity of iron obtained at Furness also formed the most valuable part of the booty carried off by the Scots in their raid in 1316.[2] But the large production of iron in the northern counties was absorbed by their own local requirements, and this was still more the case with the smaller quantities smelted in Northamptonshire and Rutland. Derbyshire must have been another important centre, for as early as 1257 four or five forges in the Belper ward of Duffield Frith were yielding about £10 each yearly, and in 1314 two forges in Belper accounted for £63 6s. 8d. in thirty-four weeks, and there was a third, yielding nearly £7 10s. for only eleven weeks work,[3] but there is nothing to show that Derbyshire iron was ever sent south, and from the middle of the fourteenth century such English iron as was used in London was almost entirely drawn from the Weald.

In order to understand how Sussex and Kent, where no iron has been worked for the last hundred years, came to be the centres of a great iron industry in mediaeval times, it must be borne in mind that charcoal was the only fuel used for iron working [4] until Dud Dudley discovered a method of using pit coal, about 1620, a date which may be considered to mark the end of the mediaeval period in iron mining. The earliest and most primitive method of smelting iron was by setting a

---

[1] *Furness Coucher* (Chetham Soc.), pt. III, Introd.

[2] Holinshed, *Chron.*, sub anno.   [3] *V. C. H. Derby*, ii. 357.

[4] Peat was mixed with the charcoal in Lancashire, and doubtless elsewhere, when available. *V. C. H. Lancs.*, ii. 361. An iron-mine at Alston in Cumberland was returned in 1292 as only worth 15s. because there was no wood available for smelting the ore. Assize R., 135, m. 26 d.

hearth of wood and charcoal on a wind-swept hill
or in some other draughty position, heaping upon it
alternate layers of ore and charcoal, and covering the
whole with clay, to retain the heat, leaving vents at the

FURNACES—old type with foot-blast (above), and Burckhard's
furnace blown by water-power (below)

base for the wind to enter and the iron to come out.[1]
A slight advance on this substituted a short cylindrical
furnace of stone for the containing layer of clay, and an
ingenious device for increasing the draught was used

[1] This process was used by the Romans at Beaufort, near Battle,
in Sussex, amongst other places. *Suss. Arch. Coll.*, xxix. 173.

by the Romans at Lanchester, in Durham, where two narrow tunnels were made on the side of a hill, with wide mouths facing to the west, the quarter from which the wind blows most frequently in this valley, tapering to a narrow bore at the hearth.[1] Even under the most favourable conditions such a furnace would reduce a very small percentage of the ore to metal,[2] and the use of an auxiliary blast, produced by bellows, must have been resorted to at a quite early date. Prior to the fifteenth century such bellows were almost invariably worked by hand, or rather by foot, for the blowers stood upon the bellows, holding on to a bar ; but during the fifteenth century water power was introduced in many parts of the country, and the bellows were driven by water-wheels. Such was apparently the case in Weardale in 1408,[3] probably in the Forest of Dean about the same date, and clearly in Derbyshire by the end of the century.[4]

In several early charters granting mineral rights to Furness Abbey, mention is made of the privilege of using water from the grantor's streams ; but where particulars are given, as in the case of the charter of Hugh de Moresby made in 1270, the water is always stated to be for the washing of the ore, and not for power.[5] The ore, or ' mine ', to use the more common mediaeval term, was sometimes dug on the ' open-cast ' system, but more usually by a series of bell or beehive pits.[6] It

---

[1] *Journ. of Brit. Arch. Ass.*, xxix. 124.

[2] Even after the introduction of the footblast the ' cinders ' or slag contained about half the original iron, according to Dud Dudley (*Metallum Martis*), and were worth resmelting in the improved furnaces of later times.

[3] *Eng. Hist. Rev.*, xiv. 513. [4] *V. C. H. Derby*, ii. 358.

[5] *Furness Coucher* (Chetham Soc.), pt. III, Introd., and pp. 261–6.

[6] See above, p. 7.

was then roughly cleansed by washing on a coarse sieve, and was next subjected to a preliminary burning, or ' elyng ',[1] as it was termed at the Tudeley forge in the fourteenth century.[2] The burnt ore was then broken, and carried to the furnace. In the sixteenth century this was a building in the shape of a truncated cone, about twenty-four feet in diameter, and not more than thirty feet high, in the base of which was a cupped, or bowl-shaped, hearth of sandstone; and such we may assume the earlier furnaces also to have been. Alternate charges of mine and charcoal were fed into the furnace from the top, the iron settling down into the bowl of the hearth, from which it was taken as a lump or ' bloom '. From the sixteenth century, when by the use of a more powerful blast a higher temperature was obtainable and cast iron was produced, the molten iron was drawn off from time to time through a vent at the bottom of the hearth into a bed of sand. In Sussex and Gloucester-shire it seems to have been usual to form in the sand one large oblong depression in the direct course of the flow of the iron with a number of smaller depressions at right angles to the first, the large mass of iron thus moulded being known as a ' sow ', and the smaller blocks as ' pigs '.

There were in the earlier periods of the industry a very large number of smelting hearths, consisting

[1] The same term is used in connexion with burning tiles, and is no doubt derived from the same root as anneal.

[2] This account of the process of manufacture is compiled from several sources, the chief being : (1) the accounts of Tudeley Forge, Tunbridge, for the reign of Edw. III, in the P. R. O. ; (2) the accounts of Bedbourne Forge, Durham, in 1408, *Engl. Hist. Rev.*, xiv. 509–29 ; (3) several Sussex accounts summarized by the present writer in *V. C. H. Sussex*, ii. 244–5.

practically of an ordinary blacksmith's forge with
a cup-shaped hearth, or crucible, in the bottom of which
the imperfectly molten iron accumulated. Such were
the itinerant forges (*fabricæ errantes*) in the Forest of
Dean, of which there were as many as sixty in blast
at the end of the thirteenth century.[1] Early in that
century, in 1229, the king, hearing that iron ore could
be found in Chippenham Forest, ordered John de Mune-

BLACKSMITHS. 12th cent.

muth to search for it and if he found it to cause forges
to wander about (*itinerare*) in the forest to make iron ; [2]
and in the previous century when the monks of Fountains Abbey were given forges in Nidderdale they were
expressly given the right to move them from one place
to another.[3] The buildings attached to such a forge
would naturally be merely temporary sheds, such as
were referred to by the Earl of Richmond in 1281, when
he gave leave to the monks of Jervaux to cut wood in
his forest to smelt iron and to make two small sheds

[1] Nicholls, *Iron Making in the Forest of Dean*, 20.
[2] Close R., 14 Hen. III, m. 21.   [3] *V. C. H. Yorks.*, ii. 343.

(*logias*) 'without nail, bolt, or wall', so that if the smelters moved to another place (as these itinerant forges did when the ore or the fuel became exhausted) they should pull down the sheds and erect others.[1] In this instance the grant of two sheds may imply two smelting-houses, but it seems more probable that one

IRON MILL—diagrammatic drawing of a water-hammer

was the 'bloomery', or smelting forge, and the other the smithy, which invariably accompanied the bloomery.[2] With this simple type of forge the product was a lump of malleable iron, which was purified by hammering and worked up at the smithy, but the pig iron produced by the larger high-blast furnace required more elaborate

[1] *Cal. Chart. R.*, iii. 95–6.
[2] *V. C. H. Glouc.*, ii. 219, n. 5. Cf. the twelfth-century grant to the monks of Louth Park of 'duas fabricas, id est duos focos . . . scilicet unam fabricam blomeriam . . . unam operariam.' *V. C. H. Derby*, ii. 356.

treatment. The sow was carried from the furnace to the forge, ' finery ' or ' strynghearth ', where it was heated on an open hearth and reduced by the sledge, or by the water-hammer [1] when available, to a large ingot or ' bloom '.[2] The latter was, as a rule, reheated, divided, and worked into bars, the completion of which was usually carried out in the seventeenth century at a third hearth, the ' chafery ', but this appears to have been an elaboration of post-mediaeval date. The sows naturally varied in size according to the capacity of the furnace, and this, it may be observed, was much greater at the end of a ' blowing ' than at the beginning, owing to the fire eating away the hearth, especially if too large a proportion of intractable ' hot ' ore were used ; [3] but the blooms were made of standard weight. At the same time the weight of the bloom, though constant in any given district, varied in different parts of the country. In Weardale it seems to have been about two hundred-weight, being composed of fifteen stones, each of thirteen pounds ; [4] and in Furness it was about the same weight, but contained fourteen stones of fourteen pounds.[5] On the other hand, we find blooms selling at the Kentish ironworks of Tudeley for 3s. 4d. in the reign of Edward

[1] The date of the introduction of hammers driven by water power is problematic : a ' great waterhamor ' was working in Ashdown Forest, Sussex, in 1496. Misc. Bks. Exch. T. R., 8, f. 49.

[2] The unworked bloom was called a ' loop ', which appears to be derived from the French *loup*, which was applied to such a mass of iron. Swank, *Iron in All Ages*, 80.

[3] A furnace once lit might be kept in blast sometimes for as much as forty weeks, in the seventeenth century, but the periods usual in earlier times were no doubt much shorter.

[4] *Engl. Hist. Rev.*, xiv. 529.

[5] *Furness Coucher*, pt. iii, Introd. The word used is ' band ', but it is apparently equivalent to ' bloom '.

III,[1] when iron bought for repairs to Leeds Castle cost about 7s. the hundredweight,[2] which, allowing for cost of carriage, agrees fairly well with the three-quarters of a hundredweight attributed to the Sussex bloom in the seventeenth century.[3] As regards the price of iron, it was always high during the mediaeval period, but naturally varied with conditions of demand and supply, cost of carriage, and the quality of the iron. To take a late instance : in Staffordshire in 1583, ' coldshear,' or brittle iron, fetched only £9 the ton when tough iron fetched £12.[4] In Sussex[5] in 1539 iron sold on the spot for from £5 to £7 the ton, allowing a profit of 20s. the ton, and ten years later £8 at the forge and about £9 5s. in London, the cost of carriage to London being 9s. the ton.[6]

The number of workmen employed at the different works naturally varied, but the surveyor of the iron mills in Ashdown Forest in 1539 laid down the rule : [7] ' That to melt the sowes in ij forges or fynories there must be iiij persones, and at the forge to melt the blomes there must be ij persones. So are there at every forge ij persones whereof the oone holdeth the work at the hamor and the second kepeth the work hot. Md that oone man cannot kepe the hamor bicause the work must be kept in such hete that they may not shifte handes.'

At the Bedburn forge in 1408,[8] there were a ' blomer ' or ' smythman ', a smith and a foreman, as well as a ' colier ' or charcoal burner. The blomer was paid 6d.

---

[1] Exch. K. R. Accts., 485, no. 11.   [2] *Ibid.*, 466, no. 20.
[3] *Suss. Arch. Coll.*, ii. 202.   [4] Exch. K. R. Accts., 546, no. 16.
[5] *V. C. H. Sussex*, ii. 246.   [6] Exch. K. R. Accts., 483, no. 19.
[7] *V. C. H. Sussex*, ii. 245.   [8] *Engl. Hist. Rev.*, xiv. 509–29.

for every bloom smelted, of which the average production was six in a week, the largest output recorded in any week being ten blooms. For working up the bloom at the forge, the smith received 6*d*. and an extra penny for cutting it up into bars, while the foreman, who in spite of his name does not seem to have had any staff of workmen under him, received 2*d*. a bloom when he assisted at the smelting, and 3*d*. at the reworking. Such additional labour as was required was supplied by the wives of the smith and foreman, who did odd jobs, breaking up the ore, attending to the bellows, or helping their husbands, earning wages paid at first on a vague but rather high scale, but falling afterwards to the settled rate of a halfpenny a bloom. An allowance of one penny a week was made for ale for the workmen ; and a similar munificent allowance was made ' for drink for the four blowers ' at Tudeley in 1353.[1] At this Tudeley forge in 1333 the workmen were paid in kind, receiving every seventh bloom,[2] a payment roughly equivalent to 6*d*. a bloom, but by 1353 this system had been dropped, and they were paid from $7\frac{1}{2}d$. to $9\frac{1}{2}d$. a bloom. In addition to the ' seventh bloom ', we find mention in 1333 of a customary payment to the ' Forblouweris '[3] of $2\frac{1}{4}d$. a bloom, and in the 1353 account we find ' rewards ' paid to the master blower and three other blowers ; no other workmen are mentioned by name, and as the whole process of making the blooms is here referred to as ' blowyng ' we may probably assume that the staff of these Kentish works consisted of four men. The Sussex

---

[1] Exch. K. R. Accts., 485, no. 11.
[2] Mins. Accts., 890, no. 25.
[3] Latinized in one place as ' *anteriores flatores* '.

BELLOWS driven by water-power.   16th cent.

iron mills at Sheffield in Fletching in 1549 [1] employed one hammerman and his assistant, two fyners and their two servants, a founder, and a filler,[2] the business of the latter being to keep the furnace charged. Here the founder was paid 8s. and the filler 6s. for each ' foundye ' or working week of six days, and the hammerman and fyners received between them 13s. 4d. a ton, about three tons being produced each ' foundye '. At a mine at Llantrisaint in Glamorganshire in 1531 there were five men at the forge, paid 12d. a day—the rate prevalent in the Forest of Dean among the ' free miners ' and therefore more or less equivalent to the ' trade union rates ' of modern times; there were also four blowers, paid $7\frac{1}{2}d.$, of whom ' 3 blows at a tyme and one of them stond voyd to refrechesse the other ', the period of blowing being six or seven hours for each ' gad ' of about a hundred-weight.[3]

In addition to the actual ironworkers every forge afforded employment to a number of charcoal-burners and miners. At Llantrisaint there were three men in the mine, one hewing, one timbering (this mine was five fathoms deep), and one bringing the ore up—the hewer receiving 12d. and the others 6d.—also a man with a horse carrying the ore to the furnace.[4] For the most part these workmen, as was the case with the coal miners, ranked as ordinary labourers, but in the Forest of Dean they formed a close corporation of ' free miners ',

[1] *Suss. Arch. Coll.*, xiii. 128.

[2] At some iron mills near Teddesley in Staffordshire in 1583 the filler and fyner were identical, and there was a hammerman and a founder. Exch. K. R. Accts., 546, no. 16.

[3] *L. and P. Hen. VIII*, v. 261.

[4] *Ibid.*

possessing an organization and privileges of considerable importance and antiquity.[1] So far as can be judged, the customs of the free miners were traditional, based on prescription, recognized as early as the time of Henry III, and officially confirmed by Edward I. By these customs the right of mining was restricted to the free miners resident within the bounds of the Forest, and they had also control of the export of the iron ore, all persons carrying it down the Severn being bound to pay dues to the miners under penalty of forfeiture of their boat. The free miners had also the right of digging anywhere within the Forest, except in gardens, orchards, and curtilages ; the lord of the soil, who might be the king or a private landowner, was entitled to a share as a member of the fellowship, almost always consisting of four ' verns ' or partners. Besides the right thus to open a mine, the miners had a claim to access thereto from the highway, and to timber for their works. In return, the king received from every miner who raised three loads of ore in a week one penny, which was collected by the ' gaveller ' every Tuesday ' between Mattens and Masse '. He had also the right to certain quantities of ' law-ore ' from the different mines every week, for which the miners were paid at the rate of a penny a load ; and if he was working an itinerant forge they were bound to supply ore therefor at the same rate ; and finally there was a royal export duty of a halfpenny on every load of ore taken out of the Forest.[2]

[1] Nicholls, *Ironmaking in the Forest of Dean* ; *V. C. H. Gloucs.*, ii. 219–23.

[2] This was farmed in 1280 for £23, so that the amount exported annually must have been well over 10,000 loads. About sixty years

The right of mining within the forest was restricted, as we have already said, to the resident free miners, and they might only employ the labour of their own family or apprentices. These rights to their mines, or shares therein, were definite, and could be bequeathed by will; and in order to prevent trespass the rule was laid down that no man should start a fresh working near that of another miner 'within so much space that the miner may stand and cast ridding [1] and stones so far from him with a bale, as the manner is'. When disputes arose between the miners, they were settled at their own court, held every three weeks at St. Briavels, under the presidency of the Constable, appeals being made, if necessary, from the normal jury of twelve miners to juries of twenty-four or forty-eight. These Mine Law Courts continued to be held until the latter half of the eighteenth century; but we are not here concerned with

THE NEWLAND BRASS

A contemporary representation of a 15th-century free miner.

later the average amount received yearly from this source was some £3 10s., equivalent to rather under 1,700 loads. Memo. R., K. R., 45 Edw. III, Hil.

[1] The surface material which has to be removed before the ore is reached.

their later proceedings and constant endeavours to maintain restrictions which had long passed out of date ; endeavours which seem to have resulted chiefly in promoting ' the abominable sin of perjury ', so that it was found necessary to ordain that any miner convicted thereof should be expelled and ' all the working tooles and habitt burned before his face '. What those tools and costume were in the fifteenth century, and until modern times, may be seen on a brass in Newland Church, whereon is depicted a free miner wearing a cap and leather breeches tied below the knee, with a wooden mine-hod slung over his shoulder, carrying a small mattock in his right hand, and holding a candlestick between his teeth.[1]

Although not so intimately connected with iron working as the smiths, smelters, and miners, the charcoal-burners were auxiliaries without whom the industry could not have existed, and who in turn derived their living largely from that industry. The amount of wood consumed by the iron works was enormous. As an example we may take the case of the two Sussex mills of Sheffield and Worth for 1547–9.[2] At Sheffield 6,300 cords of wood were ' coled ' for the furnace, and 6,750 cords for the forge ; at Worth the amounts were respectively nearly 5,900 and 2,750 cords ; the cords being 125 cubic feet, this represents an expenditure of about 2,700,000 cubic feet of timber for these two works alone in less than two years. In 1553 when Sir George Harper and Thomas Culpepper took a lease of ironworks in South Frith Chace (in Tonbridge Forest)—consisting of

---

[1] *Arch. Cambr.* (S. 3), iii. 418.
[2] *V. C. H. Sussex*, ii. 247.

a furnace, a finery, a house, and seven cottages for the labourers—for forty years with the option of breaking it in twenty-one years, it was expected that they would avail themselves of the option as the wood would probably be used up by that time.[1] Later, in 1580, it was stated that a beech tree of one foot square ' at the stubbe ' would make one and a half loads of charcoal, and the ironworks at Monkswood, near Tintern, would require 600 such trees every year,[2] while some thirty years later Norden referred to the fact that there were in Sussex alone about 140 forges using two, three, or four loads of charcoal apiece daily. Acts were passed in 1558, 1581, and 1585 regulating the cutting of wood for furnaces and prohibiting the use of timber trees for charcoal, but they were evaded, and the destruction of trees continued until, in the eighteenth century, charcoal was supplanted by mineral coal, the first successful use of which for iron smelting, by Dud Dudley in 1620, marks, as we have said, the termination of the mediaeval period.

[1] Exch. Spec. Com. 1093.
[2] Exch. Dep. by Com., 22 Eliz., Trin. 4.

III

MINING—LEAD AND SILVER

THE lead mining industry in England is important and interesting from its antiquity, the value of its produce, large quantities of silver being obtained from this source during the mediaeval period, and the organization of its workers. Although lacking the completeness of organization which rendered the tinners of Cornwall and Devon almost an independent race, the lead miners of Alston Moor, Derbyshire, and the Mendips, the three great mining camps of England, were more highly organized than the iron miners of Dean, who form the lowest class of privileged ' free miners '.

The lead mines of Britain were worked by the Romans from the earliest days of their occupation of the island, pigs of lead having been found in the Mendips stamped with the titles of Britannicus (A. D. 44–8) and Claudius (A. D. 49).[1] Mines of this period exist at Shelve and Snailbeach in Shropshire and elsewhere, and smelting hearths have been found at Minstreley in the same county and at Matlock.[2] Nor was the industry discontinued after the departure of the Romans. Lead mines at Wirksworth in Derbyshire were leased by the Abbess of Repton to a certain Duke Humbert in 835,[3] and a ' leadgedelf ' at Penpark Hole in Gloucestershire is

[1] *Journ. Brit. Arch. Ass.*, xxxi. 129–42. For a list of Roman pigs found in England, see *ibid.*, liv. 272.

[2] *Ibid.*

[3] Birch, *Cart. Sax.*, i. 579.

mentioned in 882,[1] though that county was not a great centre of lead production at a later date. In the time of Edward the Confessor the Derbyshire mines of Bakewell, Ashford, and Hope yielded £30, besides five wainloads of lead, but in 1086 their yearly value had fallen, for some reason, to £10 6s. Besides these three mines Domesday Book alludes to others at Wirksworth, Metesford, and Crich.[2]

During the twelfth century the output of lead was considerable. The ' mines of Carlisle ', that is to say of Alston Moor, on the borders of Cumberland, Yorkshire, and Northumberland, occur on the Pipe Roll of 1130, and were farmed during the reign of Henry II[3] at an average rent of £100; during the same reign large quantities of lead from Derbyshire were carried across to Boston and shipped to London and the Continent : the Shropshire mines were also active, one hundred and ten loads of lead being sent down to Amesbury in 1181 alone. King Stephen granted to the Bishop of Durham certain mines in Weardale, probably of silver-bearing lead, as the non-precious minerals already belonged to the bishopric; and during the vacancy of the see of Durham in 1196 considerable issues of silver were accounted for.[4] A similar grant of lead mines in Somerset was made to Bishop Reginald of Bath by Richard I.[5] How soon the three great mining camps acquired their privileges and organization cannot be definitely stated : some of the regulations seem to have been traditional from very early times, even in the case

[1] *V. C. H. Gloucs.*, ii. 237.   [2] *V. C. H. Derby*, ii. 323.
[3] Pipe Rolls of Hen. II.   [4] *V. C. H. Durham*, ii. 348.
[5] *V. C. H. Somers.*, ii. 363.

of the Mendip mines, of which the laws were largely
based upon the Derbyshire code. So far as the northern
mines are concerned, we find Henry III in 1235 confirming to the miners of Alston the liberties and privileges
' which they used to have '.[1]

Of the regulations in force at Alston Moor [2] we have
but few details, but of the laws of Derbyshire [3] and the
Mendips [4] we have ample information. In each case
there was a mine court, known in Derbyshire as the
' berghmote ' or ' barmote ', of which the ordinary
meetings were held every three weeks and special
sessions twice a year, at Easter and Michaelmas. The
' body of the court ' consisted of twelve, or in the ' great
courts ' twenty-four, miners of good standing, and the
presiding officer was in Derbyshire the barmaster and
in Somerset the lead-reeve : at Alston [5] he appears as
bailiff, ' king's serjeant,' and steward. Associated with
this official was the coroner : [6] the two offices indeed
seem to have been combined at Alston during the
thirteenth century, as in 1279 complaint was made that
the coroners of the Scottish king's liberty of Tindale
(that portion of the present county of Northumberland
which adjoins Alston Moor) were acting in the mine
' where the serjeant of the mine appointed by the
English king ought to exercise the office of coroner in all
things ' : [7] by 1356, however, it was the custom for the

[1] Pat., 20 Hen. III, m. 13.   [2] *V. C. H. Cumberland,* ii. 339.
[3] *V. C. H. Derby,* ii. 326.   [4] *V. C. H. Somers.,* ii. 367–9.
[5] *V. C. H. Cumb.,* ii. 340.   [6] Pat., 15 Edw. IV, pt. i, m. 22.
[7] Assize R., 143, m. 1. The Scottish king's dominial rights over
Alston, apart from the mines, seem to have been well established.
William the Lion granted land at Alston as ' in Tyndale ', to
William de Vipont, and later to his son Ivo de Vipont, the latter

Alston miners to elect a coroner separate from the bailiff or king's serjeant.[1] In Somerset the miners seem to have dispensed with a coroner in cases of fatal accidents, as it was laid down that if any man ' by thys doubtfull and daungerous occupasyon tack his deth and ys slayne by faulyng of the yerth upon hym, by drownyng, by styffyng with fyer or wother wyse, as in tymes past meny hath ben so murthryd,' the coroner shall not intervene but the miners shall take up his body—even if he be killed 60 fathoms down—and bury him at their own costs.[2] The exact degree of independence possessed by these mine courts is difficult to determine. During eyres in Cumberland it was customary to send special justices to Alston to hold the pleas of the Crown. This was already an old-established custom in 1246,[3] and we find that Robert de Vipont, who about the beginning of the reign of Edward I had formed a manor out of what had been moor and waste, had usurped the right to try thieves in his manor court when they ought only to be tried in the mine court.[4] Even in Derbyshire there was a tendency to use the courts of the Duchy of Lancaster instead of, or to overrule, the mine courts, at least in the sixteenth century.[5]

By the Derbyshire mine law a small trespass was punishable by a fine of 2*d.*, but if this was not paid at

grant being confirmed by King John in 1210. Finally, after the whole matter had been carefully examined, Edward I gave the manor of Alston in 1282 to Nicholas de Vipont to hold of the King of Scotland, reserving, however, the liberty of the mines. Assize Rolls, 143, m. 1 ; 132, m. 34 ; Chanc. Misc. 53, file 1, nos. 20, 22.

[1] *V. C. H. Cumb.*, ii. 340.   [2] *V. C. H. Somers.*, ii. 368.
[3] Assize R., 143, m. 1.   [4] Assize R., 132, m. 34 ; 143, m. 1.
[5] *V. C. H. Derby*, ii. 339.

once the fine was doubled each successive day until it reached the sum of 5s. 4d. This same sum of 5s. 4d.[1] (doubled in a similar way up to 100s.) was the fine for bloodshed, or for the offence of encroaching upon another man's claim underground. For a thrice-repeated theft of ore the offender's hand was pinned with a knife to the uprights of his windlass, and if he succeeded in getting free he had to forswear the mine for ever. A similarly savage and primitive measure of justice was meted out to the Mendip miner who stole lead worth $13\frac{1}{2}d.$: his property was forfeited, and the bailiff was to bring him ' where hys howse or wore [i. e. ore] hys, hys work and towlls with all instruments belongyng to that occupacyon and then put hym in hys howss or working place and set fyer yn all together about hym and banyshe hym from that occupacyon for ever by fore the face of all the myners there '. Both methods of punishment are clearly of early origin, and it seems probable that they originally involved the death of the thief, though a later and more humane generation connived at his escape while retaining the ancient form of punishment. If the burnt thief did not dread the fire, but returned and stole again, he was handed over to the sheriff's officers and committed to prison, being no longer one of the privileged community. It is worth noting that the great mining camp on the borders of Cornwall and Devon, though not apparently possessing any mine court, had, as we might expect, certain control over the excesses of the miners, as in 1302 there was made ' a pit in the mine by way of prison to frighten (*ad terrorem*)

---

[1] Evidently four ores of 16d., the ore being a monetary unit in use in the districts of England influenced by the Danes.

evil doers and bad workmen '.[1] The Devon miner, as
we have just said, had no code of laws or privileges ;
at Alston the code applied only to the miners actually
living in the collection of ' shiels ' or huts on the Moor ;
in Derbyshire the full system of regulations was confined
to the royal ' field ', though a few private owners of
mining fields established barmotes on similar lines ; [2]
but the customs of the Mendips appear to have applied
throughout the district, whoever might be lord of the
soil.

By mining law the miner had the right to prospect
anywhere except in church-yards, gardens, orchards, and
highways ; on the Mendips, however, he had first to go
through the formality of asking leave of the lord of the
soil, or of his lead-reeve, who could not refuse their
permission ; he might then pitch where he pleased and
break ground as he thought best. In Derbyshire, when
the prospector had struck a promising ' rake ' or vein,
he cut a cross in the ground and went to the barmaster,
who came and staked out the claim into ' meers ', each
being four perches of twenty-four feet : the first two
meers were given to the finder, the third to the king, as
lord of the soil, and the others to those miners who first
demanded them. Within three days the owner of a meer
must set up a ' stow ',[3] a wooden frame with two uprights joined by a bar or spindle placed at the top of the
shaft, and serving as a windlass. If the claim was not
then worked, the barmaster nicked the spindle, and if
this were done three times, and the claim was still

---

[1] Exch. K. R. Accts., 260, no. 19.

[2] E. g. at Eyam and Litton. *V. C. H. Derby*, ii. 338.

[3] Until the nineteenth century the would-be miner had to set up
a model stow, fastened with wooden pins and not with nails.

A TIMBERED SHAFT. 16th cent.

unworked, it was declared forfeit and granted to the
first applicant. The regulations in use on the Mendip
field were rather different. There the pitches or claims,
instead of being of one standard size, were decided by the
throw of the ' hack ' or small pick, weighing 3 lb. 14 oz.
' Every man when he doth begyn hys pyt, otherwyse
callyd a grouff, shaull have hys haks throw ij weys after
the rake,[1] so that he do stand to the gyrdyl or wast in
the gruff ' ; while this decided the limits of the pitch
along the line of the vein, the pitcher had always eighteen
feet on either side of his ' grooffe or gribbe '. The hack,
however, was not thrown unless another party wished to
pitch in the neighbourhood ; in that case the new-comer,
or ' younger pitcher ', could demand that the hack be
thrown by the ' elder pitcher ' and his partners, ' when
they have their chine, rake or course,' that is to say,
when they have struck the vein. The lead-reeve then
proffered the hack to one of the elder pitchers, and if
they failed to throw it within fourteen days the younger
pitcher had the throw.[2] The rules for reserving a claim
were probably founded on those in use in Derbyshire.
' The first pytcher in any grounde muste make yt
perfecte wyth a caddel of tymber and a payre of styllyngs
within fowre and twentie howers next after the pyching.'
Although this was the strict law, custom seems to have
been content with the making of the ' caddel ', some sort
of framework of timber, the first day, and to have allowed
a month for the ' styllyngs ', or stow. If a claim lay

[1] I. e. forwards and backwards along the line of the vein.

[2] It is not quite clear whether he threw from the old pit, in which
case he would naturally throw a very short distance, or from his
own pit, in which case he might so throw as to cover much of the
vein which would have belonged to the elder pitchers.

unworked for four weeks, the lead-reeve caused proclamation to be made, and if the old partners did not
turn up within fourteen days, it was forfeited.

Besides the right of prospecting where they chose,
the miners had right of access to the nearest high road,
and in Derbyshire if this were refused them the barmaster and two assistants might walk abreast with arms
stretched out, and so mark out a way direct from the
mines to the road, even through growing corn. They
were also privileged to take timber from the neighbouring
woods for use in the mines, and in Cumberland, where
fuel was scarce, they might even prevent the owners of
the woods from cutting them until they had obtained
a sufficient supply for the furnaces. Their proprietary
rights in their mines were recognized, and they could
dispose of them, wholly or in part, without licence.
They might also take their ore to what ' myndry ' they
pleased, to be smelted, and the only restriction upon the
sale of the ore or lead was that in some places the king,
or other lord of the soil, had ' coup ', that is to say,
pre-emption, the right of buying the ore at the market
price before it was offered to any other purchaser, and
in 1295 we find the Derbyshire miners paying 4*d.* a load
in respect of ' coup ' for licence to sell to whom they
pleased.[1]

The terms upon which the miners held their mines
varied. On private lands, when the owner did not work
the mines himself by hired labour, he usually bargained
for some proportion, an eighth, a tenth, or a thirteenth,
of the produce. On the Mendips the lord of the soil
received the tenth part as ' lot '; on the royal field of

[1] *V. C. H. Derby,* ii. 328.

Derbyshire the king had the thirteenth, and at Alston the ninth dish of ore, the dish in the latter case being ' as much ore as a strong man can lift from the ground '.[1] At Alston the king had in addition the fifteenth penny from the other eight dishes, but had to provide at his own expense a man called ' the driver ', who understood how to separate the silver from the lead.[2] This method of paying a proportion of the produce was clearly the fairest to all concerned, for, as the Cumberland miners said in 1278, though

they knew that there was ore enough to last to the end of time, no one could tell the yearly value of the mines, as it depended upon the richness of the ore they struck,[3] and in the same way when Robert de Thorp was made warden

DISHES (*alvei*) hollowed out of solid wood. 16th cent.

of the Devon mines in 1308,[4] it was expressly stated that no definite sum was to be demanded of him, because the silver-bearing ore, the refined lead, and the reworked slag all had ' diversetez de bonntez et quantitez de respouns '. In addition to the payment of lot ore, the miners had to give tithes to the Church. In some cases these tithes originated in a definite grant, more often they seem to have been regarded as compensation for the tithes of

[1] The Derbyshire standard dish made in 1512 and still preserved at Wirksworth contains about sixty pounds of ore.

[2] Assize R., 132, m. 34.   [3] *Ibid.*

[4] Memo. R., K. R., Mich., 2 Edw. II, m. 55.

crops which would otherwise have grown on the ground taken by the mines ; but the strangest reason for claiming them was that lead was itself a titheable crop, because it ' grew and renewed in the veins '.[1]

While many small mines were worked by parties of free miners under these conditions, for their own profit and at their own risk, there must have been from early times a large number of poor men who worked for the king, the lord of the soil, or capitalist adventurers, receiving wages either by piece or by time. The regulations for the payment of these hired miners in the royal mines of Beer Alston, in Devonshire, drawn up in 1297 are of considerable interest.[2]

' As to the piecework of the miners, those who can find ore in their diggings shall receive for piecework as before, that is to say 5s. for the load,[3] as well of black as of white ore, if the white cannot reasonably be put lower. And those who are engaged in " dead " (i. e. unremunerative) work, and cannot find ore in their diggings, and yet work more, for some dead work is harder than (digging in) the vein, shall be at wages (*a lour soutz*) until they reach the ore, so that all piecework be undertaken by two or three gangs who divide the profits between themselves, as well to those doing dead work as to the others.'

Towards the end of the reign of Edward I the keeper of the Devon mines tried to increase their profitableness by refusing to pay the miners their 5s. for the king's tenth load. The result was to cause so much hardship

---

[1] *V. C. H. Derby*, ii. 332.

[2] Memo. R., L. T. R., 25–6 Edw. I, m. 51.

[3] The load, or lade (*lada*), contained nine dishes (*disci, scutella*).

and discontent that by 1307 out of 700 miners that had been working there only 60 remained, and they only stayed because the new keeper, Robert de Thorp, promised to support their petition for the restoration of payment for the tenth load, which he duly and successfully did.[1]

That the price of 5s. a load was calculated to pay the miners for their preliminary unproductive ' dead ' work may be gathered from the fact that ' tithe ore ', that is to say, the ore paid to the Church, was bought back from the rector of Beer at 2s. the load, and a further 9d. was deducted from this sum for washing the ore.[2] At the same time it is clear that where the ' dead ' work was exceptionally heavy or the eventual yield small this system of payment would not work; and in 1323 we find that the ' dead work ' of clearing, searching, and digging into an old mine in Devon was paid at the rate of 3s. 4d. the fathom, and that two gangs of six men were paid at the daily rate of 7d. to 9d., about 1½d. a head, for searching for the vein and for piercing the hard rock to follow up the vein in hope of finding a richer vein.[3]

By the Ordinance of 1297 wages were to be paid every Saturday, though as a matter of fact we find that they were constantly falling into arrears.

' All the ore of each week shall be measured before the Saturday and carried to the boles or other places where it is to be smelted. And knowledge shall be taken each Saturday or Sunday of the issues of each week in all things. And the payments shall be made to the miners

---

[1] Memo. R., K. R., 1 Edw. II, 53.
[2] Exch. K. R. Accts., 260, no. 19.   [3] *Ibid.*, 261, no. 25.

and other workmen the same Saturday. And no miner shall remain in a market town under colour of buying food, or in other manner after the ninth hour on Sunday, without leave.'

Besides their wages the miners received such iron, steel, and ropes as they required, free of charge, and had the use of a forge for the repair of their tools.[1] At Beer, in 1297, there were three forges, one for each of the three mines into which the field was divided,[2] and each worked by a man and a boy. In addition to the smiths[3] there would be, as auxiliaries, one or more candlemakers, carpenters, charcoal-burners, and woodcutters. In many mines it was also necessary to employ a number of hands in baling water out of the pits with leathern bodges or buckets ; during April 1323 an average of twenty persons were so engaged at Beer Alston, and during one week the number rose to forty-eight.[4] So greatly did the accumulation of water in the pits interfere with work, that in early times the Devon mines were closed down during the winter ;[5] and it was not until about 1297 that means were found of dealing with this evil. About that date the plan of draining the pits by means of ' avidods ' or adits, that is to say, horizontal galleries driven from the bottom of the pits to a level of free drainage on the surface, was introduced into the lead mines. The ordinances of 1297 arranged for one hundred tinners to work in ' avidods ', and the accounts of the working of

[1] Memo. R., L. T. R., 25–6 Edw. I, m. 51.

[2] In 1302 there were four mines : the South Mine, the Middle Mine, the Mine of Fershull, and the Old Mine. Exch. K. R. Accts., 260, no. 22.

[3] The smiths were paid 12d. to 18d. a week. *Ibid.*

[4] Exch. K. R. Accts., 261, no. 25.   [5] Anct. Corresp., xlviii. 81.

DRIVING AN ADIT. 16th cent.

these mines for the same year show payments averaging
£12 10s. to ' William Pepercorn and his partners ', and
to six other gangs ' for making avidods '.[1] It was
probably in the following year that Walter de Langton,
the Treasurer, reported that the yield of the Beer
mine had been doubled by the new method of draining,
as they could now work as well in the winter as in the
summer.[2]

The ore having been raised was broken up with
a hammer, no mechanical stamps being used apparently
before the sixteenth century,[3] though there is mention
in 1302 of a machine (*ingenium*) for breaking ' black
work ' or slag.[4] It was then washed in ' buddles ' or
troughs, with the aid of coarse sieves, women being
frequently employed for this process. The washed ore,
separated as far as possible from stone and other impurities, was then carried to the smelting furnace. The
commonest type of furnace was the ' bole ', a rough
stone structure like a lime-kiln, with an opening at the
top, serving as a chimney, and also for charging the
furnace, and one or more vents at the base for the blast.
These boles were usually built in exposed and draughty
positions, and could only be used when the wind was
favourable. At an early date they were supplemented
by ' slag-hearths ' or furnaces (*fornelli*) possessing an
artificial blast and closely resembling blacksmiths'

[1] Exch. K. R. Accts, 260, no. 16.
[2] Anct. Corresp., xlviii. 81.
[3] In an account of Irish mines in Wexford in 1557 it is stated that
the two labourers employed in breaking the ore and the two women
washing it may be dispensed with when the stamping mill is installed,
which will do more in one day than they in ten. *Cal. S. P. Carew*,
i. 268.   [4] Exch. K. R. Accts., 260, no. 22.

forges. The bottom of the hearth was hollowed out into a sort of bowl, from 12 to 18 inches in depth, to receive the molten lead, and as the stone burnt away rapidly it had to be constantly renewed.[1] The bellows of these

STAMP FOR BREAKING ORE, worked by water-wheel. 16th cent.

hearths were usually driven by the feet of men or women, but a water-mill was in use in Devon at least as early as 1295,[2] and at Wolsingham, in Durham, in 1426, water power was used when available, the footblast being used

---

[1] Exch. Spec. Com. 1955.   [2] Pipe R., 28 Edw. I.

during dry seasons.[1] The report on the Wexford mines
made in 1557 discusses the question of the best method
of smelting. The use of a bole depending on the wind,
'after the manner of the bollars of Derbyshire,' by which

WOMAN WASHING ORE. 16th cent.

6 fother (each of 20 cwt.) could be made in one 'boyle'
of two days and two nights, is condemned as costly and
uncertain, as they have to wait for a south-west wind, that
being the steadiest and most to be relied on. If a close
furnace is used it must be blown by very great bellows
by water power with an instrument called a 'sleagyll'

[1] *V. C. H. Durham,* ii. 349.

(evidently the wooden channel, with sluices, &c., carrying the water), and this will also work the stamp and wash the ore. With this type of furnace high wages must be paid, as the labour is great and painful owing to the heat.[1] The fuel of the boles was brushwood, and that of the hearths charcoal, with peat and, for the remelting of the lead, sea-coal.

In Devon mention is made of a third type of smelting house, the ' hutte ', the nature of which is obscure. The huttes are usually classed with the boles ; [2] thus it was noted in 1297 that ' from each load of black ore smelted at the huttes and boles there come $3\frac{1}{2}$ feet of silver-lead, each foot containing 70 lb. of lead, each pound weighing 25*s.* sterling. And from a load of black ore smelted by the mill furnace come 3 feet of silver-lead. And from a load of white ore smelted by the furnace or elsewhere come $1\frac{1}{2}$ feet of silver-lead. Moreover, a pound of lead made from black ore smelted by the boles and huttes and by their furnaces yields 2 dwt. of silver ; a pound of lead from black ore smelted by the mill furnace yields 3 dwt. of silver ; and a pound made from white ore $1\frac{1}{2}$ dwt.' In the same way the ' black work ' or slag of both boles and huttes were reworked at the furnaces.[3] A possible hint is found in the fact that large quantities of refined lead had to be put into the hutte when it was first lit, ' as the huttes cannot burn ore or smelt lead without the addition of sufficient melted lead at the start to roast (*coquenda*) the ore in the lead so added '.[4] This certainly suggests some sort of cupellation furnaces ; but even with the boles a certain proportion of incom-

[1] *Cal. S. P. Carew*, i. 268. [2] Pipe R., 28 Edw. I.
[3] Exch. K. R. Accts., 260, no. 6. [4] Pipe R., 28 Edw. I.

pletely smelted ore seems to have been added, as in a report on methods of lead-working made in 1582 it is said that after as much lead as possible has been got out of the ore by ' bolling ', they smelt the ' slagges ' or black work on another hearth, leaving, however, enough to cover their blocks at the next ' bolling '.[1]

Yet another type of furnace was the ' turn-hearth ' used in the Mendips ; the construction of this, again, is obscure, but it seems to have derived its name from some portion of the hearth being movable and adjustable to changing winds, while it would seem that the ordinary furnace could only be used when the wind blew from a particular quarter.[2]   There are references in 1302 to a ' *fornellus versatilis* ' used in the Devon mines, and one entry speaks of making the furnace ' upon the turning machine ' (*super ingenium versatile*).[3]   At the time of the revival of mining in Elizabeth's reign it was reported that on the Mendips for the past forty years the only hearths used had been those which could be turned about as the wind changes, but in early days they had been made on the ground, immovable, so that when the wind shifted the workers ' were enforced to remove their bellowes to other hearthes '.[4]

The bolers and furnacemen, who were paid about 12*d*. to 16*d*. a week, their assistants receiving about half those amounts, having cast the lead into pigs and stamped it, handed it over to the wardens of the mine. The next process was the refining of the silver from the lead by cupellation.   When an alloy of silver and lead

[1] *Cecil Papers* (Hist. MSS. Com.), ii. 523.
[2] *V. C. H. Somers.*, ii. 373.   [3] Exch. K. R. Accts., 260, no. 22.
[4] Exch. Spec. Com. 1955.

is melted on an open hearth with free access of air, the lead is oxidized and in the form of litharge can be removed either by skimming it off or by absorption by the porous body of the hearth, leaving the silver in a more or less pure form. By adding more lead and repeating the process the silver can be further refined. In England it seems to have been usual to remove the litharge by absorption; in the case of the Romano-British refinery at Silchester,[1] the absorbent material used was bone ash, which was also used in Wales in the sixteenth century,[2] but in the mediaeval refineries at the Devon mines charred ' tan turves ',[3] or refuse blocks of oak bark from the tanneries, were used, and probably the same material was used in Derbyshire, the southern mines being largely worked by Derbyshire miners. A thick bed of this tan-ash was made with a dished hollow in the middle, in which was placed the fuel and the lead; the hearth was then fired, and blast supplied from the side: when the whole was melted, the fire was raked aside and the blast turned on to the upper surface of the molten metal, which was thus rapidly oxidized and so refined.

But first, as soon as the mass of silver-lead was in a fluid state, ' before the ash has absorbed any of the lead, the lead is to be stirred and mixed so that it is of equal quality throughout, and a quantity of the lead amounting to about 6*s.* weight shall be taken out, and

---

[1] *Archæologia*, lvii. 113–24.

[2] Payments to men for collecting bones on the mountains and from towns and for burning them. *Cecil Papers* (Hist. MSS. Com.), ii. 185.

[3] E. g. ' In 6510 turbis tannitis emptis ad inde faciendos cineres pro plumbo affinando.' Exch. K. R. Accts., 260, no. 4.

this shall be divided into two parts, half being given to
the refiner, ticketed with his name and the date and
sealed by the wardens, and the other half shall be assayed
by the king's assayer in the presence of the wardens and
of the refiner, and the refiner shall answer for the whole
of that refining at the rate of the assay, as nearly as is
reasonable, having regard to the fact that there is
greater waste and loss in the big operation of refining
than in the assay. And when the silver has been fully
refined it shall be given by the refiners to the wardens
for a tally (or receipt) of the weight, so that there shall
be neither suspicion nor deceit on either side. . . . And
the lead that remains in the ash after the refining shall
be resmelted at a suitable time '.[1] These ordinances of
1297, just quoted, arranged for there being five skilled
refiners at the Devon mines, and the account rolls show
that they received from 18*d.* to 2*s.* a week.

The silver seems to have been cast into plates or
ingots varying from ten to twenty pounds in weight and
value (for the monetary pound was simply the pound
weight of standard silver). Its purity probably varied,
for while in 1296 the pound of refined silver was mixed
with 14*d.* of alloy to bring it to the standard,[2] a few
years later silver weighing £132 5*s.* was worth only
£131 13*s.* 7$\frac{1}{4}$*d.* in coined money,[3] and 370 lb. of silver
sent up from Martinstowe in 1294 had to be further
refined in London before it could be made into silver
vessels for the Countess of Barre.[4] In the case of the
lead we have the usual mediaeval complexity of weights.

[1] Memo., L. T. R., 25–6 Edw. I, m. 51.
[2] Exch. K. R. Accts., 260, no. 7.   [3] *Ibid.*, no. 19.
[4] Pipe R., 28 Edw. I.

MEN WORKING AT FURNACES. 16th cent.

An early entry [1] records that ' a carretate (or cartload) of lead of the Peak contains 24 fotinels, each of 70 lbs., and the fotinel contains 14 cuts [2] of 5 lbs. A carretate of London is larger by 420 lbs.'. The London weight appears to have gained the day, as a later entry gives $13\frac{1}{2}$ lb. to a stone, 6 stones to a foot, and 30 feet (or 2,430 lb.) to a carretate ' according to the weight of the Peak '.[3] In Devon we find in 1297 carretates of 24 feet and 32 feet in use simultaneously, the foot being 70 lb. here as in Derbyshire.[4]

In no other part of England had the lead-mining industry so continuous a history of steady prosperity as in Derbyshire. The Devon mines seem to have been richer and more productive during a short period, but the half century, 1290–1340, practically covers the period of their boom. During the five years, 1292–7, these mines produced £4,046 of silver, and about £360 worth of lead ; next year the silver amounted to £1,450. Then in April 1299 the king leased the mines to the Friscobaldi, Italian merchants and money-lenders, with whom he had many dealings.[5] They agreed to pay 13s. 4d. a load for the ore, but after about a year, during which time they drew some 3,600 loads of ore,[6] they found that they were losing heavily, the ore not being worth more than 10s. a load, and the costs of

[1] *V. C. H. Derby,* ii. 324.

[2] It is possible that ' cut ' is the Celtic word ' *cwt* ', meaning a piece, and dates back to British times. *Ibid.*

[3] *V. C. H. Derby,* ii. 324.   [4] Pipe R., 28 Edw. I.

[5] Pat., 27 Edw. I, m. 28. Italians were possibly exploiting the northern mines at this time, as in 1290 we find Henry Pisan, a Lombard, brought from Durham to assay a mine at ' Hardeshull' in Warwickshire. Chanc. Misc., bdle. 4, no. 5.

[6] Exch. K. R. Accts., 126, no. 9.

working being higher than they had expected.[1] The mines, however, continued to yield well when worked by the king for his own benefit, as much as £1,773 of silver and £180 from lead being obtained in 1305 : this, however, seems to have been the high-water mark, the yield for 1347 being only £70.[2] After this the mines were let to private adventurers from time to time ; but such records as we have do not suggest that many fortunes were made from them : in 1426 the yield for the previous two and a half years had been 39 ounces of silver,[3] for the year 1442 it was £17,[4] but for the six years, 1445–51, the average output rose to 4,000 ounces.[5] At the beginning of the boom in 1295 it was found necessary to recruit labour from the older lead-mining districts, and commissioners were appointed to select miners for Devon from Cheshire, Earl Warenne's liberty of Bromfield in Shropshire, the Peak, Gloucester, Somerset, and Dorset.[6] The ordinances of 1297 stipulated for 150 miners from the Peak, and an equal number of local men from Devon and Cornwall, though the accounts show that there were that year 384 miners from the Peak and 35 from Wales.[7] On the other hand, in 1296, while we have over 300 miners coming from the Peak, a twelve days' journey, we also find four picked men sent from Devon to the king's court, and thence to Ireland to prospect on the king's behalf.[8]

The prosperity of the Devon mines caused an increase of activity in those of Somerset, where a number of fresh strikes were reported during the early years of the

[1] Pat., 35 Edw. I, m. 19.   [2] Mins. Accts., 826, no. 12.
[3] *Ibid.*, no. 11.   [4] Exch. K. R. Accts., 265, no. 9.
[5] *Ibid.*, no. 10.   [6] Close 24 Edw. I, m. 11 d.
[7] Pipe R., 28 Edw. I.   [8] *Ibid.*

fourteenth century, about one of which an optimistic leadreeve wrote to the Bishop of Bath and Wells as follows : [1]

Know, my lord, that your workmen have found a splendid mine [2] of lead on the Mendips to the east of Priddy, and one that can be opened up with no trouble, being only five or six feet below the ground. And since these workmen are so often thieves, craftily separating the silver from the lead, stealthily taking it away, and when they have collected a quantity fleeing like thieves and deserting their work, as has frequently happened in times past, therefore your bailiffs are causing the ore to be carried to your court at Wookey where there is a furnace built at which the workmen smelt the ore under supervision of certain persons appointed by your steward. And as the steward, bailiffs, and workmen consider that there is a great deal of silver in the lead, on account of its whiteness and sonority, they beg that you will send them as soon as possible a good and faithful workman upon whom they can rely. I have seen the first piece of lead smelted there, of great size and weight, which when it is struck rings almost like silver, wherefore I agree with the others that if it is faithfully worked the business should prove of immense value to yourself and to the neighbourhood, and if a reliable workman is obtained I think that it would be expedient to smelt the ore where it is dug, on account of the labour of carrying so heavy material such a distance. The ore is in grains like sand.

There is no evidence that this mine fulfilled the sanguine expectations of its discoverers, but about the same time, in 1314, we find Herman de Alemannia and other adventurers working a mine in Brushford, near

---

[1] Anct. Corresp., xlviii. 177.
[2] ' Minera ' may also bear the sense of ' ore '.

Dulverton.[1] The Germans were for many centuries the most skilled miners, and English mining owes much to their enterprise. As an instance of their greater skill we may take the case of Thomas de Alemaigne, silver finer,[2] who being out of work, petitioned the king to grant him the refuse and slag (*les aftirwas et les remisailles*) thrown aside at the mines in Devonshire, which had been refined so far as those at the mines could refine them : no one else would touch them, so the king would get no gain unless he granted them to Thomas, who was willing to pay 20*s.* a year for the right to re-work them. This same Thomas de Alemaigne was appointed in 1324 to dig, cleanse, and examine the king's mines in Cumberland and Westmorland.[3] Probably these mines had not been worked for some time previous, as in 1292 the total issues of the Alston mines for the last fourteen years were said to have been £4 0*s.* 2*d.*, possibly owing to the absence of fuel, which is given as the reason for an iron mine there being worth only 15*s.* a year.[4] Later, in 1359, Tilman de Cologne was farming the Alston mines ; and in 1475, as a result apparently of a report by George Willarby[5] that there were in the north of England three notable mines, one containing 27 lb. of silver to the fodder of lead with a vein half a rod broad, another 18 lb. with a vein five rods broad, and a third 4 lb. with a vein $1\frac{1}{4}$ rods broad, the mines of Blaunchlond in Northumberland, Fletchers in Alston, Keswick in Cumberland, and also the copper mine near Richmond, were granted for fifteen years to the Duke of Gloucester,

---

[1] Close 7 Edw. II, m. 6.
[2] Anct. Pet., 13552.
[3] Pat., 17 Edw. II, p. 2, m. 15.
[4] Assize R., 135, m. 26d.
[5] Pat., 14 Edw. IV, p. 1, m. 7d.

the Earl of Northumberland, William Goderswyk, and John Marchall.[1] The two noblemen were presumably sleeping partners, and appear to have abandoned the arrangement, as soon afterwards, in 1478, William Godereswyk, Henry Van Orel, Arnold van Anne, and Albert Millyng of Cologne, and Dederic van Riswyk of England, received a grant for ten years of all mines of gold, silver, copper, and lead in Northumberland, Cumberland, and Westmorland, paying one-fifteenth of the profits.[2] Mining at this time was far from flourishing. It was said in 1492 that the silver mines were not being worked[3] and in 1538 that the lead mines ' are now dead '[4] —though there had been a certain revival of activity in 1528, when Joachim Hochstetter was appointed chief surveyor and master of the mines in England and Ireland. He arranged to make a start with a thousand men, under the supervision of six German experts, and advised that a foundry should be erected at Combe Martin.[5] It was not, however, until the latter part of Elizabeth's reign that mining, under the joint auspices of English capitalists and German engineers, took on a fresh lease of life.

Although gold is mentioned in a number of grants of mines in the fifteenth century, and though Galias de Lune and his partners were licensed in 1462 to dig ores containing gold in Gloucestershire and Somerset,[6] gold does not appear to have been worked in paying quantities in England. In 1325 John de Wylwringword was sent down to the mines of Devon and Cornwall to seek for

---

[1] Pat., 15 Edw. IV, p. 1, m. 22.
[2] Pat., 18 Edw. IV, p. 2, m. 30.
[3] *Middleton MSS.* (Hist. MSS. Com.), 614.
[4] *L. & P. Hen. VIII*, xiv (1), 946.
[5] *Ibid.*, iv. (2), 5110.   [6] Pat., 2 Edw. IV, p. 1, m. 7.

gold : he obtained from the Devon mines 22 dwt., of which he refined 3 dwt. at Exeter ; this yielded 2½ dwt. of pure gold.[1] The remainder was sent up to the Exchequer and eventually refined at York ; but this is almost the only note we have of gold being found, though no doubt small quantities were found from time to time in the Cornish stream tinworks. In 1545 one St. Clere declared that certain gold called ' gold hoppes and gold oore ' in every stream tinwork in Devon and Cornwall was by ignorance of the tinners molten with the tin, and so conveyed abroad ; certain persons were appointed to test his statement,[2] but nothing more seems to have been heard of the matter.

A few years earlier an astonishing report that gold had been found in Suffolk seems to have gained credence, as in 1538 Richard Candishe and others were appointed to have the oversight of the king's mines of gold in Suffolk, and workmen were actually sent there from Cornwall and worked at the mine from July to September ; [3] but of the output I have found no record. The actual site of this remarkable mine is not mentioned, though it is possibly referred to in a contemporary complaint made to Cromwell of certain persons who had dug for gold and treasure at Brightwell in Suffolk.[4] Just a hundred and fifty years earlier, in 1388, Richard II had sent a man down into Essex to inquire about a gold mine said to have been found there ; but in this case also we hear nothing of any yield of gold.[5]

[1] Exch. K. R. Accts., 262, no. 2.
[2] *Acts of Privy Council*, 1542–7, p. 367.
[3] *L. & P. Henry VIII*, xiii (1), 1280.
[4] *Ibid.*, App. 41.   [5] *Issue Rolls of Exch.*, 238.

IV

MINING—TIN

Tin mining claims an antiquity unsurpassed by any other industry in this country, but with what degree of justice may well be doubted. The claim of the western promontory of Britain, later known as Cornwall and Devon, to be the Cassiterides or Tin Islands whence the Phoenicians obtained their stores of that metal at least five hundred years before the Christian era rests upon rather shadowy grounds.[1] Diodorus Siculus, who wrote about 30 B.C., is the first writer definitely to connect Britain with the tin trade, and his statements appear to be based rather upon a doubtful understanding of earlier topographers than upon actual knowledge. According to him the tin was produced in the promontory of ' Bolerium ' and brought to the island of ' Ictis ', whence it was transported to Gaul. If ' Bolerium ' is Cornwall, then there is some reason to believe that ' Ictis ' is ' Insula Vectis ', or the Isle of Wight, which was apparently at that date still connected to the mainland by a narrow ridge of rock, covered at high-water but dry at low-water, as ' Ictis ' is said to have been.[2] It is certainly strange, if an ancient and well-established trade in tin really existed in Britain when the Romans came over, that that race, with its keen eye for metallic wealth, should have made no use of the tin

---

[1] *Journ. of Brit. Arch. Ass.*, lxii. 145–60.
[2] *Archæologia*, lix. 281–8.

mines of Cornwall. Yet there is no reference to these mines in the literature of the period of the Roman occupation, nor are there traces of anything approaching an organized occupation of Cornwall by the Romans, who appear to have almost ignored this corner of Britain. After the departure of the Romans, and before the Saxons conquered this district, which did not happen till the middle of the ninth century, there is some evidence of tin being worked here, as Cornish tin is said to have been carried over to France in the seventh century, and in a life of St. John of Alexandria, who died in 616, there is a story of an Alexandrian galley coming to Britain for tin.[1] That the Saxons worked the tin seems probable from the discovery of Saxon remains in the St. Austell tin grounds and elsewhere,[2] but the industry can hardly have been of any great importance at the time of the Norman Conquest, as there is no reference to it in the Domesday Survey.

While the history of tin mining in Britain prior to the middle of the twelfth century is problematical, there is from that time onwards an immense mass of material bearing upon the subject. This material has been patiently examined by Mr. George Randall Lewis, and summarized in his work on *The Stannaries*,[3] a book so full and complete that I have saved myself much labour by basing this chapter almost entirely upon it.

There are, as might be expected, many analogies between the mining of tin and the mining of lead.

---

[1] *V. C. H. Cornwall*, i. 524.   [2] *Ibid.*

[3] Vol. iii of *Harvard Economic Studies*. The same writer has contributed a valuable article on tin-mining to *V. C. H. Cornwall*.

The processes were very similar, and the laws governing the workers had much in common, but it is in the case of the Stannaries that we find the full development of the ' free miner ', so far as England is concerned. Certain initial differences in the methods employed are observable owing to the form in which tin is obtained. Tin, like other metals, exists in veins or lodes embedded in the rock at various depths ; where these veins outcrop on the banks of a stream they are broken up by the action of the water and climatic variations, the resultant pile of stanniferous boulders being known as ' shode ' ; the waters of the stream constantly wear away small pieces of the tin ore and carry them downwards until, owing to its heavy specific gravity, the tin sinks, forming a deposit in the bed of the stream which may sometimes be as much as twenty feet thick. It was this third class of alluvial tin which was alone worked in prehistoric and early mediaeval days. This might safely be assumed, but rather remarkable confirmation is obtained from an account of tin worked for Edmund of Cornwall in 1297. From this it appears that twenty-eight and a half ' foot-fates ' of ore produced a thousand-weight (1,200 lb.) of ' white tin ', the proportion corresponding pretty closely with those—three ' foot-fates ' of ore to yield 150 lb. of metal—given in the sixteenth century by Thomas Beare for alluvial or ' stream ' tin, which was far richer than mine tin.[1] It cannot have been very long before the miners realized that the stream tin was carried down by the water, and started to search for its source. The ' shode ', or boulder tin, must therefore have been worked almost as early as the alluvial deposits, and the

[1] Lewis, *op. cit.*, 5.

final stage was the working of the ' lode '. In this lode mining the first workings were no doubt shallow trenches and confined to places where the ore lay close to the surface ; a somewhat greater depth was obtained by ' shamelling ', the trench being carried down in stages, a ' shamell ' or platform being left at each stage at the height to which the miner could throw his ore ; finally came the deep shaft with galleries. But here, as in all mining, the question of drainage came in. Where the workings were quite shallow the water could be baled out with wooden bowls, or a ' level ', or deep ditch, could be dug. For greater depths the adit, or drainage gallery (see above, p. 53), was available, and although Mr. Lewis [1] cannot find any record of the use of the adit in tin mining before the seventeenth century, it does not seem reasonable to doubt that it was in use much earlier, especially as the tinners were employed to make the avidods in the Devon mines in the thirteenth century, as we have seen. Exactly when pumps and other draining machines were introduced into the tin mines is not clear, but probably they were little used during our mediaeval period, when few of the mines were of any great depth ; [2] though as early as 1474 Thomas Nevyll had a tinwork in Cornwall, called ' the myne of the Cleker ', in which his miners dug 12 fathoms deep before they came to ' the proper beame ' or vein. [3]

The primitive miner, when he had got his ore with

---

[1] *Ibid.*, 11.

[2] A case of a London goldsmith making engines and instruments to drain a deep mine near Truro occurs in first quarter of the sixteenth century. Early Chanc. Proc., 481, no. 46.

[3] Coram Rege, 852, m. 37.

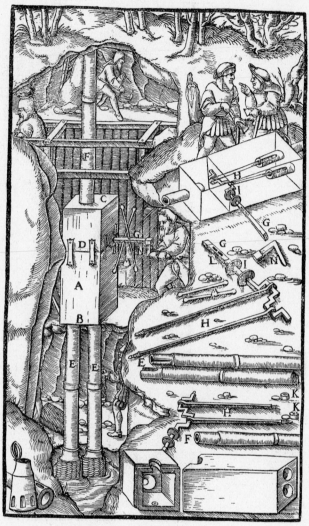

PUMP, in two stages. 16th cent.

the aid of his simple tools, a wooden shovel and a pick,
also in earliest times of wood but later of iron, constructed a rough hearth of stones on which he kindled
a fire. When it was burning strongly he cast in his ore
and afterwards collected the molten tin from the ashes.

BREAKING AND WASHING THE ORE.　16th cent.

The next stage was to construct a regular furnace,
exactly similar in type to the boles or furnaces used
for lead-melting (see above, p. 55). These furnaces were
enclosed in a building, the 'blowing-house', in early
times a rough thatched shanty, which was burnt from
time to time to obtain the metallic dust which had

lodged in the thatch, but afterwards more substantial.
The cost of a ' melting howse ' (80 feet by 20 feet) built
at Larian in Cornwall by Burcord Crangs, a German,
in the time of Queen Mary, was about £300, composed
as follows : [1]

	£	s.	d.
For the ryddyng, clensing and leveling of the ground for setting of the foundacon therof	23	6	8
For making foundacon of the walls and the poynyons of the meltyng howse . .	120	0	0
For making of the audit [2] to build the fornas and meltyng chymney upon . . .	30	0	0
For tymbering and covering the howse with esclattes	50	0	0
For dores, windows, locks, and barres . .	6	0	0
The whele, exultree and the stampers . .	10	0	0
For 4 paire of grete bellowes wt their geames and other necessaryes	20	0	0
For makyng of the Colehouse . . .	15	0	0
For makyng of the Rostingehowse [3] . .	20	0	0
For makyng of the lete and dyke comyng to the meltynghowse	66	0	0
For the hatt and the crane . . .	20	0	0

The lumps of ore were first broken up with hammers
or in a mill ; the powdered ore was then washed to free
it as far as possible from earthy impurities. Sometimes
this was done with a ' vanne ', or shovel, the heavy
ore remaining at the point of the shovel and the lighter
impurities being washed away. An elaborate process
was also used, in which the water containing the powdered
ore was allowed to run over pieces of turf, the metallic

[1] Memo. R., L. T. R., 9 Eliz., Mich. 3.

[2] Either the channel by which the blast was admitted, or else
the channel conveying water to the wheel.

[3] The ore was sometimes roasted before smelting.

portion sinking and becoming entangled in the fibres. The usual method, however, was by means of troughs or ' buddles '. This washing was not only a necessary preliminary to the smelting, but had an economic importance, as it was at the wash that the ore was divided when a claim was worked by partners, and the tribute or share due to the lord of the soil was apportioned ; it was also, towards the end of the mediaeval period, the only place where the ore might be bought by dealers.[1] To prevent fraud it was therefore enacted that due notice should be given of washes, and no secret buddles should be used.

Ancient block of tin

When we first get any details of tin-working, in 1198, it was usual for the tin to be smelted twice, the first being a rough process performed near the tinfield, but the second, or refining, being only permitted at special places and in the presence of the officers of the stannaries. The tin from the first smelting had to be stamped by the royal officers within two weeks of smelting, a toll being paid to the king at the same time of 2s. 6d. per thousand-weight in Devon, and of 5s. in Cornwall. Moreover, by the regulations of 1198, within thirteen weeks the tin had to be resmelted and again stamped, this time paying a tax of one mark.[2] The double smelting possibly ceased before the end of the thirteenth century. In any case the fiscal arrangement was altered, and in 1302, not long after the stannaries had reverted to the

---

[1] *V. C. H. Cornwall*, i. 539.   [2] Lewis, *op. cit.*, 133–4.

Crown, after being in the hands of the Earls of Cornwall from 1231 to 1300, we find the stampage dues consolidated into a single coinage duty. Under this system of coinage all the tin smelted had to be sent to certain specified towns, those for Cornwall being Bodmin, Liskeard, Lostwithiel, Helston, and Truro; and for Devon, Chagford, Tavistock, Plympton, and Ashburton. Here the tin remained until the two yearly visits of the coinage officials, at Michaelmas and Midsummer, when each block, weighing roughly 200 to 300 lb., was assayed, weighed, and taxed: it was then stamped and might be sold. At some time during the mediaeval period it became the custom to cast the tin into standardized blocks, which in Devon

Seal of the Pewterers' Company showing ' strakes ' of pewter

weighed 100 lb. and in Cornwall 250 lb., and which were accepted by the collector of export duties as being of those weights. In order to evade these duties the merchants persuaded the tinners to increase the size of the blocks until they contained nearly twice their nominal weight of metal, the revenue being thus defrauded of half its dues.[1] These large ingots seem from the earliest times to have been cast in the shape of an astragalus (flat oblong blocks, of which

[1] S. P. Henry VIII, cxiii. 132.

the sides were prolonged, like a butcher's meat-tray), probably for convenience of carriage by pack-horses, one ingot being hung on each side of the horse.[1] For retail purposes the tin was recast in ' strakes '—grilles, or rectangular lattices,[2] which were easily divided for customers who wished to buy small quantities— and these strakes figure in the arms of the Pewterers' Company. To prevent fraud an elaborate system of marking was gradually introduced during the sixteenth and seventeenth centuries, and the use of private marks by the owners of the blowing-houses was probably of much earlier origin. These marks were designed not only to protect the merchant, but also to act as a check on smuggling, of which an immense amount undoubtedly went on.[3]

One result of the coinage system, by which tin might not be sold until stamped, and could only be stamped twice a year, was that the smaller tin-workers inevitably fell into the hands of the capitalists. The small independent tinner, with no reserve of capital to draw upon, had almost always to pledge his tin in advance to the adventurers and tin-dealers, and as a result he was often worse off with his theoretical independence than he would have been as a recognized wage-labourer. The wage work system must have been introduced into the stannaries at quite an early period. Even in 1237

[1] *Arch. Journ.*, xxviii. 196.

[2] Solder was cast in the same way, a portion of one of these harrow-like strakes having been found at Westminster. *Proc. Soc. Antiq.*, 1898, p. 21.

[3] W. de Wrotham, when appointed warden of the stanneries in 1198, ordered all masters of ships in Cornwall and Devon to swear not to take unstamped tin out of the country.—Lewis, *op. cit.*, 337.

there are references to servants who worked the mines
for the tinners.[1] In 1342 certain of the wealthier Cornish
tinners endeavoured to force their poorer brethren to
work for them at a penny a day, when they had been
working tin worth 20*d*. or more daily, and it is said that
Abraham the tinner in 1357 was actually employing
three hundred persons on his works. Side by side
with these hired workmen were the independent tinners,
working either separately or, more usually, in partnerships ; but from the small amounts which many of
these tinners presented for coinage, Mr. Lewis has
concluded that they may have been only partly dependent upon their mining.[2] There is, however, the complication that the small amounts presented may in
part have been due to their having sold their ore to
the larger dealers, but it is clear that some of the tinners
did also carry on farming.

While the economic position of the smaller tinners
must often have been little, if at all, superior to that
of ordinary labourers, their political position was
remarkable. They constituted a state within a state ;
the free miner ' paid taxes not as an Englishman, but
as a miner. His law was not the law of the realm,
but that of his mine. He obeyed the king only when
his orders were communicated through the warden of
the mines, and even then so long only as he respected
the mining law. His courts were the mine courts, his
parliament the mine parliament.' [3] The tinner was a free
man and could not be subjected to the system of villein-

[1] Lewis, *op. cit.*, 190. [2] *Op. cit.*, 187.
[3] *V. C. H. Cornwall*, i. 523. The fourteenth-century seal of the
community of tinners of Cornwall is illustrated in *Arch. Journal*,
v. 65.

age. He had the right of prospecting anywhere within the two counties, except in churchyards, highways, and gardens, and might 'bound' or stake out a claim by the simple process of cutting shallow holes and making piles of turf at the four corners of his claim, and such claim would be his absolute property provided that he worked it (the exact amount of work necessary to retain a claim varied in different places and at different periods). For his claim he paid to the lord of the land, whether it were the king or a private lord, a certain tribute of ore, usually the tenth or the fifteenth portion. He had, moreover, the right to divert streams, either to obtain water for washing his ore or to enable him to dig in the bed of the stream, and the important privilege of compelling landowners to sell him fuel for his furnace. Further, he had his own courts, and was under the sole jurisdiction of the warden-officers of the stannaries. Each stannary, of which there were five in Cornwall and four in Devon, had its own court, presided over by a steward, and no tinner might plead or be impleaded outside his court, from which the appeal lay to the warden, or, in practice, to the vice-warden. How and when these privileges were obtained must remain a matter for speculation, but they can be traced when William de Wrotham was appointed warden in 1198, and were definitely confirmed to the tinners by King John in 1201.

By development, apparently, from the two yearly great courts of the stannaries, arose the 'stannary parliaments'. The parliament for Cornwall consisted of twenty-four members, six being nominated by the mayor and council of each of the four towns of Lost-

withiel, Launceston, Truro, and Helston ; that of Devon
contained ninety-six members, twenty-four from each
of the stannaries. Those parliaments were summoned,
through the lord warden, by the Duke of Cornwall, in
whom the supreme control of the stannaries was vested
from 1338 onwards, and had power not only to legislate
for the stannaries, but to veto any national legislation
which infringed their privileges. When the parliaments
originated is not known, but they were certainly established before the beginning of the sixteenth century,
prior to which date all records of their proceedings are
lost.

With all these privileges, to which may be added
exemption from ordinary taxation and military service,
though the tinners were liable to be taxed separately
and enrolled for service under their own officers, it was
natural that the exact definition of a tinner should have
given rise to much dispute. On the one hand, it was
argued that these exemptions and privileges applied
only to working tinners actually employed in getting
ore ; on the other, the tin dealers, blowers, and owners
of blowing-houses claimed to be included. Eventually
the larger definition was accepted, and, indeed, it was
almost entirely from the capitalist section of the industry
that the parliaments were elected, from the sixteenth
century, if not earlier.

It is rather remarkable that when the stannaries
first come into evidence, in the reign of Henry II, the
chief centre of production appears to have been Devon
rather than Cornwall.[1] So far as can be estimated the
output during this reign rose gradually from about

[1] Lewis, *op. cit.*, 34.

70 tons in 1156 to about 350 in 1171. Richard I, with his constant need of money, reorganized the stannaries in 1198, and at the beginning of John's reign the output was between 400 and 450 tons. The issue of the charter to the stannaries in 1201 does not seem to have had any immediate effect on the industry, but about ten years later there was increased activity, the output rising in 1214 to 600 tons.[1] During the early years of Henry III the tin revenues were farmed out, and no details are available either for these years, or for the period 1225–1300, during which time the stannaries were in the hands of the Earls of Cornwall. Two things only are clear : that the total output had fallen off, and that Cornwall had now far outstripped Devon. The grant of a charter confirming the privileges of the stannaries in 1305 seems to have marked the beginning of a more prosperous era, and by 1337 the output had reached 700 tons. The Black Death, however, in 1350 put an end to this prosperity, and with the exception of a boom during the reign of Henry IV, tinning did not recover until just at the end of our mediaeval period. Even at its worst, however, the industry was a source of considerable revenue, the coinage duties [2] never falling below £1,000, and amounting in 1337 and 1400 to over £3,000, in addition to which there were other smaller payments and perquisites.[3] The royal privileges of pre-emption was also of value to needy kings, who frequently availed themselves of it to grant this pre-emption, or virtual monopoly, to wealthy foreign merchants and other money-lenders in return for substantial loans.

---

[1] For output, see Lewis, *op. cit.*, App. J.
[2] Lewis, *op. cit.*, App. K.   [3] *Ibid.*, Apps. L–T.

Before leaving the subject of the tin mines of Cornwall and Devon, it is perhaps worth while noting that there is virtually no documentary evidence of the working of the copper deposits of Cornwall prior to the late sixteenth century, and it would seem that most of the copper used in mediaeval England must have been imported.

V

QUARRYING—STONE, MARBLE, ALABASTER, CHALK

STONE-QUARRYING is an industry to which the references in mediaeval records are more numerous than enlightening. It would be easy to fill pages with a list of casual references to the working of quarries in all parts of England, and after struggling through the list the reader would know that stone was dug in quite a lot of places at different times, which he might have assumed without the documentary evidence. It is natural that when a castle, an abbey, a church, or other stone building is to be erected, the stone, whose cost lies mainly in transport, should be obtained from the nearest possible source. Founders of monasteries frequently made grants either of existing quarries or of the right to dig stone for the monastic buildings, and the discovery of a bed of suitable stone close to the site selected for the Conqueror's votive abbey of Battle was so opportune as to be deemed a miracle.[1] When a monastery was founded in a district where stone could not be found, it was almost essential that its supplies should be drawn if possible from some place from which the stone could be carried by water, and it was no doubt the position of Barnack between the Welland and the Nene that made its quarries so important to the monks of the Fenland.[2] The abbeys of

[1] *Chron. of Battle Abbey*, 11.   [2] *V. C. H. Northants.*, ii. 293–5.

Peterborough, Ramsey, Crowland, Bury St. Edmund, and Sawtry all held quarries in Barnack, and quarrelled amongst themselves over their respective rights. The monks of Sawtry, for instance, had made a canal for carrying stone to their abbey by way of Wittlesea Mere by permission of the abbey of Ramsey, a permission which they seem to have abused, as in 1192 orders were given to block all their lodes except the main one leading to Sawtry, and they had to promise to put up no buildings except one rest house for the men on their stone barges.[1]

For York Minster[2] stone was brought from the quarries of Thevesdale, Huddleston, and Tadcaster down the Wharfe, and from Stapleton down the Aire into the Ouse, and so up to St. Leonard's wharf, whence it was carried on sleds to the mason's yard. Westminster and London were mainly supplied from Surrey— from the Reigate, Merstham, and Chaldon quarries—and Kent, from the Maidstone district. The tough ' Kentish rag ', which was used by the Romans for the walls of London, was much in demand for the rougher masonry,[3] and in a contract for building a wharf by the Tower in 1389, it was stipulated that the core of the walls should be of ' raggs ', and the facing of ' assheler de Kent '.[4] The Reigate stone, on the other hand, was of superior quality and more suited for fine work, and we find it constantly used for images, carved niches, and window

---

[1] *V. C. H. Northants.*, ii. 295.

[2] *York Fabric Rolls* (Surtees Soc.), *passim*.

[3] e. g. at the Tower in 1324, ' one boatload of Aylesford stone called rag, 6s.'—Exch. K. R. Accts., 469, no. 7. And in 1362 ' 8 boatloads of stone called ragg, with carriage from Maidstone, £10 13s. 4d.' *Ibid.*, 472, no. 9.   [4] *Ibid.*, 502, no. 10.

tracery.[1] It was much used at Windsor for the more decorative features, stone from the local quarries of Bisham and Eglemunt being chiefly employed for ordinary building purposes.[2]

The most accessible stone not always being the most suitable for the varying requirements of architecture, it was necessary to find other stone possessing the desired qualities, and certain quarries at an early date acquired renown. Setting aside the famous Norman quarries of Caen, whose stone appears in greater or less quantities in hundreds of buildings and of records, there are a number of English quarries of more than local repute in mediaeval times. Such were the quarries of Beer in Devonshire, from whose labyrinthine galleries stone was carried to Rochester in 1367,[3] to St. Stephen's Westminster in 1362,[4] and elsewhere. The fine limestone, later known as Bath Stone, was quarried to a large extent at Haslebury in Box in Wiltshire, from which place it was sent in 1221 to the royal palace at Winchester for the columns of the hall and for chimney hoods,[5] Richard Sired receiving 23s. 4d. for cutting 105 blocks

Men cutting marble with a saw.
11th cent.

---

[1] See the Westminster building accounts, *passim*.

[2] See Hope's *Windsor Castle, passim*.

[3] *Arch. Cant.*, ii. 112.

[4] ' 20 tontightes de peers de Beer.'—Exch. K. R. Accts., **472**, no. 8.   [5] Exch. K. R. Accts., **491**, no. 13.

of stone in the quarry of Hesalburi.[1] For these same works at Winchester much stone was brought from the Hampshire quarry of Selbourne, and from the better known quarries of the Isle of Wight, while a stone-cutter was sent to procure material from the quarry of Corfe. This latter was no doubt the same as the ' hard stone of Corfe ' bought for Westminster in 1278.[2] With Corfe and Purbeck is associated Portland stone, which attained its greatest fame in the hands of Wren after the Fire of London, but was already appreciated in the fourteenth century, when it was used in Exeter Cathedral and at Westminster.[3] Further east Sussex possessed a number of quarries of local importance,[4] and the quarry of green sandstone at Eastbourne, from which the great Roman walls of Pevensey and the mediaeval castle within them were alike built, probably provided the ' 28 stones of Burne, worked for windows of the vault under the chapel ' at Shene in 1441.[5] Another Sussex quarry, that of Fairlight, near Hastings, supplied large quantities of stone for Rochester Castle in 1366 and 1367.[6] The list of stone brought in the latter year at Rochester is of interest as showing the various sources from which it was derived.[7] There were bought 55 tons of Beer freestone at prices varying from 9*s*. to 10*s*. the ton,[8] 62 tons of Caen stone at 9*s*., 45 tons of Stapleton free-

[1] For some fourteenth- and fifteenth-century references to the Haslebury quarries, see *The Tropenell Cartulary* (Wilts. Arch. Soc.), ii. 148–50.

[2] *V. C. H. Dorset*, ii. 333.   [3] *Ibid.*, 339.

[4] *V. C. H. Sussex*, ii. 230.

[5] Exch. K. R. Accts., 305, no. 12.

[6] *Ibid.*, 502, no. 3.   [7] *Arch. Cant.*, ii. 112.

[8] The ' pondus dolii ', anglicized in other entries as ' tuntight ', seems to have been about 40 cubic feet.

stone [1] at 8*s.*, 44 tons of Reigate stone at 6*s.*, 195 tons
of freestone from Fairlight at 3*s.* 4*d.*, 1,850 tons of rag
from Maidstone at 40*s.* the hundred tons, and a large
quantity [2] of worked stone from Boughton Monchelsea.

The Kentish quarries seem to have been especially
favoured for the manufacture of the stone balls flung
by the royal artillery in early days by mangonels,
balistae, and other forms of catapults, and in later days
by guns. Thus in 1342 the sheriff of Kent accounted
for £13 10*s.* spent on 300 stones dug in the quarry of
Folkestone and drawn out of the sea in various places,
and afterwards cut and hewn into round balls for the
king's machines; one hundred weighing 600 lb. each,
and the same number 500 lb. and 400 lb. respectively;
and a further £7 10*s.* for another 300 stone balls of
various weights.[3] It is true that some years earlier,
in 1333, similar balls had been obtained in Yorkshire,
the sheriff buying 19 damlades [4] and 3 tons of stone in
the quarry of Tadcaster, and setting 37 masons to work,
the result being 606 stone balls weighing 9 damlades,[5]
but casual references point to Kent as the great centre
of manufacture. In 1418 as many as 7,000 such balls
were ordered to be made at Maidstone and elsewhere,
and the Maidstone quarries were still turning out stone
shot for bombards during the early years of Henry VIII.[6]

So far we have been dealing with what may be called

---

[1] Presumably from the Yorkshire quarry referred to above; it
came via London.—*Ibid.*, 121.

[2] Apparently about 440 tons.—*Ibid.*

[3] Pipe R., 16 Edw. III.

[4] The term ' damlade ', of uncertain meaning, seems to be peculiar
to Yorkshire. See *York Fabric Rolls*.

[5] Pipe R., 7 Edw. III.   [6] Misc. Bks., Tr. of R., 4, f. 142.

block stone, but there were also in many parts of the country stones that, from the ease with which they could be split into thin slabs, were suitable for roofing purposes. How early and to what extent the true slates of Cornwall and Devon were worked it is difficult to say, but in 1296, when certain buildings were put up for the miners at Martinestowe 23,000 ' sclattes ' were quarried at Birlond, and another 10,000 at ' Hassal '.[1] For the roofing of buildings at Restormel in Cornwall in 1343 slates were employed, 19,500 being bought ' between Golant and Fowey ', at 11*d*. the thousand, and 85,500 dug in the quarry of Bodmatgan at a cost of 6*d*. the thousand.[2] So also in 1385, at Lostwithiel, it is probable that the ' tiles ', of which 25,400 were bought ' in the quarry ' at 3*s*. 4*d*. the thousand, were true slates,[3] and the same material is probably referred to in the ' 400 of blew helyng (= roofing) stone ' bought at Bridport in 1465.[4] But besides the real slates, which in their modern uniformity of perfection render so many towns hideous, there were many quarries of stone slates, of which the most famous were at Collyweston in Northants.[5] The Collyweston stone, after being exposed to the influence of frost, could easily be split into thin slabs,[6] and seems to have been used for roofing purposes as early as the times of the Romans. During the mediaeval period there are numerous references to these Collyweston slates, and about the end of the

---

[1] Exch. K. R. Accts., 476, no. 5. [2] *Ibid.*, 461, no. 11.

[3] *Ibid.*, no. 12.

[4] *Hist. MSS. Com. Rep.*, vi. 494.

[5] *V. C. H. Northants.*, ii. 296–7.

[6] A similar method of splitting was employed in the case of the slates of Stonesfield in Oxfordshire.—*V. C. H. Oxon.*, ii. 267.

fourteenth century they seem to have fetched from
6s. to 8s. the thousand.[1] Other similar quarries of more
than local fame were situated round Horsham in Sussex,[2]
and Horsham slates continued in demand from early
days until the diminished solidity of house construction
made a less weighty, and incidentally less picturesque,
material requisite for roofing.

The work of quarrying stone counted as unskilled
labour, and the rate of pay of quarriers is almost
always that of the ordinary labourer. At Martinstow
in 1296, men ' breaking stone in the quarry ' received
$1\frac{1}{2}d$. to 2d. a day, and women, always the cheapest form
of labour, 1d. a day for carrying the stones from the
quarry.[3] The Windsor accounts for 1368 show quarriers
at Bisham (Bustesham) receiving $3\frac{1}{2}d$. a day, and one,
no doubt the foreman, 4d., while 65,000 blocks of stone
were cut at Collingley (in Surrey) at 10s. the thousand,
and 3,500 at Stoneden at 20s.[4] Those employed upon
shaping the rough blocks were naturally paid at a higher
rate, and in 1333, while the quarriers at Tadcaster were
paid 1s. 4d. a week, the masons employed there in making
stone balls earned 2s. 6d., and their foremen 3s. a week.[5]
Often, however, the payment was by piece work, and
in the case of the stone wrought at Boughton Monchelsea
in 1366 for Rochester Castle, we have a list of the rates
of payment : ' rough ashlar ' worked at 10s. the hundred,
' parpainassheler '—for through-stones—cut to pattern

---

[1] *V. C. H. Oxon.*, ii. 267 ; *V. C. H. Northants.*, ii. 296.

[2] *V. C. H. Sussex*, ii. 230. William Brooker, ' sclatter,' of
Horsham, was employed on the roofing of the hall of the Drapers'
Gild in 1425.—A. H. Johnson, *Hist. of Company of Drapers*, p. 304.

[3] Exch. K. R. Accts., 476, no. 5.

[4] *Ibid.*, 494, no. 4.

[5] Pipe R., 7 Edw. III.

18s. the hundred, newel pieces 12d. each, jambs 3d. the foot, 'scu' or bevelled stones 2d. the foot, voussoirs (*vausur*) 5d. the foot, and so on.[1] The tools used were of a simple nature ; the inventory of tools at Stapleton quarry in 1400 [2] shows a number of iron wedges, iron rods, 'gavelokes' or crowbars, iron hammers, 'pulyng axes ',[3] ' brocheaxes,' and shovels.

Purbeck columns in Lincoln Cathedral. 12th cent.

So far we have been dealing with stone as a building material, but there were two varieties of stone worked in England in mediaeval times whose value was artistic rather than utilitarian. These were marble and alabaster. PURBECK MARBLE,[4] a dark shell conglomerate capable of receiving a very high polish, came into fashion towards the end of the twelfth century,[5] and continued in great demand for some two

---

[1] Exch. K. R. Accts., 502, no. 3.   [2] *Fabric. R. of York*, 19.

[3] A fifteenth-century account for Launceston mentions the purchase of 'An iron tool for breaking stones in the quarry, called a polax, weighing 16½ lb., and two new wedges weighing 10 lb.'— Exch. K. R. Accts., 461, no. 13.

[4] For a fuller history of the Purbeck marble quarries, see *V. C. H. Dorset*, ii. 331–8, from which the details given below are taken when other references are not given. A similar marble was quarried in Sussex : *V. C. H. Sussex*, ii. 229.

[5] A marble quarry near Worth Maltravers is mentioned in a deed of about 1190.—*Middleton MSS.* (Hist. MSS. Com.), 30.

hundred years. The biographer of St. Hugh[1] waxes
eloquent over the beauties of the Purbeck marble
introduced so effectively into the work in Lincoln
Cathedral executed under the saintly bishop's direction

at the end of the twelfth
century : ' the work is supported by precious columns
of swarthy stone, not confined to one sole colour,
nor loose of pore, but
flecked with glittering
stars and close-set in all
its grain. This stone dis-
dains to be tamed with
steel until it have first
been subdued by art ; for
its surface must first be
softened by long grinding
with sand, and its hardness
is relaxed with vinegar.
Moreover, it may suspend
the mind in doubt whether
it be jasper or marble ; it
is dull indeed for jasper,
yet, for marble, of a most

Purbeck marble figure of Archbishop Grey. 13th cent.

noble nature. Of this are formed those slender columns
which stand round the great piers, even as a bevy of
maidens stand marshalled for a dance.' Not only was it
used in 1205 at Chichester Cathedral, but it would seem
that some thirty years earlier it was sent to Dublin and to
Durham. All the evidence goes to show that the marble

[1] Coulton, *Social Life in Britain*, 472.

was not only quarried at Purbeck, but worked into columns
and carved upon the spot. Thus in 1279 the sheriff of
Dorset bought 300 columns of marble and 200 capitals for
the Countess of Arundel for her nunnery of Marham ;[1]
and it is probable that most, if not all, of the scores of
marble effigies which still remain in churches, such as the
figures of knights in the Temple Church and the tomb
of King John at Worcester, were carved by members
of the Purbeck school[2] and usually at the quarries ;
though in some cases it would seem that the carver was
called upon to do his work at the place where it was to
be used, and under the eye of his patron. But however
much we may admire the execution of these Purbeck
effigies, we must not hastily assume that they bear any
particular resemblance to the persons whom they com-
memorate ; for although the Purbeck carvers were no
doubt capable of executing portrait sculpture, a large
proportion of their work was undoubtedly conventional.
Thus in 1253 we find Henry III ordering the sheriff of
Dorset to cause ' an image of a queen ' to be cut in
marble and carried to the nunnery of Tarrant Keynston,
there to be placed over the tomb of his sister, the late
Queen of Scots.[3] The actual tomb had apparently been
made of marble in 1239 under the direction of Elias
de Derham, the famous architect of Salisbury.[4]

Corfe was the great centre of the Purbeck marble
industry. William of Corfe, who executed the tomb of
' Henry the King's son ' at Westminster in 1273,[5] was

[1] Lib. R., 8 Edw. I, m. 5.
[2] See E. S. Prior, *Mediaeval Figure Sculpture in England*.
[3] Liberate R., K. R., 37 Hen. III, m. 13.
[4] *Cal. Lib. R.*, i. 316.
[5] Exch. K. R. Accts., 467, no. 6 (2).

probably William le Blund, brother of Robert le Blund, also called Robert of Corfe, who supplied marble for the Eleanor crosses at Waltham, Northampton, and Lincoln; and one Adam of Corfe settled in London early in the fourteenth century, and died there in 1331.

SCULPTORS from 13th-century stained-glass window

This Adam ' the marbler ' seems to have carried out several large contracts, including the paving of St. Paul's, and in 1324 supplied great quantities of marble for the columns of St. Stephen's, Westminster, at 6*d.* the foot.[1] The same price was paid in 1333 for similar columns bought from Richard Canon,[2] one of a family which for a century and a half played a prominent part as carvers

[1] Exch. K. R. Accts., 469, no. 8.   [2] *Ibid.*, no. 12.

and marble merchants, particularly in connexion with Exeter Cathedral.[1]

Monumental effigies of Purbeck marble went out of fashion about the time of the Black Death, but the architectural features of tombs continued to be made in that material. For the splendid tomb of Richard II and Queen Anne of Bohemia, which the king prepared in his lifetime, Henry Yevele and Stephen Lote undertook to make the marble portion—the figures were of bronze—for the sum of £250 ;[2] and sixty years later, in 1457, John Bourde, marbeler, of Corfe, was employed to make a tomb of marble to be set on the grave of the Earl of Warwick.[3]

By the sixteenth century, and probably for some time earlier, the ' Marblers and Stone Cutters of Purbeck ' had formed themselves into a company. By their rules the industry was restricted to freemen of the company, and regulations were laid down as to the number of apprentices that might be employed. These apprentices, in turn, could become freemen at the end of seven years upon payment to the court held at Corfe Castle on Shrove Tuesday of 6s. 8d. and the render of a penny loaf and two pots of beer. The wives of freemen were also allowed to join the company on payment of 1s., and in that case might carry on the trade, with the assistance of an apprentice, after their husband's death. At the time, however, that this company was formed, it is probable that the greater part of their business was concerned with building stone, as the marble had gone

---

[1] G. Oliver, *Exeter Cathedral, passim.*

[2] *London and Middlesex Arch. Soc.*, ii. 263.

[3] Add. MS. 28564, f. 263.

out of fashion and been largely superseded by alabaster in the fifteenth century for sepulchral monuments.

ALABASTER appears to have been dug in the neighbourhood of Tutbury in very early times, some of the Norman mouldings of the west door of Tutbury Church being carved in this material.[1] It is in the same neighbourhood, at Hanbury, that the earliest known sepulchral image in alabaster is to be found : this dates from the early years of the fourteenth century, but it was not until the middle of that century that the vogue of alabaster began. From 1360 onwards there exists a magnificent series of alabaster monuments which bear striking testimony to the skill of the mediaeval English carvers,[2] and it is clear from records and the evidence of such fragments as have survived the triple iconoclasm of Reformers, Puritans, and Churchwardens, that these monuments found worthy companions in the statues and carved reredoses scattered throughout the churches of England.[3] One of the finest of these reredoses must have been the ' table of alabaster ' bought in 1367 for the high altar of St. George's, Windsor. For this the enormous sum of £200 (more than £3,000 of modern money) was paid to Peter Mason of Nottingham, while some idea of its size may be gathered from the fact that it took ten carts, each with eight horses, to bring it from Nottingham to Windsor, the journey occupying seventeen days.[4] Five years earlier Queen Philippa had

---

[1] *Arch. Journ.*, x. 116.

[2] *Ibid.*, lxi. 221–40.

[3] See, e. g., the Flawford and Breadsall figures, *ibid.* ; and the catalogue of alabaster carvings exhibited at the Society of Antiquaries in 1910.

[4] Pipe R., 41 Edw. III.

caused six cartloads of ' alebaustre ' to be brought from
Tutbury to London for some unspecified work.[1]

All the evidence points to Nottingham having been
the great centre of the industry, the material being
brought from the Derbyshire quarries of Chellaston.
The stone and the workmanship alike found favour
outside this country, and in 1414, when the abbot of
Fécamp required alabaster, he sent his mason, Alexander
de Berneval, to England to procure it ; and it was from
Thomas Prentis of Chellaston that the stone was bought.[2]
The alabaster tomb of John, Duke of Bretagne, which
was erected in Nantes Cathedral in 1408, was made in
England by Thomas Colyn, Thomas Holewell, and
Thomas Poppehowe,[3] but it is not certain that they
belonged to Nottingham. Various customs accounts [4]
show that carved alabaster figures were often exported
to the Continent. The Prior of Modbury in 1441 sent
a table of alabaster from Poole to the abbey of St. Pierre-
sur-Dives,[5] and the frequent export of alabaster carvings
from Poole suggests that the Purbeck carvers may have
worked alabaster, which is found in the district,
though only in small quantities and of poor quality.
A number of carvings still to be seen in the churches of
France, and even of Iceland,[6] have the green background,
with circular groups of red and white spots, peculiar to
the Nottingham school,[7] and many of them, as well as
of those that remain in England, possess great artistic
merit. Besides the elaborate ' tables '—reredoses, or

[1] Pat. R., 36 Edw. III, pt. 2, m. 37.
[2] *Arch. Journ.*, lxiv. 32. [3] *Ibid.*, lxi. 229.
[4] *V. C. H. Dorset*, ii. [5] *Hist. MSS. Com. Rep.*, viii. 352.
[6] Some of these no doubt were sold at the time of the Reformation.
—*Arch. Journ.*, lxi. 239. [7] *Ibid.*, 237–8.

altar-pieces—there were smaller stock pieces in great demand, such as the representations of St. John the Baptist's head on a charger, flanked by angels, and tablets with a figure of the Trinity (one of which was in

An alabaster Trinity
15th cent.

the chapel at Stonor in 1474 [1]), of which a good many examples have survived. Occasional references also occur to secular objects made of this material, such as the covered cup of 'albastre' which figures in a London will of 1352,[2] or the bedstead of 'alblaster' which was among the furniture of the magnificent Cardinal Wolsey in 1530.[3]

Thomas Prentis, who is mentioned above, is found in 1419 in company with Robert Sutton [4] covenanting to carve, paint, and gild the elaborate and beautiful tomb of Ralph Green and his wife, which may still be seen in Lowick Church, Northants, for a sum of £40. An examination of this tomb makes it almost certain that the glorious monuments of the Earl and Countess of Arundel at Arundel, Henry IV and Queen Joan at Canterbury, and the Earl of Westmorland and his two wives at Staindrop, were all from the same workshop. During the last twenty years of the fifteenth and the first thirty years of the sixteenth century, we have

[1] *Stonor Papers* (Camden Soc.), i. 146.
[2] *Cal. of Wills in Court of Hustings*, i. 667.
[3] *L. & P. Hen. VIII*, iv. 6184.　　　　[4] *Arch. Journ.*, lxi. 230.

the names of a number of ' alablastermen ' and ' image-
makers ' in Nottingham,[1] Nicholas Hill in particular
being prominent as a manufacturer of the popular
St. John the Baptist heads,[2] and during the same
period we find a number
of ' alblasterers ' at
York.[3] Richard Couper,
' corver of alablaster ',
occurs at Coventry in
1444,[4] and alabaster-
men were included with
painters, gilders, and
stainers in the gild of
St. Luke founded at
Lincoln in 1525.[5] At
Burton-on-Trent, also,
where Leland in the
sixteenth century men-
tions ' many marbellers
working in alabaster ',
the trade was evidently
established in 1481,
when Robert Bocher

1475 R

St. John's Head.   15th cent.

and Gilbert Twist were working for a number of religious
houses ; and it still flourished there in 1581 and 1585,
when Richard and Gabriel Royley undertook contracts
for elaborate tombs of alabaster ; [6] but for all practical
purposes the English school of alabaster carvers ceased

[1] *Ibid.*, 234–5.
[2] For an account of these, see Mr. Hope's article in *Archaeologia*,
xli.   [3] *Arch. Journ.*, lxiv. 239.
[4] Pat. R., 22 Hen. VI, pt. 1, m. 27.
[5] *Hist. MSS. Com. Rep.*, xiv (8), 54.   [6] *Arch. Journ.*, x. 120.

to exist when the Reformation put an end to the demand for images and carven tables.

The alabaster, or gypsum, when not suitable for carving, was still valuable for conversion into plaster by burning, the finer varieties yielding the so-called Plaster of Paris and the coarser the ordinary builders' plaster. References to the actual burning of plaster seem practically non-existent, but it is noteworthy that one of the places from which Plaster of Paris was obtained for the works at York Minster was Buttercrambe,[1] where there is a large deposit of gypsum which probably furnished the York alabasterers with their material. In the Isle of Purbeck, also, where, as we have seen, alabaster may perhaps have been worked, plaster was evidently burnt, as in the well-known list of English places and their specialities (dating from about 1300) ' Plastre de Nower ' (Nore Down, Purbeck) comes immediately after ' Marbre de Corf ',[2] and ' plaster de Corf ' was used at Windsor in 1362.[3] In the same way CHALK, though to some extent used for masonry, was most in demand for conversion into lime. When building operations of any importance were undertaken, it was usual to build a limekiln on the spot for the burning of the lime required for mortar. In earlier times the kiln seems to have taken the form of a pit, ' lymeputt ' or, in Latin, *puteus*, being the term usually employed, as for instance in 1396 in a lease of cliffs at Sarre in Thanet with ' a lymhows and a lympette ',[4] but in 1236 we find a regular kiln (*torale*) built at the large cost of £14 8s., and another,

---

[1] *York Fabric Rolls*, 74, 78, 84, 90, 106.
[2] *Engl. Hist. Rev.*, xvi. 501.   [3] Hope, *Windsor Castle*, 186.
[4] Anct. D., C. 5364.

still larger, costing £20 in 1240,[1] while in 1400, for the building of one at York, 3,300 bricks and 33 loads of clay were purchased.[2] Where lime was burnt commercially, that is to say for sale and not merely for use on the spot, the kilns would naturally be larger and more permanent, and a sixteenth-century account of the erection of eight such kilns[3] at a place unnamed—probably Calais—shows that each kiln was 20 feet high, with walls 10 feet thick, and an average internal breadth of 10 feet, and cost over £450.

When wood was plentiful it was naturally employed for burning the lime, and a presentment made in 1255 with regard to the forest of Wellington mentions that the king's two limekilns (*rees calcis*) had devoured 500 oaks between them.[4] But it was soon found that pit coal was the best fuel for the purpose, and it was constantly used from the end of the thirteenth century onwards, as much as 1,166 quarters of sea coal being bought in 1278 for the kilns (*chauffornia*) in connexion with the work at the Tower.[5] For the most part, chalk and lime required for work at London or Westminster was brought from Greenwich. Kent has indeed always been one of the great centres of the trade, both home and foreign, and in 1527,[6] to give but one instance, we find six ships from Dutch ports taking out of Sandwich port chalk to the value of £20.[7] In the chalk hills round Chislehurst, labyrinthine galleries of great extent bear

---

[1] Hope, *Windsor Castle*, 72.
[2] *York Fabric Rolls*, 15.
[3] Exch. K. R. Accts., 504, no. 4.   [4] *Hundred R.*, ii. 56.
[5] Exch. K. R. Accts., 467, no. 4.
[6] Customs Accts., 124, no. 30.
[7] Probably chalk may be taken at about 4*d.* the quarter.

witness to the flourishing state of chalk-quarrying in
this district in former times ; [1] smaller quarries of a
similar type exist in the ' caverns ' at Guildford.   Kent,
Surrey, and Sussex [2] were indeed busily employed in
quarrying chalk during the mediaeval period, and for
long afterwards, down to the present day.

[1] *Brit. Arch. Ass. Journ.*, lx.
[2] *V. C. H. Sussex*, ii. 231.

VI

BUILDING

In treating of the mediaeval builders' craft, one of the first points to arise is the interesting question, how far is it correct to speak of ' architects ' in the Middle Ages ? It has sometimes been stated that there was no such person as a real architect before the period of the Renaissance. To my mind such a statement can only be upheld by something almost indistinguishable from a quibble. Certainly the word architect is not found in English before Tudor times—the earliest date given by the Oxford Dictionary being 1563—and it is rare in Latin, though it is found in a metaphorical sense occasionally and in a technical sense at least as early as the twelfth century.[1] Certainly, also, we do not find in early times any sharp dividing line between builders and architects, or any class of men who earned a living by drawing plans for buildings with only, at most, a theoretical knowledge of the constructional methods by which the plans would be converted into realities—a mediaeval Pecksniff is unimaginable. But equally certainly there were men who could conceive a work of architecture, such as Salisbury Cathedral, as a whole ; could set down in writing the exact dimensions of such a building in full detail before beginning to work upon it ; could copy, usually in spirit rather than in slavish facsimile, existing work, or originate designs of their own ; and could

[1] Orderic Vitalis applies the term to Lanfred, who was made master of the works for the building of the castle of Ivry.—Mortet, *Textes relatifs à l'histoire de l'Architecture*, 276.

prepare estimates, ground-plans, working-drawings,[1] and models.[2] If these were not architects merely because they were also practical masons and carpenters, then the word must bear a different meaning from that which most people attach to it.

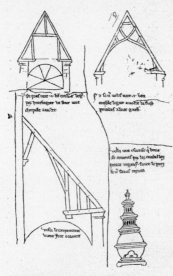

Diagrams of construction of roofs
13th cent.

One of the earliest architects of whom we have any record in England was the Frenchman, William de Sens, who rebuilt Canterbury Cathedral after it had been burnt in 1174. After the fire the monks had called in French and English masons to consult, but they had not been able to agree whether it was necessary to pull down such parts of the church as were still standing or not. Finally

---

[1] See the *Note Book of Villard de Honnecourt* (ed. by Professor Willis). The drawings of architectural details by this French architect of the thirteenth century are of extraordinary interest ; they are, however, unique not for their skill (plenty of contemporary architects must have done similar work) but for their fortunate survival.

[2] For the use of models in the case of foreign Gothic buildings, see *Trans. Roy. Hist. Soc.* (N.S.), vii. 21 ; I do not know of any cases in England in which models were used except for details of mouldings, &c. What appears to be the original model for the church of St. Maclou at Rouen still exists ; Perrot et de Lasteyrie, *Mons. et Mems.*, xii. 211–24.

BUILDING. 15th cent.

the monks wisely put themselves in the hands of William
of Sens, 'a most skilled craftsman in wood and stone',
who caused the ruined church to be pulled down and
rebuilt on a new design. In addition to conceiving and
carrying out that main design, he attended to such details
as inventing special cranes for discharging the boatloads

BUILDING OPERATIONS in the reign of Henry III

of stone brought from the famous Norman quarries of
Caen, and providing the workmen with models for
mouldings. Owing to the use of these models the
arcades at Canterbury are so exactly like those which
William had built at Sens that the same working drawings might have been used for both.[1] Just a century
earlier than William of Sens was Robert, who was given
land at St. Albans by the monks whom he served,
because he excelled all the masons of his time; and

---

[1] *Archaeologia*, xliii. 81.

BUILDING showing tilers at work on roofs. 15th cent.

a little later, in 1113, Arnold, a lay brother of Croyland Abbey, was reckoned ' a most scientific master of the art of masonry '.[1]

During the twelfth century we have frequent mention of a military architect in the person of Ailnoth ' the engineer ' (*ingeniator*), whose name shows him to have been a native Englishman. He was surveyor of the king's buildings at Westminster and the Tower in 1157, and was in charge of building operations at Windsor from 1166 to 1173; the following year he carried out repairs at Westminster Abbey after a fire, and he also superintended the destruction of the castles of Framlingham and Walton.[2] Early in the reign of Henry III we meet one of the great architects of the Middle Ages, Elias de Derham,[3] who was in charge of the building of the new cathedral of Salisbury from its start in 1220 till his death in 1245. In 1220 he was employed with that other ' incomparable artist ', Walter de Colchester, sacrist of St. Albans, on the shrine of St. Thomas at Canterbury, where he was again employed by Archbishop Edmund in 1239. From 1230 to 1235 he was in charge of building operations at Winchester; he was also connected for a while with Wells Cathedral, and there is some reason to believe that he may have done some work at Lincoln. In Elias de Derham we have an unusually close approach to the modern architect, as he was a clerk, a canon of Salisbury, and therefore had probably not had the practical training in mason-craft which most mediaeval architects possessed; at the same

---

[1] *Roy. Inst. of Architects*, 1862, 37.

[2] Hope, *Windsor Castle*, 19; cf. Maurice ' the engineer ', who worked on the castles of Newcastle (1174) and Dover (1181–2).

[3] *Arch. Journ.*, xliv. 365–71.

BUILDING. 15th cent.

time, he is not to be confused with such clerks of the works as William de Wykeham—whose supervision of building operations seems to have been purely financial, the actual architect of his college at Winchester (and possibly of the works associated with Wykeham's name

BUILDING A TOWER. 15th cent.

at Windsor) being the master mason William Winford, whose portrait may still be seen in one of the windows of Winchester College.[1] More typical of the Middle Ages is Henry Yevele.[2] He first occurs as a working free-

---

[1] *Roy. Inst. of Architects*, 1860, 48.

[2] *London and Middlesex Arch. Soc.*, ii. 259–63 ; Lethaby, *Westminster Abbey*, 212–19 ; for other master masons, or architects, of the Abbey, see *ibid.*, 150–227. In 1435 the Chapter of Canterbury appointed Master Richard Beck, mason, to the control of all their work ; he was to have 4s. weekly, a house, clothes, and an allowance for fuel, and a pension if he became blind or bedridden.—*Hist. MSS. Com. Rep.*, ix. 113. He was evidently a man of some fame, as the

mason in London in 1356. Six years later he is called
' deviser of masonry ' and in 1365 he became master
mason of the king's works at Westminster and the Tower,
at a wage of 1s. a day, being sent the following year to
carry out work at Rochester Castle. He also acted as

BUILDING A CASTLE. 15th cent.

consulting architect to Lord Cobham for work at Cowling
Castle, and drew up plans for a south aisle to St. Dunstan's
Church in Thames Street, to be built at Lord Cobham's
expense. From 1388 onwards he was chief mason at
Westminster Abbey and probably designed the portion
of the nave begun in that year; and although he was
at this time ' of great age ' he, in conjunction with
mayor and aldermen of London wrote to the prior of Canterbury
when the arches of London Bridge were in a dangerous state asking
leave to have Beck's advice, as he was considered very expert.—
Ibid., 102.

Stephen Lote, undertook to make the marble portion of the tomb which Richard II was preparing for himself and his queen, Anne of Bohemia, in 1394; and in the following year he prepared the 'forme et molde' for the raising of the walls of Westminster Hall and the insertion of twenty-six corbels of Caen stone.

In accordance with the usual mediaeval practice of keeping different branches of crafts separate,[1] we find that the mason's and carpenter's crafts were always distinct, and we must so far modify our conception of the mediaeval architect as to allow that, except in the case of a wooden building, it usually, if not invariably, took two of him to complete the plans. In the instance of the raising of Westminster Hall, just alluded to, while the masonry was designed by Yevele, the magnificent roof was the work of Master Hugh Herland, the king's carpenter.[2] When a house was built entirely of wood its construction was naturally in the hands of the carpenters,[3] and by the end of the fifteenth century the Carpenters' Company in London had obtained such complete control over the industry that licence had to be obtained from them to put up a house, a shed, or even a pen for swans.[4] In return they saw that the buildings that they licensed were properly constructed, as for

[1] At York in 1413 it was agreed that if a plasterer undertook tiling work he should pay 3*d.* to the tilers' pageant and his work should be supervised by the tilers' searchers.—*York Memorandum Book*, i. xliii. In London no carpenter might do any 'masonrie, plommery, dawbyng, or tilyng'—except repairs to his own house.— Jupp, *Hist. of Carpenters' Co.*, 350.

[2] Lethaby, *Westminster Abbey*, 217.

[3] A specification by a carpenter for building a house in 1308.— Riley, *Mems. of London*, 65.

[4] Jupp, *Hist. of Carpenters' Co.*, 135.

instance in 1543, when a house built for Mr. Cowper by Thomas Sherman and William Becham fell down owing to defective workmanship : the two carpenters had to share the cost of its being properly rebuilt, ' as well for ther own honystie as the honystie of the crafte.' [1]

BUILDING A CHURCH.   15th cent.

Although the London carpenters exercised a certain amount of control over the erection of wooden buildings, the town authorities generally drew up building regulations.   As early as 1189 London possessed an elaborate series of by-laws with regard to party walls of masonry,[2] and in the sixteenth century when a house was set up at Newport (Isle of Wight) without consulting the burgesses they insisted upon its being shifted.[3]   At York

[1] *Ibid.*, 136.   [2] *Liber Albus*, 319–332.
[3] *Cal. of Anct. Deeds*, A. 12443.

when questions of boundaries, rights in party walls, and so forth arose, the mayor appointed two masons and two carpenters as joint searchers to decide the matters in dispute.[1]

Rules for the mason's craft were drawn up in London in 1356.[2] Of these the most interesting is one which provides for a guarantee of ability and joint responsibility for contracts : any one undertaking a contract was to come before the good man for whom he was going to work, with four or six experienced masons who should swear that he was capable of doing the job and that if he failed they would themselves complete the work on the same terms. There was no regular gild with wardens and other officers, so masters were elected whenever building operations were in progress to see that the work was properly done, and that the workmen were paid according to their deserts and not outrageously—for complaints of the extortionate wages demanded by masons were frequent, and they seem to have been more successful than most crafts in obtaining higher rates of pay.

These rules of 1356 were compiled by a commission of six mason hewers and six mason setters. The setters, wallers, or layers, were those who built walls and did other work of what we may call solid masonry ; the hewers are more usually called free masons, from their working free stone (i. e. blocks of stone shaped or carved separately, such as arch mouldings, window tracery, and so forth). The constant use of the term free mason led, as so often happens in folk-etymology, to the invention

[1] *Engl. Miscellanies* (Surtees Soc.), 11–22.
[2] Riley, *Mems. of London*, 280.

of a legendary origin for it, and the free mason became in popular imagination possessed of mysterious privileges of freedom derived from Euclid, Solomon, or Adam. Into the thorny question of the secret society of free-masonry I shall not adventure. There certainly were on the continent gilds of builders—notably the Comacine Masters, whose centre was on the Island of Comacina—whose influence was very widespread and has been claimed even to be traceable in pre-Conquest England.[1] So far as England is concerned, it is sufficient for our purpose to say that by the beginning of the fifteenth century there was some kind of general fellowship of masons in existence. A rhymed set of rules for the craft of masonry,[2] of that date, speaks of a yearly assembly of the whole craft, and such ' general chapters and assemblies ' were strictly forbidden, as subversive of the law, by an Act of Parliament in 1424. The conditions of employment in the building trade made the normal local craft gild an unsuitable form of union : unlike other craftsmen, comparatively few masons were permanently resident and employed in one spot. Wherever big building operations—a castle, a cathedral, or a monastery—were in progress, thither would come masons of all classes from all parts of the country. Just as the great archi-tects, as we have seen, travelled from place to place, so did their humbler followers. During the building of the Round Tower at Windsor in 1344 the average number of men employed was for many weeks as high as 500,

[1] Ravenscroft, *Notes on the Comacine Masters* ; Leader Scott, *Cathedral Builders*.

[2] Quoted in Coulton, *Social Life*, 482–9, from Halliwell's *Early Hist. of Freemasonry*.

and in one week it rose to no less than 720.[1] Naturally one of the first considerations when building operations on a large scale were undertaken was to find accommodation for the workmen—the town of Roslyn was said to have originated in the houses built as lodgings for the men working on the wonderful chapel, begun in 1446.[2] In particular the masons' lodge figures prominently in all building accounts. This building, with which was associated the ' trasour ', ' tracyng house ' or drawing office of the master mason, was the main workshop of the masons. It was also the place where they met for meals and for their midday nap.[3] It, therefore, became the centre of the life of the craftsmen and their temporary gild hall. Being to a large extent foreigners—in the sense in which the word was always used in mediaeval times and is still used in country districts, namely, persons from another part of England—the masons were in some degree isolated, and this fact, combined with their trade interests, would tend to form them into a close society ; the temporary nature of their residence in any one spot and their habit of travelling about prevented such a society becoming a local gild and rendered it national. This helps to explain the remarkable rapidity with which fashions in architecture spread, and the way in which a particular moulding or ornament is found all over the country at the same time ; it also

[1] Hope, *Windsor Castle*, 115.

[2] Britton, *Architectural Antiquities*, iii. 51. When Vale Royal Abbey was built in 1278, the first payments to the carpenters were ' for making lodges and dwelling-houses for the masons and other workmen '.—*Vale Royal Ledger-Book* (Lancs. & Chesh. Rec. Soc.), 203.

[3] *York Fabric R.* (Surtees Soc.), 172, 182 ; Coulton, *Social Life*, 486.

helps to explain why the mason's craft developed those features of universal brotherhood and secrecy which are associated with mystic freemasonry, and why the centres of that society should be termed lodges.

Rules for the conduct and control of workmen were drawn up wherever a large number were employed, and three typical ordinances for the lodge of York Minster (compiled in 1352, 1370, and 1409) have fortunately been preserved.[1] In summer (from Easter to Michaelmas) they were to begin work at sunrise and continue till a bell rang, when they adjourned for breakfast; after ' the tyme of a mileway ' (the time it takes to walk a mile—about twenty minutes) the master mason rapped on the door of the lodge and they returned to work. At noon they had an hour's interval for dinner,[2] and, between May and August, about half an hour for sleep, and then worked on till the first bell for vespers, when they broke off for a drink, returning when the third bell rang and working on till sunset. During the winter they started ' als erly als thai may see skilfully by day lyghte for till warke ' and went on without a break till noon; then after a reasonable interval for dinner they went back and worked, with a break for a drink at vespers, so long as there was light. On holy days—the greater feasts of the Church and the days of various saints specially venerated in the particular place where they were working—no work was done, and on vigils (days

---

[1] *York Fabric R.*, 171, 181, 199.

[2] References to the nuncheons, or luncheons, of builders are not infrequent: e. g. at Canterbury in 1398—' pro nonschenchis datis carpentario in fabricacione molendini et cloace, 12d.' (*Hist. MSS. Com. Rep.*, ix. 137) ; at Oxford in 1372—' pro nonshyns ad eosdem stonemasons, 3d.' (*ibid.*, ii. 140).

preceding festivals) work ceased at noon. As these holidays were so numerous that they would have seriously diminished the wages of the workmen, it was customary to pay wages for alternate festivals.[1] Wages were also affected by the season, being diminished by a penny (reduced from an average of 5*d.* to 4*d.* a day) about 1 November, owing to the shortness of the days, and restored to the higher rate about the beginning of February, as the days grew longer.[2] The frosts of winter also put a complete stop to work in the open, and unfinished masonry had to be protected by a covering of turf, heather, or tiles.[3] For lack of such protection the west front of their church, which gave the monks of St. Albans so much trouble at the beginning of the thirteenth century, crumbled into ruin.[4]

The fifteenth-century rhyming rules, already referred to, are interesting as containing one of the earliest direct references to the ' food basis ' of wages :

> And pay thy fellows after the coste
> As vytaylys goth thenne, wel thou woste ;
> And pay them truly, upon thy fay,
> What that they deserven may.

In actual practice the price of food was not much, if at

---

[1] At Exeter in 1380 in Easter week 4½ days' wages were paid ' as is the custom here and elsewhere and according to the agreement between the chapter and the workmen that festivals shall be divided equally between them ' : Oliver, *Exeter Cath.*, 385. At Westminster the workmen claimed by ancient custom that wages should be paid them for every alternate feast day—except Sundays—that fell while they were resident in the king's service.—Exch. K. R. Accts., 467, no. 7.

[2] *Ibid.* ; and *Vale Royal Ledger-Book*, 205, 206.

[3] Hope, *Windsor Castle*, 118, 134, 182.

[4] *Gesta Abbatum*, i. 219.

all, taken into consideration; but the deserts of the workmen were, fines being enforced for coming late, hindering
other workmen, quarrelling, losing or damaging tools,
and so forth. At Eton, when the College was in building

STONECUTTERS AND MASONS. From 13th cent.
stained-glass window

in 1448, one man was docked of a week's wages, 'for
he wol not do labor but as he list himself,' and Robert
Goodgrome was fined 'for he wold kepe his ouris and
never go to werke till the clock smyte '—in other words,
for insisting on taking the full hour which was the
maximum time allowed for dinner.[1] Such deductions
and differentiation between good and bad workmen seem
to have been resisted by the masons as a rule, and they

[1] Willis and Clark, *Arch. Hist. of Univ. of Cambridge*, i. 383.

appear to have anticipated modern trade unions in fixing a minimum wage and in adopting a policy of ' ca' canny '; for Wyclif, singling out the free masons as typical men of subtle craft who conspire to support each other even in wrong and oppress others, says that they ' conspire together that no man of their craft shall take less for a day than they fix, though he should by good conscience take much less—that none of them shall do good steady work which might interfere with the earnings of other men of the craft, and that none of them shall do anything but cut stone, though he might profit his master twenty pounds by one day's work by laying a wall, without harm to himself.' [1]

Before beginning any architectural undertaking it was, of course, necessary to have a clear idea of what the finished building was to be like. Sometimes the design would, no doubt, be left entirely to the master mason, but more often the patron gave at least general instructions as to what was required ; the Liberate and Close Rolls of Henry III are full of orders for alterations and additions to the royal castles and palaces, often giving details of measurements, fittings, and particularly of such artistic features as paintings and stained windows. In other instances the design was to follow that of some existing building ; the first cathedral of Hereford was built after the model of the famous church of Charlemagne at Aix,[2] the chapel at Windsor in 1243 was to have a high wooden roof ' made after the manner of the roof of the new work at Lichfield, so that the stone-work may be seen ',[3] and in 1448 when the tower of Totnes

[1] Coulton, *Social Life*, 491.
[2] William of Malmesbury, *Gesta Pontificum*, 300.
[3] Hope, *Windsor Castle*, 56.

Church was to be built, the overseers of the work were
sent to inspect the towers of Kelington, Buckland,
Tavistock, and Ashton, to decide which was the best
design to follow.[1] Usually a contract would be drawn up
by the architect (mason or carpenter), and although the
majority of these have disappeared, a large number still
remain, often elaborately minute in their specification of
details.[2] How far it was customary to submit ground
plans and working drawings of details it is difficult to
say. In the contract for the beautiful stone roof of
King's College Chapel at Cambridge in 1512, it was
expressly stipulated that the work should be carried out
' accordyng to a platt therof made and signed with the
handes of the lordes executours unto the kyng of most
famous memorye Henry the vij[th] ',[3] and a few years
earlier we have a carpenter complaining to King
Henry VII that whereas ' your Grace had a sight bi
picture of the ruffe (roof) of your halle of Woodstoke '
and had approved it, the plans had been altered so that
the timber which he had shaped would be wasted.[4]
In 1448 a plan (*portratura*) for the completion of Eton
Chapel was submitted to the king.[5] That such plans

[1] *Hist. MSS. Com. Rep.*, iii. 345.

[2] A number relating to collegiate buildings, especially King's
College and Eton, will be found in Willis and Clark, *Arch. Hist. of
Univ. of Cambridge* ; Fotheringay Church, 1435—Dugdale, *Monasti-
con* ; Catterick Bridge—*Arch. Journ.*, vii, 56 ; a timber-framed
house, 1308—Riley, *Mems. of London*, 65 ; shops in London, 1370
and 1410—*Hist. MSS. Com. Rep.*, viii. 12, 20 ; a wharf, 1390—
Exch. K. R. Accts., 502, no. 10.

[3] Willis and Clark, *op. cit.*, i. 608. A drawing of a tower, said to
be a design for the belfry at King's College, exists in Cott. MS.
Aug. I. 1. 3 and has been reproduced in Lysons, *Cambridgeshire*, 116.

[4] *Hist. MSS. Com. Rep.*, iii. 318.

[5] Willis and Clark, *op. cit.*, i. 398, and *Report Hist. Mon. Com.
Bucks.*, i. 142.

and drawings were made for working purposes is
sufficiently clear, and it is well known that details of
mouldings were prepared, as, indeed, was necessary
seeing that the moulded blocks were carved as a rule
at the quarries. When Sir William Sinclair built Roslyn
Chapel in 1446—' he first causd the draughts to be
drawn upon Eastland boords,[1] and made the carpenters
to carve them, according to the draughts theron, and
then gave them for patterns to the masons that they
might therby cut the like in stone.'[2] This was the
usual procedure, and we have seen that William de Sens
supplied such models for the mouldings at Canterbury.
At Ely in 1313 we find boards bought ' for making molds
for the masons ',[3] and at Westminster in 1330 boards
and laths bought for the same purpose.[4] Sometimes the
shapes were drawn out on canvas instead of cut in wood ;
for instance, in 1314 at Westminster three yards of canvas
were bought ' for false molds sent to Caen for stones
there to be shaped according to the said molds '.[5]

Of the first process in building—the laying of foundations—little need be said. In the account of the building
of the glorious octagonal lantern of Ely,[6] under the
direction of Alan of Walsingham, we have an account
of how he set the workmen to dig and search until they
found solid and secure ground for the foundations of his
eight pillars, which they dug out and firmly founded
with stones and sand ; and we may note that where
such firm ground could not be found the soil was rein-
forced with wooden piles, such piles of beech being

---

[1] Deal boards, imported from the Eastlands of the Baltic.
[2] Britton, *Arch. Antiq.*, iii. 51.
[3] Willis, *Archit. Nomenclature*, 22.
[4] Exch. K. R. Accts., 469, no. 12.   [5] *Ibid.*, no. 8.
[6] Coulton, *Social Life*, 480.

granted to the Friars Minor of Winchester for the
foundation of their church in 1239.[1] The walls were
usually faced with ashlar (i. e. rectangular blocks of
dressed stone) and filled with rubble, flints, 'lomp-
stanes,' broken tiles, and mortar. Besides ordinary
mortar, a cement of wax and pitch was occasionally
used for the masonry.[2]
The walls were divided
for decorative purposes by
horizontal lines of flat
stones—often projecting to
a greater or less degree :
these were known as
' tables ', the lowest being
the ground-, earth-, or
grass-table, and those
above this being termed
' leggements '.[3] At the top
of the wall would come the
corbel-table, with its row
of corbels, or stone blocks,
usually carved into quaint

BUILDING.   Rough scaffold of
tree trunks.   11th cent.

and fantastic forms, acting as brackets for the support of
the roof timbers or of a parapet. From the roof and
parapet-walks (*alure*) the rain-water would be carried off
by gutters with spouts or gargoyles, and occasionally by
leaden pipes.[4]

[1] *Cal. Liberate R.*, 394. 'A machine carrying a ram for driving
piles ' occurs in 1330 : Exch. K. R. Accts., 467, no. 7.

[2] Lethaby, *Westminster Abbey*, 365.

[3] Willis, *Archit. Nomenclature*, 25–9.

[4] At Westminster in 1330 there is mention of ' a leaden pipe for
carrying off the rain-water, to preserve the timber, on which the
water used to fall '.—Exch. K. R. Accts., 467, no. 7.

In order to work at the higher parts of the walls scaffolds were necessary. They were composed in much the same way in mediaeval times as at present; saplings or firs were used for the uprights, the shorter logs used

BUILDING. 15th cent.

as horizontal cross-pieces were bound to them with withies and made more secure by driving in wedges, or 'warokkes'.[1] Across the horizontal pieces were laid hurdles to form platforms.[2] Use was also made of

[1] 'Talwode (small pieces of wood) pro warrokis ad scaffotam'.—*Ibid.*, 468, no. 13. 'Warrokis ad scaffotam ligandam'.—*Ibid.*, no.11.
[2] 'Pro 24 crat' pro via super scaffota facienda'.—*Ibid.*, 467, no. 3.

' cradles ', or swinging platforms, suspended by ropes, for doing repairs : at Berwick Castle in 1422 there were made ' two credill for the workmen to stand and make holes in the town walls to insert corbels ',[1] ten years later at York we find mention of ' two cords with which to hang the plumbers' cradell ',[2] and at Windsor in 1534 there was ' a great rope for the glasyers to hange ther cradelles on the owtsyde of the wyndowes to make clene the glasse '.[3] A windlass, ' wyndas ' (*verna*), is another instrument that is constantly alluded to in building accounts. For instance, in 1330 we find an entry of the cost of constructing a wyndas ' or machine for raising and winding up timber : 2 iron rings to bind the heads of the axle, 2 iron rods for the *hauka* of the wyndas on which rods the trendels have to turn or rotate, and an iron band 3 feet long and 3 fingers broad to bind and strengthen the rod of the wyndas which is partly broken, with 18 nails called spikyngs to fasten the band onto the rod '.[4] Of the other tools used in building—including an infinite variety of nails—nothing need be said.

Inside, the walls, alike of churches and living rooms, were usually plastered and either whitewashed or painted, either with subjects—sacred, historical, legendary, and allegorical—or with patterns—stencilled with stars, masonried or painted to look like marble, for such devices were used in mediaeval times—even the terrible Victorian practice of ' graining ' wood has, I believe, been found in those good old days, and appears to be indicated in a payment made in 1353 to Richard Assheby for

[1] Foreign R., 9 Hen. V, m. G.   [2] *York Fabric R.*, 54.
[3] Hope, *Windsor Castle*, 250.
[4] Exch. K. R. Accts., 467, no. 7.

painting the woodwork of the canons' chambers at Windsor ' according to his own devising with varnish and ochre '.[1] Walls were also often ' ceiled ', or panelled, either with oak or with ' wainscot ' (deal).[2] Floors, as every one knows, were strewn with rushes, though we find matting coming into use in the time of Henry VIII, Thomas Awnsell, ' matlayr,' in 1544 providing 36 dozen mats for the royal lodging at 4s. the dozen, as well as 12 lb. of ' handylband' for sewing the said mats.[3] With furniture we are not concerned, as that hardly comes under the head of building. One feature of domestic interiors which should be mentioned, as figuring constantly in building accounts, is the fireplace. Generally speaking this consisted of a hearth of stone, usually composed of one large slab,[4] with a back of tiles—purchases of ' Flanders tiles ' in early times and of bricks at a later date for fireplaces being of common occurrence—and a projecting hood or mantel of either stone or plaster. This mantel was, and still is, where it remains, a decorative architectural feature, and was often highly ornamented—sometimes with carving, as in the case of one in the queen's hall at Clarendon which was rebuilt in 1250 with marble columns on either side and carved with the symbols of the twelve months.[5] More frequently the decoration of the mantel was in

[1] Hope, *Windsor Castle*, 148.

[2] ' Norway boards of fir ' were used for wainscotting Prince Edward's room in Winchester Castle in 1253.—Liberate R., 37 Hen. III. Fir was used for the doors and windows of Windsor Hall in 1234.—Hope, *Windsor Castle*, 72.

[3] Exch. K. R. Accts., 504, no. 2.

[4] ' for an awterstone to the same furneys '—at the Dolphin Inn, in London.—Exch. K. R. Accts., 474, no. 5.

[5] Liberate R., 35 Hen. III.

painting, Henry III ordering one in his chamber at
Clarendon to be painted with a Wheel of Fortune and
a Tree of Jesse,[1] and one at Westminster with ' a figure
of Winter, which by its sad countenance and by other
miserable contortions of the body may be deservedly
likened to Winter itself '.[2]   One at Nottingham was
exceptionally provided with a fire-screen, boards being
bought in 1313 to make ' a screen hanging over the
fireplace between the hearth and the king's bed '.[3]   In
halls where the fire was made on a central hearth, the
smoke found its way out through a louvre or turret with
open sides in the centre of the roof, but where there was
a fireplace in the wall it was carried up the flue, which
usually terminated in a stone chimney of a more or less
ornamental character.[4]   A reference in 1278 to the
purchase of an earthen chimney (*chymenea terr'*) from
Ralph de Crokerelane [5] (of Crockers' or Potters' Lane)
suggests something in the nature of the modern chimney-
pot, but is exceptional and, so far as I know, unique.

[1] *Ibid.*, 32 Hen. III.   [2] *Ibid.*, 24 Hen. III.

[3] Exch. K. R. Accts., 478, no. 1.

[4] One of Norman date was found during excavations in the
castle of Old Sarum, where it may be seen.

[5] Exch. K. R. Accts., 467, no. 6.

VII

METAL WORKING

THE English craftsmen were renowned for their
metal work from the days of St. Dunstan downwards.
St. Dunstan was the patron of the goldsmiths, his
image being one of the chief ornaments of their gild hall
in London, and a ring attributed to his workmanship
was in the possession of Edward I in 1280,[1] while his
tools, including the identical tongs with which he pulled
the devil by the nose, may still be seen at Mayfield.
Coming to later times and the less questionable evidence
of records, we may probably see in Otto the Goldsmith,
whose name occurs in the Domesday Survey of 1086, the
progenitor of the family of Fitz-Otho, king's goldsmiths
and masters of the Mint from 1100 to 1300.[2] The names
of many early goldsmiths [3] have survived, and the
beautiful candlestick given to St. Peter's Abbey at
Gloucester in 1110, and now in the South Kensington
Museum, is evidence of their mastery of the art.

In early days, when the modern system of investments
and vicarious commercial enterprise was unknown, the
surplus revenues of the wealthier classes were largely
expended on plate and jewels—a form of investment
which at once lent a welcome splendour to the owner and
was easily realized when its possessor required money.
The goldsmith's trade therefore flourished in all the

---

[1] Chaffers, *Gilda Aurifabrorum*, 19.   [2] *Ibid.*, 23–5.
[3] A long chronological list of English goldsmiths is given by
Chaffers, *op. cit.*

great towns, and nowhere more than in London. Here by the end of the twelfth century the goldsmiths had constituted themselves a gild of such wealth and importance that in 1180, when Henry II inflicted fines amounting to £120 on eighteen 'adulterine' or unlicensed gilds, a quarter of the whole amount— £30—was assessed on the gild of the goldsmiths, of which Ralph Flael was alderman.[1] The largeness of the fine proved more of a tribute to the pre-eminence of the gild than a tax upon its resources, as it was not paid. The long reign of Henry III must have given the craft a fresh impetus, as that pious, artistic, and extravagant king was continually ordering costly jewels to be made for the adornment of royal or monastic altars or as gifts for his too numerous favourites and foreign friends,[2] and we may safely assume that his example was followed by the

The Gloucester Candlestick. 12th cent.

nobles of his court. If Henry's son Edward I was less of an artist, he possessed a taste for solid magnificence that must have proved equally remunerative to the court goldsmiths. In 1290, when his daughters Joan and Margaret were married, he spent £500 on silver plate for Joan alone, and other large sums on splendid girdles and

[1] Pipe R., 26 Hen. II.   [2] Close and Liberate Rolls, *passim.*

chaplets, covered with precious stones, and other ornaments for the two princesses.[1] Inventories of the royal treasure leave the same impression of splendour : long lists of gold and silver vessels ; the great crown (valued at £4,000), four other crowns, besides coronets, garlands,

ANATHEMA CUP of Pembroke College, Cambridge [4]

and chaplets ; a girdle of red silk with twenty-five cameos ; rings, brooches, and so forth.[2] Some of this treasure was no doubt of foreign manufacture, but the great bulk of it was certainly the work of English goldsmiths—one of whom, Thomas Frowick, in 1303 made a golden crown for Queen Margaret and, incidentally, had a good deal of trouble over getting his bill paid.[3]

The high position held by England in the realm of Art during the Middle Ages is apt to be forgotten. We hear so much of the skill of the French and Italian craftsmen that many people are inclined to overlook the existence of a flourishing school of English art. We have seen in the last chapter something of the native schools

[1] Chanc. Misc., bdle. 4, no. 5.
[2] Exch. K. R. Accts., 354, no. 12.
[3] Herbert, *Hist. of Livery Companies*, ii. 127.
[4] The earliest secular piece with date letter.

of carvers at Purbeck and Nottingham, whose products were appreciated outside their own country; in embroidery the *opus Anglicanum* was justly famous throughout Europe; students of manuscripts know the beautiful work produced by the English school of miniaturists; the existence of a great native school of painters is less well known but not less certain.[1] So too the English goldsmiths could produce not only massive cups and services of plate but more ornate fancy pieces, such as the gold-mounted hunting knife and horn which John Bottesham made for King Richard II,[2] or the laver, enamelled with portraits of the Nine Worthies, which was made in 1334 for Edward III as a present for his mother.[3] It is natural, but not the less lamentable, that only an infinitesimal portion of the products of these artists should have survived, and of those practically none can be assigned to definite makers. There is, however, one branch of the art of which we can still study innumerable examples. In the Middle Ages, when reading and writing were far from being universal attainments, the essential proof of the authenticity of a deed was not the signature of the executant but his seal. Consequently every man of rank, every corporation, and practically every landed proprietor, possessed a seal; of these, numbers of actual matrices and thousands of impressions have survived, and attest the skill of the engravers. In the case of many of the royal seals the names of the makers are known. Thus in 1299 William

---

[1] See, e. g., *V. C. H. Norfolk*, ii. 529–54; Lethaby, *Westminster Abbey*, ch. xiii.

[2] Devon, *Issue Rolls*, 231.

[3] Wardrobe Enrolled Accts., ii. m. 35.

de Keyles made for Queen Margaret a great seal in silver and a privy seal in gold,[1] John de Chichester made two privy seals for Edward III,[2] and John Bernes made seals for Henry V [3] and for his successor.[4] All of these were London goldsmiths, but a provincial craftsman who

SEAL OF QUEEN MARGARET. Made in 1299

evidently made a speciality of this branch of the art occurs in 1333, when Hugh le Seler of York made a new seal for the bishopric of Durham.[5] Edward II, whose example was in most matters one to be avoided, seems to have employed a foreigner, as shortly after his accession £4 was paid ' to Reynold de Berewic, a German gold-

[1] Exch. K. R. Accts., 355, no. 17.
[2] Devon, *Issue Rolls*, 175. ' Hist. of the Great Seal ', *Arch. J.*, ii, 14 seq.
[3] *Ibid.*, 322.   [4] *Ibid.*, 382.   [5] *Ibid.*, 143.

smith ', for making his privy seal.[1] The question of the
relative skill of English and German craftsmen came up
in 1464 as the result of a dispute between Oliver Davy,
citizen of London, and White Johnson, a German; it
was agreed that each should cause four steel puncheons
or dies to be made by a compatriot—two of the dies to
be engraved and two embossed, the designs being a cat's
face and a naked man. Davy duly brought his four
puncheons, made by Thomas Cotterell, his apprentice,
to Goldsmith's Hall on the appointed day ; Johnson
came six weeks late and then brought only the two
engraved dies ; the jury compared the exhibits and
decided that Davy's were ' better kunynger wrought '.[2]

The cat's face device alluded to in the last entry was
no doubt chosen in allusion to the royal stamp of the
leopard's head, which has been the guarantee of standard
purity of metal for centuries. In addition to this universal stamp, objects of gold or silver made in any town
had to bear the particular device or ' touch ' of that
town. References to ' a saltcellar of the touch (*de tactu*)
of London ' and another ' of the touch of Paris ' occur
in 1323,[3] and in the charter of Edward III to the goldsmiths' gild of London in 1327, by which the gild were
granted the right to search and examine goldsmiths'
wares throughout England, it was specified that all the
trading cities and towns should send up to London and
register their particular ' touches ' and should receive
a punch with the stamp of the leopard's head, ' as of old
ordained.' [4] This charter of 1327 marks the important

[1] Exch. K. R. Accts., 373, no. 15.
[2] Herbert, *Hist. of Livery Companies*, ii. 197.
[3] Wardrobe Enrolled Accts., ii. m. 23.
[4] Herbert, *Hist. of Livery Companies*, ii. 288.

position occupied by the London gild, and its growth
in size and wealth during the reign of Edward III seems
to have been particularly rapid. In 1340 there were
about 25 apprentices,[1] but in 1360, in spite of the Black
Death having occurred in the interval, the number had
risen to about 60.[2] Eight years later one of the gild
ordinances was sworn to by 135 goldsmiths [3]—a remarkable number, considering that the total population of
London was then about 40,000. It is not surprising,
therefore, that the goldsmiths took a prominent part in
the struggle of the trading gilds against the victualling
gilds (headed by the fishmongers), which is the chief
feature of London municipal history during the first
half of the reign of Richard II.[4]

It was in this reign that the goldsmiths were incorporated and became the first of the City Companies under
royal charter in 1393.[5] Their wealth and popularity
at this time are shown by the premiums which they were
able to exact from apprentices, namely a minimum of
100s. for a ten years' apprenticeship and 10 marks
(£6 13s. 4d.) for one of seven years.[6] While, generally
speaking, the Company was concerned with the control
of trade and the maintenance of discipline and of a high
standard of workmanship, it is clear that it occasionally
undertook work in its corporate capacity, as in 1475
the Company of Goldsmiths made the shrine of St. Os-
mund for Salisbury Cathedral.[7]

The great religious houses were foremost patrons of
the craft, many of them, as the Abbey of St. Albans,

---

[1] Prideaux, *Mems. of Goldsmiths' Company*, 4.
[2] *Ibid.*, 5.   [3] *Ibid.*, 7.
[4] Unwin, *Gilds of London*, c. vi.   [5] *Ibid.*, 159.
[6] Prideaux, *op. cit.*, 15.   [7] Herbert, *op. cit.*, 185.

numbering amongst their inmates artists of great repute.
The famous college of Beverley included a goldsmith in
its household,[1] but in 1292, when it was determined to
erect a new shrine for the relics of St. John of Beverley,
the chapter did not entrust the work to their own craftsman, but sent up to London to the establishment of
William Faringdon, the greatest goldsmith of that time.
The contract between his servant, Roger of Faringdon,

St. Eligius making a silver shrine. 15th cent.

and the Chapter of Beverley is still extant.[2] By it the
chapter were to provide the necessary silver and gold ;
Roger was to refine it, if needful, and to supply his own
coals, quicksilver, and other materials. The shrine was
to be 5 ft. 6 in. long, 1 ft. 6 in. broad, and of proportion-
ate height : the design was to be architectural in style,
and the statuettes, the number and size of which were
to be at the discretion of the chapter, were to be of
cunning and beautiful work, the chapter reserving the
right to reject any figure or ornament and cause it to
be remade. For his work Roger was to receive the weight

[1] *Beverley Chapter Act Book* (Surtees Soc.), ii. lxv.
[2] *Cal. of City of London Letter Books*, A, 180.

in silver of the shrine when completed, before gilding. No very general rule can be laid down as to the proportion between the intrinsic value or weight of metal and the cost of workmanship, but roughly in the case of simple articles of plate the cost of manufacture may be set at

GOLDSMITH'S ROW, CHEAPSIDE, 1547

approximately half the weight. Thus in the case of the plate presented by the City to the Black Prince on his return from Gascony in 1371 [1] we find six chargers, weight £14 18s. 9d., amounting with the making to £21 7s. 2d. ; twelve 'hanappes', or handled cups, weight £8 12s., amounting to £12 7s. 7d. ; and thirty saltcellars, weighing £15 6s. 2d., amounting to £21 17s. 8d. The charge for making silver basins and lavers in the

[1] Riley, *Mems. of London*, 350.

same list amounts to about two-thirds of the weight. The rate appears to have remained fairly constant, as in 1416 William Randolf made four dozen chargers and eight dozen dishes of silver for King Henry V at 30s. the pound.[1]

· The demand for silver plate during the later mediaeval period must have been brisk, for every house of any

THE ROCHESTER MAZER

pretension had its service of plate standing on the cupboard or dresser. Nothing more astonished the Venetian travellers in England in 1500 than this extraordinary profusion and display; they noted that,[2] 'In one single street, named the Strand, are 52 goldsmiths' shops[3] so rich and full of silver vessels, great and small, that in all the shops in Milan, Rome, Venice, and Florence put together I do not think there would be found so many of the magnificence that are to be seen in London. And

[1] Foreign R., 4 Hen. V, m. A.

[2] *Camden Soc.*, xxxvii. 42.

[3] For an inventory of a jeweller's goods, valued at over £600, in 1398, see Riley, *Mems. of London*, 550; cf. *ibid.*, 455, 470.

these vessels are all either saltcellars or drinking-cups
or basins to hold water for the hands, for they eat off
that fine tin which is
little inferior to
silver.' Although the
home of the gold-
smiths is here stated
to be the Strand,
their chief centre was
in Lombard Street
and in Cheapside,
where, just about the
time that this Vene-
tian account was
written, Thomas
Wood built Gold-
smiths' Row, with its
ten fair houses and
fourteen shops and
its four-storied front
adorned with allusive
wild men of the wood
riding on monstrous
beasts.[1] The charter
of 1327, already re-
ferred to, set forth

Bronze jug of the time of Richard II

that hitherto the goldsmiths had all kept to ' the high
street of Cheap ', where alone gold and silver ought to
be sold, but that now many goldsmiths had set up in
obscure streets, where they bought stolen plate and
made false jewellery. At a later date, in the fifteenth

[1] Chaffers, *Gilda Aurifabrorum*, 38.

century, many of these fraudulent craftsmen established themselves in the sanctuaries or privileged districts round St. Martin-le-Grand and St. Bartholomew's, where they were exempt from the ordinary jurisdiction of the City. On one occasion the wardens of the Company went to the Prior of St. Bartholomew's and complained of the mal-practices of John Tom-kins, a clever but fraudu-lent goldsmith; the prior took them to Tomkins's room, where they found bands of latten (a kind of bronze) for use on bowls and, hidden in the bed straw, a piece of copper, all of which had been sil-vered over.[1] The plating of base metal and the use of silver below the standard of the Mint had been for-bidden in the earliest surviving ordinances of the gold-smiths, in 1238,[2] in order that customers should know exactly what they were getting for their money. With the same object an ordinance in 1370 [3] forbade the use of hollow work for rings and buckles, the setting of false jewels in gold or (except in the case of church work) of real stones in copper or latten, or the placing of tinfoil

THE PEWTERER. 16th cent.

---

[1] Herbert, *Hist. of Livery Companies*, ii. 179.
[2] Close R., 22 Hen. III, m. 7.
[3] Prideaux, *Mems. of Goldsmiths' Co.*, 9.

behind real stones—a method of increasing their lustre that was in later times regarded as legitimate. The records of the Company show that all types of fraud were, as we might expect, at least as numerous in this profitable craft as in the poorer trades, and explain the necessity of keeping the craftsmen together in a main street where they were under the eye of the public and more especially of the Company.

Next in interest and importance among the metal-working crafts stands that of the PEWTERERS. And, indeed, in some respects this craft might take precedence of goldsmithery, for, while the working of gold and silver was an art which England shared with the rest of Europe, the working of pewter was an essentially English art and one which brought considerable fame and wealth to the country. In the Venetian account quoted in the last paragraph pewter is referred to as ' that fine tin which is little inferior to silver ', and the terms tin and pewter are often used indiscriminately for the alloy. Harrison,[1] writing early in the reign of Elizabeth, says : ' Our pewterers . . . have grown unto such exquisite cunning that they can in manner imitate by infusion any form or fashion of cup, dish, salt, bowl, or goblet which is made by goldsmiths' craft. . . . Such furniture of household of this metal as we commonly call by the name of vessel is sold usually by the garnish,[2] which doth contain twelve platters, twelve dishes, twelve saucers, and those are either of silver fashion or else with broad or narrow brims and bought by the pound, which is now

[1] *Description of England,* bk. iii, c. 18.

[2] Mention of ' half a garnish of pewder ' in a will of 1477—just a century before Harrison's *Description* was published : *Ripon Chapter Acts* (Surtees Soc.), i. 179.

valued at six or seven pence or peradventure eightpence.
. . . It consisteth of a composition which hath thirty
pounds of kettle brass to a thousand pounds of tin,
whereunto they add three or four pounds of tin-glass ; [1]
but as too much of this doth make the stuff brickle, so
the more the brass be the better is the pewter. . . . In
some places beyond the
sea a garnish of good flat
English pewter . . . is
esteemed almost so pre-
cious as the like number
of vessels that are made
of fine silver.'

The importance and
extent of the foreign trade
in pewter vessels is shown
by the customs accounts
of the fifteenth and six-
teenth centuries, and by
Soranzo's report to the
Venetian Senate in 1554,
in which he states that
100,000 ducats worth of

BASIN-MAKERS. 16th cent.

wrought tin were exported yearly, mostly to Spain.[2]
Injury to our foreign trade, with consequent unemployment and loss of wealth to the nation, was
also the chief argument put forward by the pewterers
in 1533 when pleading, successfully, for protection.
They stated that their craft had suffered through the
unpatriotic action of certain men who had gone abroad

[1] i. e. bismuth. The proportion of brass to tin appears to be
too small ; see below.   [2] *Cal. S. P. Venice,* v. 543.

and taught the trade secrets to aliens, so that much tin-ware, often of bad quality, was now imported. As a result of their petition the purchase of such foreign wares was forbidden, and it was ordered that no alien should be received as an apprentice and that any English pewterer going abroad or failing to return at once should lose his rights of nationality and be accounted an alien.[1]

Thirty years earlier the powers of parliament had been invoked to protect honest pewterers and their customers from the frauds of wandering hawkers and pedlars, who went about the country buying stolen metal and selling vessels made of bad pewter. The sale of pewter and brass was, therefore, restricted to fairs, markets, and shops; all pewter was to be of the standard used in London, including ' hollow ware ', such as saltcellars and pots, made of ' Ley metell '.[2] Searchers, or inspectors, were to be appointed by the wardens of the pewterers' gilds, in boroughs where such gilds existed, or by the Justices of the Peace; and all vessels were to bear their maker's mark.[3] The London standard was that laid down in the ordinances of the Pewterers drawn up in 1348.[4] Flat vessels, such as dishes of all sorts, cruets, chrismatories, &c., of a square shape, were to be made of fine pewter, containing 26 lb. of copper to a hundredweight of tin; round cruets, pots, candlesticks, &c., were to be of pewter containing the same proportion of lead to tin.

Not only was the standard of London adopted through-

---

[1] Stat. 25 Hen. VIII, c. 9. [2] i. e. pewter containing lead.
[3] Stat. 19 Hen. VII, c. 6.
[4] Welch, *Hist. of Pewterers' Co.*, 3 ; Riley, *Mems. of London*, 242.

out the country, but the rules of the London gild were taken over bodily by the pewterers' gild at York, which ranked as the second centre of the trade, in 1416.[1] Moreover, the London gild—or rather Company, for the pewterers had been incorporated by royal charter in 1468—exercised the right of search and forfeiture of bad material throughout the country in 1474, at which time many provincial pewterers were enrolled therein.[2] Nor was the composition of the metal the only point regulated; in 1438 an elaborate assize of weights of different articles was drawn up : these include chargers, in various sizes from 7 pounds down to $2\frac{3}{4}$, platters, from 30 pounds the dozen down to 22 pounds, dishes, saucers, ' the Cardinals hatte and saucers,' Florentine dishes and saucers, bowls and various types of salt-cellars.[3] The price of workmanship was also fixed, in 1483, at 8s. the hundredweight for ' Normandy potts ', &c., and at 7s. for ' howssold potts, mesure potts and four-penny, three-penny and twopenny ware '.[4]

Closely allied to the pewterers by the nature of their craft were the FOUNDERS, of whom the potters (makers of brass pots), latoners (workers of latten—a variety of brass in common use in mediaeval times), and copper-smiths were specialized branches which occasionally maintained an independent existence as separate gilds. Two other branches of the founders' craft—the casting of bells and of guns—are of sufficient historic interest and importance to justify their being treated separately,

---

[1] *Memorandum Book of York* (Surtees Soc.), i. xli.
[2] Welch, *Hist. of Pewterers' Co.*, 43.   [3] *Ibid.*, 11, 12.
[4] *Ibid.*, 57. For an inventory of a pewterer's tools, including moulds, hammers, anvils, ' pryntes ' or dies, &c., see *London Letter Book K*, 65 ; also *Test. Ebor.* (Surtees Soc.), ii. ccxv.

but apart from these the only feature to which attention need be called is the great artistic and technical ability displayed by members of the craft in the execution of memorial figures for tombs. As early as 1257 we find Master Simon de Welles sent for to come to Westminster to make a figure of gilt bronze for the tomb of Katherine, the infant daughter of Henry III ; [1] though, as a matter of fact, the king changed his mind and caused William of Gloucester, the court goldsmith, to make a silver image instead.[2] The existing figures of Queen Eleanor of Castile and Henry III, both cast by William Torel, and that of Edward III, probably by John Orchard, are magnificent examples. In the case of the effigies of Richard II and his queen we have the specification for the figures to be made of copper and latten, gilded, ' with their right hands clasped and their left hands holding sceptres,' and the bill of £700 (say £9,000 of modern money) paid to Nicholas Croker and Godfrey Prest, citizen coppersmiths of London, for materials, labour, and the hire of two buildings in the parish of St. Alban's, Wood Street, where they worked at the monument for four years.[3] Another London coppersmith, William Godeyer, was paid £43 by Henry V in 1413 towards the making of an image of the king's mother to be placed over her tomb in the college of Leicester.[4]

References to BELLS [5] during Saxon times are not infrequent, but probably the earliest notice connected with their manufacture is the entry amongst the tenants of

---

[1] Liberate R., K. R., 41 Hen. III, m. 5.   [2] *Ibid.*, m. 4.

[3] Foreign R., 3 Hen. IV, m. E.

[4] Devon, *Issues of Exch.*, 321.

[5] *Church Bells of England,* by H. B. Walters, contains much valuable matter.

Battle Abbey in the late eleventh century of 'Aedric who cast the bells *(qui signa fundebat)*'.[1] It is likely that most early monastic peals were cast in the immediate neighbourhood of the monastery by, or under the supervision of, the brethren. But in the twelfth century, when Ralph Breton gave money to Rochester Cathedral Priory for a bell, in memory of his brother, the sacrist sent a broken bell up to London to be recast.[2] Possibly the craftsman who recast this bell was the Alwold 'campanarius' who was working in London about 1150.[3] Another early bell-founder was Beneit le Seynter, sheriff of London in 1216.[4] Mr. Stahlschmidt interprets this founder's name as 'ceinturier' or girdler, and there was at Worcester in the thirteenth century a family whose members bore indifferently the name of 'Ceynturer' and 'Belleyeter'.[5] The demand for bells could hardly have been large enough to enable a craftsman to specialize entirely in that branch; a bell-maker would always have been primarily a founder, and according as the main portion of his trade lay in casting buckles and other fittings for belts, or pots, or bells, he would be known as a girdler, a potter, or a bell-founder.[6] On the other hand, M. Fagniez says that 'sainterius', the title applied to Thomas de Claville, who recast a bell for Notre Dame in 1397, is 'fait sur le vieux nom français des cloches *saints* . . . qui se rattache à *signa*'.[7] This is borne out by the

---

[1] *Chron. Battle Abbey* (ed. Lower), 17.

[2] Cott. MS. Vesp. A, 22, f. 88.

[3] Stahlschmidt, *London Bell-founders*, 72.   [4] *Ibid.*, 3.

[5] Ex. inf. Mr. C. H. Vellacott, from Assize Roll.

[6] Most of the London founders recorded by Mr. Stahlschmidt as known or possible bell-founders used the title 'potter'.— *Loc. cit.*, 72–4.   [7] *Docts. relatifs à l'histoire de l'Industrie*, ii. 67.

fact that in 1250 four bells for the chapel of Windsor Castle were made, out of material left over from the casting of the great bell of Westminster, by Master John le Seynter,[1] and that two years later 1,000 pounds of copper and 500 pounds of tin, together with the metal of a broken bell, were given to Master Hugh le Seinter to make three new bells for the chapel of Dover Castle.[2]

The mediaeval English term for a bell-founder was 'bellyeter' (surviving in London as 'Billiter Street', the former centre of the industry), derived from the Anglo-Saxon *geotan*, to pour : the word is occasionally found used independently as a verb, the agreement for casting a bell for Stansfield in 1453 stipulating that it should be 'wele and sufficiantly yette and made'.[3] So far as the process itself is concerned,[4] it remained unchanged in its main features until comparatively recent times, and a considerable number of records relating to bell-founding have survived and throw a little light upon the details of the art. The first step was the formation of the 'core', an exact model of the inside of the bell, formed of clay. This was done on a rude form of lathe, the clay being placed in successive layers round a wooden bar which could be rotated between uprights. When the core had been turned into the required shape it was removed from the lathe, the bar was withdrawn, a large part of the clay was cut out from the inside, leaving it hollow—in order both to reduce the weight and to enable it to be baked through. The

[1] Hope, *Windsor Castle*, 57.

[2] Liberate R., 36 Hen. III, m. 12.

[3] Early Chanc. Proc., 24, no. 138.

[4] Particulars are given in Raven, *Bells of England*, on which this account is based.

iron staple on which the clapper was to hang was then fixed in the top of the core, inside and round which a fire was then lit. When it had been hardened by baking, the ' thickness ', corresponding exactly to the projected bell itself, was built up upon the core ; finally, over the ' thickness ' was built a thick clay ' cope '. Originally, it would seem, it was usual to make the ' thickness ' of wax, or tallow, which, melting upon the application of heat, ran out and left the space between the core and cope vacant for the molten metal to flow into : possibly some of the early uninscribed bells which still exist may have been formed in this fashion, but it seems clear that from the end of the thirteenth century the use of wax was abandoned in England, the ' thickness ' being made of loam or earth.[1] The clay cope, moulded over this, was carefully raised by a crane, the ' thickness ' destroyed, and the cope readjusted, after any inscription or other decoration had been stamped on its inner surface. In order that the metal might flow directly from the furnace into the mould, the latter lay in a pit in front of the furnace and, to prevent the cope breaking under the pressure of the molten metal, the pit was filled up with earth, leaving only a hole at the top of the cope for the entry of the metal. The furnace doors being opened, the metal, consisting of a mixture of copper and tin, flowed into the mould. If the metal was not in a sufficiently fluid state, or if any check occurred, the caster would ' lose his labour and expense ', as happened to Henry Michel when he recast the great bell of Croxden Abbey in 1313,

[1] To prevent the core, thickness, and cope sticking together, it seems to have been usual to dust them over with tan.

and the work would have to be done all over again.[1]
But if the work had been properly carried out, the
completed bell had to be tuned, unless, as was the case
at St. Laurence's, Reading, in 1596, ' not so much the
tune of the bell was cared for as to have it a loud bell
and heard far '.[2]

The tuning was done by grinding or cutting down
the rim of the bell if the note was too flat, or by reducing
its thickness, filing down the inner surface of the sound
bow, if the note was too sharp.   In order to reduce
the amount of tuning required, it was necessary to know
approximately the relation between size, or weight, and
tone, and as early as the reign of Henry III a monk of
Evesham, Walter of Odyngton, devised a system by
which each bell was to weigh eight-ninths of the bell
next above it in weight.[3]   This system, delightfully
simple in theory, could not have yielded satisfactory
results in practice, and it is probable that most founders
had their own systems, based upon experience and
practical observation.   The question of whether a bell
was correctly in tune with the others of the peal was
one which naturally led to occasional disputes.   When
Robert Gildesburgh, brazier, of London, a fifteenth-
century bell-founder, cast two bells for Whitchurch in
Dorset, the vicar refused to pay for them, as he said
they were out of tune.   Gildesburgh requested that they
should be submitted to the judgement of Adam Bugge-
berd, rector of South Petherton, who accordingly came
over and heard them rung, and decided that there was
no fault in them.[4]   At Mendlesham in 1574 the sum of

[1] Raven, *op. cit.*, 74.
[2] *V. C. H. Berks.*, ii. 418.
[3] Raven, *op. cit.*, 57.
[4] Early Chanc. Proc., 68, no. 144.

3s. 8d. was paid ' to the musicion that came to bring the sound of the bell '.[1] In the case of the bells recast for the church of St. Mary-at-Hill, London, in 1510,[2] we have first an entry of 6½d. paid ' for Reves labour and his brekefast for comyng from Ludgate to Algate to here the iiij bell in tewne ' ; and then, as apparently the churchwardens were not satisfied with his report, 8d.

paid ' for wyne and peres at Skran's howse at Algate for Mr. Jentyll, Mr. Russell, John Althorpe, John Condall and the clarkes of saynt Antonys to go and see whether smythes bell wer tewneabill or not '. Possibly the decision in the case of this fourth bell cast by William Smith was not satisfactory, as the ' great bell ' seems to

Bishop consecrating a bell.
15th cent.

have been entrusted to William Culverden, a contemporary founder, many of whose bells, bearing his rebus of the culver or wood pigeon, still exist.

The bell having been fitted with an iron clapper, swung from a staple inside the crown of the bell by a leathern baudrick, was fastened on to a massive wooden stock furnished at its ends with gudgeons, or iron pivots, to work in the bronze sockets of the frame, and was now ready to be hung in the belfry. But although it was now a finished ' trade article ', there was yet one more process

[1] *Hist. MSS. Com. Rep.,* v. 593.
[2] *Ch. Ward. Accts., St. Mary-at-Hill* (E. E. T. S.).

to be undergone before it could summon the faithful
to church : it was usual, though apparently by no means
universal, for the bells to be blessed. Thus the bells
of St. Albans Abbey were consecrated in the middle of
the twelfth century by the Bishop of St. Asaph ; [1] and
a detailed account of the dedication of the great bell
called ' Jesus ' at Lichfield Cathedral in 1477 has been
preserved.[2] In the case of the five bells of St. Michael's,
Bishop's Stortford, recast by Reginald Chirche of Bury
St. Edmunds in 1489 at a cost of £42, an extra 17s. 6d.
was paid ' for their consecration (*pro sanctificacione*) '.[3]
That the dedication ceremony included a form analogous
to baptism is clearly shown by an entry in the accounts
of St. Laurence, Reading, where, in 1508, we find ' paid
for hallowing the great bell named Harry 6s. 8d. And
over that Sir William Symys Richard Clich and Mistress
Smyth being godfather and godmother at the conse-
cracyon of the same bell, and bearing all the costs to
the suffragan '.[4]

Of the early centres of the industry London was
naturally the most important. Two early bell-founders
of this city have already been mentioned, but it is noteworthy, as showing that to a certain extent a man might
be ' jack of all trades ' even if he was master of one,
that several bells were cast for Westminster Abbey by
Edward Fitz Odo, the famous goldsmith of Henry III.[5]
That monarch, a patron of all the arts, granted 100s.
yearly to the bell-ringers' gild of Westminster for ringing

[1] Raven, *op. cit.*, 47. [2] *Ibid.*, 319.

[3] *Recs. of St. Michael's*. See also *Ch. Wardens Accts.* (Somerset
Rec. Soc.).

[4] *V. C. H. Berks.*, ii. 416. Cf. H. B. Walters, *Church Bells of
England*, ch. xii.

[5] Toulmin Smith, *English Gilds*, 295.

the great bells.[1] Mr. Stahlschmidt has shown that the
centre of the bell-founding trade was round Aldgate and
in the neighbourhood of St. Andrew Undershaft and
St. Botolph-without-Aldgate,[2] while amongst the more
prominent early founders were the family of Wimbish
at the beginning of the fourteenth century and the
Burfords at the end of the same century. Contemporary
with these last was William Founder, whose trade stamp,
bearing his name and a representation of two birds on
a conventionalized tree, occurs on a number of bells and
hints at his real surname, which, although it has hitherto
eluded historians, was clearly Wodeward. Mr. Stahlschmidt [3] noticed the entry on the Issue Rolls of 1385
recording the purchase of twelve cannon from William
'the founder', but did not notice that the very next
year sixty cannon were bought from William Wodeward,[4] while in 1417 other cannon were provided by
William Wodeward, founder.[5]

Amongst the provincial centres we may notice
Gloucester, where Hugh Bellyetare occurs about 1270,
and John Belyetere in 1346,[6] the latter being presumably
the Master John of Gloucester who with his staff of
six men came to Ely in 1342 to cast four bells for Prior
Walsingham.[7] A later bell-founder of some eminence
at Gloucester was William Henshawe, who was mayor
in 1503, 1508, and 1509.[8] Another of the craft who

---

[1] Raven, *op. cit.*, 69.
[2] *London Bell-founders*, 3.
[3] *Ibid.*, 45.
[4] *Issue R. of Exch.*, 239.
[5] *Ibid.*, 346.
[6] *Glouc. Corporation Recs.*
[7] *Sacrist Rolls of Ely*, ii. 114, 138, where details of the outlay in
the purchase of tin and copper and of clay for the moulds and other
necessaries are given.   [8] Raven, *op. cit.*, 149.

obtained more than local reputation was John de Stafford, mayor of Leicester in 1366 and 1370,[1] who was called in by the chapter of York to cast bells for the Minster in 1371.[2] This is the more remarkable as York was itself a centre of the industry, the most famous of its founders being Richard Tunnoc, who represented the city in Parliament in 1327, and dying in 1330, left behind him as a worthy memorial ' the bell-maker's window ' in York Minster.[3] In the central panel of this window Richard Tunnoc himself is shown kneeling before a sainted archbishop; the two other panels show the process of bell - making. In the one the master workman is supervising the flow of the metal into the mould from a furnace, the

Part of Bell-founder's window,
York Minster. 14th cent.

---

[1] Raven, *op. cit.*, 90.

[2] *Fabric Rolls* (Surtees Soc.), 9. Details are given.

[3] Raven, *op. cit.*, where illustrations of the three panels are given.

draught of which is supplied by bellows worked by two young men, the one standing upon them with one foot on each and the other holding the handles. The remaining panel is usually said to represent the moulding of the clay core, but it seems to me more likely to represent the finishing, smoothing, and polishing of the completed bell.[1] Richard Tunnoc is shown seated, holding a long crooked instrument (resembling a very large boomerang), and applying it with great care to the surface of the bell, or core, which an assistant is rotating on a primitive lathe consisting of two trestles and a crooked handle. The space round each panel is filled with rows of bells swinging in trefoiled niches.

The number of churches in the larger towns being much greater in mediaeval times than at the present day, and few of these churches being content with a single bell, most of the chief towns, and in particular those possessing cathedrals or important monasteries, had their resident bell-founders. In the case of Exeter, Bishop Peter de Quivil, about 1285, assured the proper care of the bells of the cathedral by granting a small property in Paignton to Robert le Bellyetere as a retaining fee, Robert and his heirs being bound to make or repair, when necessary, the bells, organs, and clock of the cathedral, the chapter paying all expenses, including the food and drink of the workmen ; and these obligations were duly fulfilled for at least three generations, Robert, son of Walter, son of the original Robert, still holding

[1] If the bell-shaped object is really the core, the ornamentation upon it must be ascribed to ' artist's licence ', as the surface of the core would in reality be quite plain.

the land on the same terms in 1315.[1] Canterbury was another local centre of the trade, and from Canterbury came the founder who in 1345 cast a couple of bells at Dover, the one weighing 3,266 lb., and the other 1,078 lb., for each of which he was paid at the rate of a halfpenny the pound.[2] In East Anglia there was an important foundry at the monastic town of Bury St.

Edmunds, one of the fifteenth-century founders using as his trade mark a shield, which is interesting as bearing on it not only a bell, but also a cannon with a ball issuing from its mouth. Norwich, again, with its seventy churches and its cathedral priory, was a busy centre of the industry. One of the later Norwich founders, Richard Brasier, seems to have been more skilful than straightforward and to have devoted some of his skill

Trade-mark of founders of Bury St. Edmunds. 15th cent.

to evading his obligations. In 1454 the churchwardens of Stansfield bargained with him to cast a bell for their church, half payment to be made on delivery and the other half at the expiration of a year and a day if the bell proved satisfactory, but if it did not he was to cast a new bell for them; he, however, taking advantage

---

[1] Inq. ad qd. damnum, File 108, no. 15.

[2] Exch. K. R. Accts., 462, no. 16. Amongst the items of expenditure are ' For eggs and ale bought for making the inscription round the bell 3*d*. For wax and cobbler's wax (*code*) for the same 5½*d*.' Possibly a mixture of eggs and ale was used to anoint the metal letter stamps and prevent their sticking to the clay of the cope.

of their being unlearned men, caused the latter clause
to be omitted from the indenture, and when the bell
proved unsatisfactory refused to make a fresh one.[1]
A few years later, in 1468, the parishioners of Mildenhall
brought an action against him for breach of contract.
It had been agreed that the great bell of Mildenhall
should be brought by the parishioners to ' the werkhous '
of the said Richard Brasier and
weighed by them, and that Brasier
should then cast from the metal of
the old bell a new tenor bell in tune
with the others then in the church
steeple, and should warrant it, as
was customary, for a year and a
day, and if it were not satisfactory
should at his own expense take it
back to Norwich ' to be yoten '.
They had duly carried the bell to
his workshop, but he had not cast
it; in defence his counsel urged that

Trade-mark of the
Brasiers of Norwich.
15th cent.

although they had brought it they had not weighed it,
and that until they did so he was not bound to cast
it. On the other side it was argued that the point was
frivolous, that he could have weighed it himself, and
that indeed the indenture implied that it was to be
weighed and put into the furnace by his men in the
presence of the men of Mildenhall.[2] A jury was summoned, but did not appear, and the case was adjourned.

The suppression of the monasteries, followed by the

---

[1] Early Chanc. Proc., 24, no. 138.
[2] De Banco, 831, m. 414 ; and Raven, *op. cit.*, 164–6, quoting
Year Book 9 Edw. IV, Easter Term, case 13.

seizure of Church goods, including large numbers of
bells, formed the rude termination of the mediaeval
period of the industry, and may be symbolized by the
death of William Corvehill, formerly subprior of Wenlock, ' a good bell founder and maker of the frame for
bells ', at Wenlock in 1546.[1]

We have seen that a cannon is shown on the shield
used as a trade mark by a fifteenth-century Suffolk
bell-founder, and the casting of ORDNANCE may rank
with the casting of bells as one of the most interesting
and important branches of the founder's craft. Cannon
seem to have been introduced into England at the beginning of the reign of Edward III. In 1339 there were
in the Guildhall ' six instruments of latten called gonnes
and five roleres for the same. Also pellets of lead weighing $4\frac{1}{2}$ cwt. for the same instruments. Also 32 lb. of
powder for the same '.[2] This same year guns are recorded
to have been used by the English at the siege of Cambrai,
and they were also used at Creçy in 1346. In 1345 there
were among the military stores provided for the French
campaign certain ' gunnis ', which shot quarrels and
lead balls, and no less than a hundred ' small machines
called ribaldis '[3]—apparently an early form of the
ribaudkins, or clustered guns, precursors of the maxim
and gatling guns of the nineteenth century. Next year
we find a reference to 10 guns *cum telariis*,[4] presumably
short bronze pieces with long wooden stocks, of the type
referred to in 1373, when payments were made to
a joiner ' for helving 8 guns '.[5] In this same account
of 1346 there is also mention of ' hand machines called

---

[1] *V. C. H. Shrops.*, i. 47.   [2] Riley, *Mems. of London*, 205.
[3] *Engl. Hist. Rev.*, xxvi. 689.   [4] *Ibid.*. 689.   [5] *Ibid.*, 693.

BOMBARD AND CANNONS. 15th cent.

gunnys,' and hand guns are evidently implied in the
account of the muster of Mancroft Leet in Norwich
in 1355, to which Adam de Porynglond and John
Spicer each brought *gunarium cum pulvere* (a gun with
powder).[1] In 1353 four guns of copper, made and worked
by William de Algate, brasier, were purchased at 13*s*. 4*d*.
each,[2] and in 1361 a small copper gun was bought by
the king from John Brasier of Cornhill as a present for
his son Sir Lionel.[3] Two large and nine small 'gunnes'
of copper were provided for Sheppey Castle in 1365 ; [4]
but these were not necessarily of native manufacture,
though a small gun sent over to Ireland in 1360 is said
to have been bought in London,[5] and had probably been
made there. In 1385, however, the sheriff of Cumberland
included in his account of repairs to the castle of Carlisle
' costs incurred in making three brass cannons which are
in the said castle ', [6] and in the same year ' William
Founder ', as we saw when considering his work as
a bell-founder, provided twelve guns. Next year the
same William Wodeward made no less than sixty cannon
for Calais.[7] Details of his account [8] show that some fifty
of these averaged about 300 lb. weight, four were half
that weight and the others about 70 lb. ; there was also
a remarkable ' large cannon ' with eleven barrels, of
which one, presumably in the middle, was of large
calibre for firing stone balls, and the other ten, clustered
round it, fired balls (of lead) or quarrels, the total weight
of this ingenious machine, without the great balk of

---

[1] *Norfolk Arch.*, xiv. 294.
[2] *Engl. Hist. Rev.* xxvi. 691.   [3] *Ibid.*, 692.
[4] Enrolled Wardrobe Accts., no. 4.   [5] *Ibid.*
[6] Foreign R., 9 Ric. II, m. A.
[7] Foreign R., 11 Ric. II, m. H.   [8] *Engl. Hist. Rev.* xxvi. 697.

timber on which it was mounted, being 665 lb. Stephen atte Marsshe at the same time supplied nine cannons of iron. Another London gunmaker of the period seems to have been Nicholas Herbert, from whom in 1384 William Spicer bought a gun at a cost of £11 for the city of Norwich.[1] The municipality of Norwich were at this

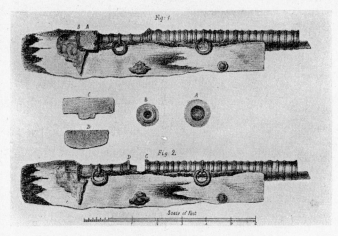

Hooped cannon, from the *Mary Rose*, sunk in 1545 [2]

time providing fire-arms for the defence of the city; but this was the only large piece bought, the other 51 guns, for which various individuals and groups of citizens were assessed, being small mobile pieces of from 16 to 24 inches in length. As Wodeward was still providing

[1] *Norf. Arch.*, xvi. 46.
[2] Fig. 1, elevation of gun with chamber forced up; the chock A and iron wedge B in rear of it. Fig. 2, elevation with chamber drawn back for loading, the chock and wedge removed. A, transverse section of gun at C; B, transverse section of chamber at D; C, elevation of chock A; D, elevation of wedge B.

ordnance in 1416,[1] we may possibly identify him with 'Master William Gunmaker', who made several small cannon in 1411, two of them being of iron.[2]

The early cannon were made of bronze of a similar composition to that used for bells, and when iron was introduced the cannon of that material were made in the form of a tube composed of long iron bars, arranged like the staves of a barrel, bound round with iron bands : the tough wrought iron was of good quality, but the weakness of this form of construction lay in the difficulty of welding the bars together and avoiding gaps between them. They were all breech-loaders, consisting of two separate parts, the barrel and the chamber ; the latter being a short cylinder, usually detachable, in which the charge of gunpowder was placed, and which was then fastened into the base of the barrel by means of a stirrup or similar apparatus. Double-barrelled cannon appear to have been fairly common, as in 1401 eight single cannon and six double (*duplices*) were sent to Dover Castle, and the same numbers to Scotland.[3] An inventory of the artillery at Berwick-on-Tweed taken at the same time [4] distinguishes between guns ' imbedded in timber bound with iron ' and ' naked ' guns ; it also mentions ' two small brass guns on wooden sticks, called handgonnes '. The same inventory refers to ' quarells for gonnes ' ; and in the previous year Henry Robertes, serjeant, dwelling near the Guildhall, was paid £8 8s. for twenty-four ' quarell gunnes ',[5] these being guns which threw quarrels or bolts similar to

[1] *Issue R. of Exch.*, 346.   [2] Foreign R., 3 Hen. V, m. C.
[3] Foreign R., 3 Hen. IV, m. G.   [4] *Ibid.*, m. I.
[5] *Issue R. of Exch.*, 277.

those used with crossbows.[1]   At the battle of St. Albans
in 1461 guns were used shooting ' arowes of an elle of
length '.[2]   The usual projectiles employed in the larger
guns were round stone balls, such as had been in use for
mangonels and catapults since the days of the Romans,
and these were supplied from the quarries of Maidstone
and elsewhere down to the time of Henry VIII.   Iron
' gunstones ' do not seem to have been made much
before the end of the fifteenth century, and the ' wooden
balls for cannon ', of which there were 350 at Dover in
1387,[3] can hardly have proved successful, but lead was
commonly employed for the smaller guns from an early
date.

London was the chief centre of the manufacture of
ordnance, but an iron cannon was made at Bristol in
1408,[4] and five years later John Stevenes of Bristol
was ordered to supervise the making of another.[5]   Just
over a century later, in 1518, Thomas Batcock of Bristol
supervised the making of a culverin for Henry VIII,
which was cast by a Genoese founder at Fontarabia in
Spain.   The details given show that the process was
very similar to that employed in bell-founding.   The

[1] An illustration of a gun firing an arrow, drawn in 1326, occurs
in the splendid manuscript of W. de Milemete's *De Nobilitatibus
Regum*, published in photographic facsimile by the Roxburghe Club.
The cannon is shown as shaped like a flask and resting on a rough
wooden stool-like mount; it is probably drawn from descriptions
rather than from an actual specimen.

[2] *Gregory's Chron.* (Camd. Soc.), 213.   ' Musquet arrowes ' were
still in store at the Tower in 1599.—*Arch. Journ.*, lxviii. 66.

[3] Foreign R., 11 Ric. II, m. G.

[4] Foreign R., 3 Hen. V, m. C.   Guns were bought at Bristol for
the city of Coventry in 1450.—*Coventry Leet Bk.*, 260.

[5] *Issue R. of Exch.*, 332.

M

core, or ' heart ', of clay, owing to its long narrow shape, had to be strengthened by an iron bar, and the outer mould, corresponding to the cope of the bell, seems also to have been bound round with iron. The king's arms and other designs on the culverin were modelled in wax. After the culverin—which was a bronze 14-pounder— had been hauled up out of the pit in which it was cast, it had to be finished off internally by boring.[1]

Early bombard or mortar.
15th cent.

In 1408 ' a certain great cannon newly invented by the king himself ' was made ; [2] this presumably was ' the great iron cannon called Kyngesdoughter ', which shortly after its birth was broken at the siege of Harlech.[3] The ' Kyngesdoughter ' was probably made at the Tower, as were three other iron cannon at the same time, four more being made in Southwark and two smaller ones by Anthony Gunner, possibly at Worcester, as one of them was tested there and broke during the trial ; of six bronze cannon made at the same time, the largest, the ' Messager ', weighing 4,480 lb., and two small ones were broken at the siege of Aberystwith. The life of a gun in those days seems to have been short, and that of a gunner precarious.[4] In 1496, when

[1] *L. & P. Hen. VIII*, ii. 4108.   [2] *Issue R. of Exch.*, 307–8.
[3] Foreign R., 3 Hen. V, m. C.
[4] In the Scottish expedition of 1496, five out of thirty-two ' faucons of brasse ', and twelve out of one hundred and eighty

the Government range was at Mile End, 13s. 4d. was
given to Blase Ballard, gunner, ' towards his leche craft
of his hands and face lately hurte at Myles ende by
fortune shoting of a gunne,' [1] and this is not the only
hint we have that these weapons were sometimes as
dangerous to their users as to the enemy.

The Germans and Dutch were particularly expert in
the manufacture of guns, and we find Matthew de Vlenk
' gonnemaker ' in the service of Richard II,[2] while
Godfrey Goykyn, one of four ' gunnemeystres ' from
Germany, who were serving Henry V during the last
years of his reign,[3] was employed in 1433 to finish off
three great iron cannon which Walter Thomasson had
begun to make.[4] These cannon threw balls of fourteen,
sixteen, and eighteen inches diameter, respectively, so
that presumably they were ' bombards ' or mortars, and
probably similar in type to one found in the moat of
Bodiam Castle, and now at Woolwich ; [5] the core of this
specimen, which is of 15-inch calibre, is of cast iron, the
outer casing being formed of a series of bands of wrought
iron, and it was probably made in Sussex. It was in
this county, at Newbridge in Ashdown Forest, that
Simon Ballard in 1497 cast large quantities of iron shot,[6]
those for ' bombardells ' weighing as much as 225 lb.
each, so that they had to be placed in the guns by means

' hakbusses of iren ' were broken in action.—Exch. Tr. of R., Misc.
Bks., 7, f. 140.

[1] Exch. Tr. of R., Misc. Bks., 8, f. 134.
[2] Early Chanc. Proc., 78; no. 81.
[3] *Issue R. of Exch.*, 382.
[4] Foreign R., 12 Hen. VI, m. D.
[5] Figured in *Suss. Arch. Coll.*, xlvi.
[6] He was paid at the rate of 16d. the hundredweight.   Exch. Tr.
of R., Misc. Bks., 8, f. 139.

of ' shotting cradles ' :[1] for ' curtows ' the shot weighed
77 lb., for ' demicurtows ' 39 lb., for ' great serpentines '
19 lb., and for ordinary ' serpentines ' 5 lb. This same
Simon Ballard was enrolled amongst the gunners at the
time of the Cornish rising under Perkin Warbeck.[2] In
the same way we find ' Pieter Robard alias Graunte
Pierre ', ironfounder of Hartfield,[3] described as a
' gonner ', and casting ' pellettes ' at 6*d.* a day in 1497.[4]
In this same year ten ' faucons ' (small guns which fired
balls of about 2 lb.) were made by William Frese,[5]
founder, at 10*s.* the hundredweight, and eight faucons of
brass were made by William Newport,[6] who was a
London bell-founder,[7] while John Crowchard repaired
an old serpentyne that John de Chalowne made, and
provided ' 10 claspis for the touche holes of diverse
gonnes with 5 oliettes and fourteen staples ', weighing
53 lb., at 2*d.* the pound, and also ' 7 bandes of yren made
for the great gonnes mouthes '.[8] Cornelys Arnoldson
at the same time was paid for mending five great serpen-
tynes and making two new chambers to them, for ' 5
forelocks with cheynes to the said gonnes ', for ' handills
made to the chambres ', and for ' vernysshing and
dressing ' the guns.[9]

At the beginning of the reign of Henry VIII large
purchases of cannon were made abroad, from Hans
Popenreuter and Lewis de la Fava of Mechlin, from
Stephen of St. Iago, from Fortuno de Catalengo, and

---

[1] Exch. Tr. of R., Misc. Bks., 8, f. 34.   [2] *Ibid.,* f. 158.
[3] Early Chanc. Proc., 222, no. 112.
[4] Exch. Tr. of R., Misc. Bks., 8, f. 132.   [5] *Ibid.,* f. 81.
[6] *Ibid.,* f. 96.   [7] Early Chanc. Proc., 376, no. 32.
[8] Exch. Tr. of R., Misc. Bks., 8, f. 136.
[9] *Ibid.,* f. 149.

from John Cavalcante of Florence, who also, in return
for a grant of alum, agreed to import saltpetre to the
value of £2,400.[1] But the English foundries were not
idle : Humphrey Walker, a London gunfounder, supplied
fifty pieces of ordnance, at 12s. the pound, as well as
much shot,[2] while Cornelys Johnson ' gonnemaker ',
made and repaired ordnance for the navy.[3] John Atkyn-
son, another founder, in 1514 was paid 2s. ' for 8 lodes
of clay to make molds for a great gun chamber ' and a
further 8d. for 5 lb. of hair ' to temper the clay withall ' ;
he was also supplied with latten and iron wire, and John
Dowson made certain iron work, including ' a rounde
plate for the bottom of the chambre, in length 4½ feet,
with 10 rounde hookes ; a rounde plate with a crosse for
the mouthe of the chambre ; 36 bandes of 4 foot in
length for to wrapp the chambre in ; . . . 6 pynnes of
hardyron, 2 hokes, a stamme, a quespile,' &c.[4]

The mediaeval period of gunfounding, so far as iron
guns are concerned, came to an end with the discovery,
about 1543, of a method of casting iron cannon in the
entire piece and then boring them in the same way that,
as we have seen, bronze pieces were treated. This
discovery is usually attributed to Ralph Hogge of Buxted
and Peter Baude, his French assistant, and resulted in
the ironmaking districts of the Weald of Sussex and
Kent becoming the chief centre of the manufacture of
ordnance.[5]

---

[1] Exch. Tr. of R., Misc. Bks., 8, f. 149, vol. vii, *passim,* and *L. & P.
Hen. VIII,* vol. i.

[2] *Ibid.,* vol. i, ff. 32, 78.   [3] *Ibid.,* ff. 57, 61.

[4] *Ibid.,* vol. iv, ff. 166, 181.

[5] See *V. C. H. Sussex,* ii. 246-9.

POTTER at his wheel, and types of kilns. 16th cent.

VIII

POTTERY, TILES, BRICKS, GLASS

THE manufacture of earthen vessels was one of the earliest, as it was one of the most widespread, industries. From the end of the Stone Age onwards, wherever suitable clay was to be found, the potter plied his trade. The Romans, who had brought the art of potting to a high pitch of excellence, introduced improved methods into Britain, where numerous remains of kilns and innumerable fragments of pottery testify to the industry and the individuality of the Romano-British potters. Several quite distinct types of pottery have been identified, and are assignable to definite localities. Great quantities of black and grey wares, consisting of articles of common domestic use, ornamented for the most part only with broad bands of darker or lighter shading, were made in Kent near the Medway, the finer specimens being associated with Upchurch.[1] From the potteries in the New Forest [2] came vases of greater ornamental and artistic execution, but it was the neighbourhood of Castor in Northamptonshire that occupied in Roman times the place held in recent times by Staffordshire. Round Castor numbers of kilns have been found,[3] and the peculiar dark ware, with its self-coloured slip

[1] C. Roach Smith, *Collect. Ant.*, vi. 173–99.

[2] *Arch. Journ.*, xxx. 319–24 ; Sumner, *Account of the Roman Pottery made at Ashley Rails* (1919).

[3] See *V. C. H. Northants*, i. 206–12.

decoration, occurs all over England, and also on the Continent.

Romano-British kilns have been found in a great number of places, some of the best preserved being at Castor,[1] in London,[2] at Colchester,[3] Radlett (Herts.),[4] and Shepton Mallet (Somerset).[5] Speaking generally they consisted of a pit—usually circular, but sometimes, as at Colchester, rectangular—about 4 to 6 feet in diameter, dug out to a depth of about 4 feet: in this was a flat clay floor raised some 2 feet from the bottom of the pit by a central pedestal. Into the space between this floor, or table, and the bottom of the pit, came the hot air and smoke from a small furnace built at one side of the pit, or kiln proper. On the clay table, which was pierced with holes for the passage of the heat and smoke, were ranged the clay vessels to be baked, and these were built up in layers of diminishing diameter into a domed or conical structure, the layers being separated by grass covered with clay; the whole was then covered in with clay, leaving only an aperture in the centre at the top,[6] and the furnace was lighted.

Roman potter's kiln

[1] *V. C. H. Northants*, i. 206–12.   [2] *Proc. Soc. Ant.*, xvi. 42.

[3] *Brit. Arch. Ass. Journ.*, xxxiii. 267. The black ware made here is indistinguishable from that made round Upchurch.

[4] *Proc. Soc. Ant.*, xvii. 261–70.

[5] *Somers. Arch. Soc.*, xiii (2), 1.

[6] The dark colour of the Castor ware seems to have been caused by ' smothering ' the kiln, by closing the vent, before the baking was complete.

The early mediaeval kilns appear to have been very similar in construction to those just described, or of even simpler construction. If we may take literally the statement that a potter at Skipton paid 6s. 8d. in 1323 'for dead wood and undergrowth to burn round his pots ',[1] it would seem that here a primitive combination of furnace and kiln in one was in use. At a later date the usual construction was probably something similar to those found at Ringmer, in Sussex,[2] which seem to belong to the fifteenth century. Here the kilns were built of bricks or blocks of clay cemented by a sandy loam which vitrified under the influence of the heat to which it was subjected. The beds of the kilns enclosed longitudinal passages covered in with narrow arches, the spaces between which served to transmit the hot air to the superimposed clay vessels. The hearths were charged through arched openings at their ends with charcoal fuel.

To render the pottery non-porous, it was necessary to glaze it,[3] and from an early period lead has been used for this purpose. A twelfth-century description of the process says [4] that the surface of the vase is first to be moistened with water in which flour has been boiled, and then powdered with lead : it is then placed inside a larger vessel and baked at a gentle heat. This process gives a yellow glaze, but if green is required—and green was the colour most often used in England in the mediaeval period, from the twelfth century onwards— copper or bronze was to be added to the lead. The

---

[1] Misc. Accts., 1147, no. 23.   [2] *Suss. Arch. Coll.*, xlv. 128–38.
[3] A Roman glazing kiln was found at Castor.—*V. C. H. North-ants.*, i. 210.
[4] Fagniez, *Docs. relatifs à l'histoire de l'industrie*, no. 133.

same authority gives a recipe for a leadless glaze : baked potter's earth is powdered and washed and then mixed with half its weight of unbaked earth, containing no sand ; this is then worked up with oil and painted over the surface of the vase.

Potters are mentioned at Bladon (Oxon.), Hasfield (Glos.), and Westbury (Wilts.), in Domesday,[1] but apart

THE POTTER.　16th cent.

from casual references in place names [2] and in descriptions of individuals [3] the documentary history of early English pottery is scanty. Kingston - on - Thames may have been an early centre of the trade, as in 1260 the bailiffs of that town were ordered to send a thousand pitchers to the king's butler at Westminster.[4] At Graffham, in Sussex, in 1341, one of the sources of the vicar's income was 'a composition from the men who made

---

[1] Dom. Bk., 65, 156, 168 b.

[2] e. g. ' Pottersfield ' at Horsham, in which parish several finds of green glazed thirteenth-century vessels have been made. *V. C. H. Sussex*, ii. 251.

[3] e. g. ' Geoffrey the potter ', who occurs in 1314 at Limpsfield, where remains of kilns have been found. *Proc. Soc. Ant.*, iv, 358 : Julian la Potere provided 300 pitchers, at a cost of 8s. 6d., for Queen Eleanor's household about 1290. *Brit. Arch. Ass. Journ.*, v. 29.

[4] Lib. R., 51 Hen. III, m. 10. Simon ' le Pichermakere ' of Cornwall is found in the fourteenth century sending his wares (presumably pitchers) to Sussex. Anct. Pet., 10357–8.

clay pots, which is worth 12*d*.',[1] but the most common form of entry is a record of sums paid by potters for leave to dig clay. Thus at Coningsborough (Yorks.) in 1348 a sum of 3*s.* yearly was paid for the digging of clay to make pots,[2] and at Hanley in Worcestershire in 1350, after the visitation of the Black Death, it is noted that the potters who used to pay 13*s.* yearly for clay are dead.[3] At Cowick, in Yorkshire,[4] in 1374, as much as £4 16*s.* was 'received from potters making earthen vessels, for clay and sand taken in the moor at Cowick'. Similar entries occur here every year for about a century, while at Ringmer, in Sussex, small dues of 9*d.* a head were paid yearly by some half a dozen potters for a period of well over two hundred years.[5] Still earlier, in 1283, a rent of 36*s.* 8*d.*, called ' Potteresgavel ', was paid to the lord of the manor of Midhurst.[6]

In dealing with the documentary history of pottery we are met by one or two complications. For instance, the term ' potter ' was, as we have seen, constantly applied to the makers of metal pots ; and it has also to be borne in mind that the commoner table utensils were often made of wood. At the election feast of the Drapers' Company in 1522 ' green pots of ale and wine with ashen cups were set before them at every mess ',[7] the green pots being presumably pottery but the cups wooden ; and the present writer, during excavations at Pevensey

---

[1] *Inq. Nonarum*, 361. Cf. the Hundred Rolls for Bucks.

[2] *Cal. Inq. p. m.*, ix. 48.

[3] *Cal. Inq. p. m.*, ix. 330. I am inclined to think that Hanley may be the place referred to in the ' poter de Hanneliam ' which occurs in the fourteenth-century list of places and their peculiar products. *Engl. Hist. Rev.* xvi. 501.

[4] Mins. Accts., 507, no. 8227.   [5] *V. C. H. Sussex*, ii. 251.

[6] *Ibid.*   [7] *Brit. Arch. Ass. Journ.*, v. 30.

Castle, found two neatly turned small beechwood bowls
or saucers, apparently of thirteenth-century date. It is
probable, therefore, that wood rather than earthenware
was the material of the 1,100 cups and 6,050 platters

MAN TURNING A BOWL ON A LATHE. 13th cent.

provided by the sheriffs of Bucks., Beds., Surrey, and
Kent for the coronation banquet of Richard I ; [1] and
also in the case of the 400 cups and 1,500 sets of dishes,
platters, and saucers supplied to Eleanore of Castile by
John le Squeler (= maker of *esqueles* or dishes),[2] and of

[1] Madox, *Hist. of Exchequer,* i. 369.
[2] *Brit. Arch. Ass. Journ.,* v. 29.

the many hundreds of cups, dishes, platters, and saucers made at Cleobury Mortimer in 1330.[1] The probability is increased by the fact that earthenware platters do not seem to have been used in mediaeval times.

The type of pottery produced does not seem to have varied to any great extent in the different districts.[2] At Lincoln it seems to have been the custom to decorate some of the vessels by means of stamps : some of these stamps, in the form of heads, may be seen in the British Museum. But the use of stamps for decorating pottery is found also at Hastings. Decoration with more or less elaborate patterns in slip—a diluted clay of a colour different from the body of the vessel—is also occasionally found, and something still more ornate seems to be suggested by the occurence of a ' pottery payntour ' at Canterbury in 1430.[3] One distinctive variety of earthenware, however, arose about the beginning of the sixteenth century : it is a thin hard pottery, dark brown in colour, well glazed, and usually decorated with elaborate patterns in white slip. From its being found in large quantities in the Cistercian abbeys of Yorkshire —Kirkstall, Jervaulx, and Fountains—it has received the name of ' Cistercian ware ', but there is at present no direct evidence of its place of manufacture.[4]

Closely connected with pottery is the manufacture of Tiles, the material being in each case clay, and the kilns used being practically identical. At what period the manufacture of tiles, which had ceased with the Roman occupation, was resumed in England is not

[1] Min. Accts. (P. R. O.), 965, no. 10.
[2] *Arch. Journ.*, lix. 1–16.   [3] *Hist. MSS. Com. Rep.*, ix. 138.
[4] *Proc. Soc. Ant.*, xv. 5–11.

certain, but from the beginning of the thirteenth century they play an increasing part in the records of building operations. The frequency and devastating effect of fires, where thatched roofs were in use, soon led to the use of tiles for roofing purposes in towns, even when the authorities did not make their use compulsory, as was done in London in 1212, and at a much later date, in 1509, at Norwich.[1] The importance, for the safety of the town,

TYPICAL MEDIAEVAL POTS

of having a large supply of tiles accessible at a low price was recognized, and in 1350, after the Black Death had sent the prices of labour and of manufactured goods up very high, the City Council of London fixed the maximum price of tiles at 5s. the thousand,[2] and in 1362, when a great tempest had unroofed numbers of houses and created a great demand for tiles, they ordered that the price of tiles should not be raised, and that the manu-facturers should continue to make tiles as usual and expose them for sale, not keeping them back to enhance

[1] *Rec. of Norwich*, ii, no. 193. In the fifteenth century 'redethek' (reed thatch) was one of the peculiarities of Norwich. Wright, *Reliq. Ant.*, ii. 178.

[2] Riley, *Mem. of London*, 254.

the price.[1] It was probably the same appreciation of the
public advantage that led the authorities at Worcester
in the fifteenth century to forbid the tilers to form any
gild, or trade union, to restrain strangers from working
in the city, or to fix a rate of wages.[2]

The Worcester regulations also ordered that all tiles
should be marked with the maker's sign, so that any
defects in size or quality could be traced to the party

TYPICAL MEDIAEVAL POTS

responsible. Earlier in the same century, in 1425, there
had been many complaints at Colchester of the lack of
uniformity in the size of the tiles made there.[3] The
tilers of London, like those of Worcester, had been
declared to be mere labourers and forbidden to form
a gild in 1461,[4] but seven years later the good men of
the mistery of tilers successfully petitioned for their

---

[1] Riley, *Mem. of London*, 309. The monks of Boxley got as
much as 10s. the thousand for some of the tiles from their tilery
this year. Mins. Accts., 1253, no. 13.

[2] Toulmin Smith, *English Guilds*, 399. At Lincoln, on the other
hand, the tilers had formed a gild in 1346, and no tiler not belonging
to the gild might stay in the town. *Ibid.*, 184.

[3] *V. C. H. Essex*, ii. 456.   [4] *London Letter Book L.*, 12.

restoration to the status of a craft with leave to elect wardens, on the ground that tiles were being made so badly that they only lasted three or four years instead of forty or fifty.[1] They laid down that, ' the clay therof shulde be diged and caste at Mighelmasse and soo lye open to Cristmas thanne next folowing, and thanne to be turned and caste agen wherby the marle and chalke shulde breke out like as chalkestones and cloddes liyng in the frost ar woned to doo. And thanne in the March thanne next ensuyng therof shulde be made tyles goode and profitable like as it have been of olde tyme '. These representations were evidently borne in mind when at last it was considered necessary in 1477 to pass an Act of Parliament to regulate the manufacture.[2] By this Act it was provided that the clay to be used should be dug, or cast, by 1st November, that it should be stirred and turned before the beginning of February, and not made into tiles before March, so as to ensure its being properly seasoned. Care was to be taken to avoid any admixture of chalk or marl or stones. The standard for plain tiles should be $10\frac{1}{2}$ inches by $6\frac{1}{4}$ inches with a thickness of at least $\frac{5}{8}$ inch ; ridge tiles or crests should be $13\frac{1}{2}$ inches by $6\frac{1}{4}$, the gutter tiles $10\frac{1}{2}$ inches long, and of sufficient thickness and depth. Searchers were to be appointed and paid a penny on every thousand plain tiles, a half-penny on every hundred crests, and a farthing for every hundred corner and gutter tiles examined. Infringement of the regulation entailed fines of 5s. the thousand plain, 6s. 8d. the hundred crest, and 2s. the hundred corner or gutter tiles sold. ' The size of the tiles is probably a declaration of the custom, the fine

[1] *London Letter Book L.*, 77. [2] Stat. 17 Edw. IV.

is the price at which each kind was ordinarily sold in the fifteenth century.'[1]

These regulations throw a certain amount of light upon the processes employed in tile-making, and further details are obtainable from the series of accounts relating to the great tileworks in the Kentish manor of Wye,[2] extending from 1330 to 1380. In 1355 the output of ten kilns (*furni*) was 98,500 plain, or flat tiles, 500 'festeux'[3] (either ridge or gutter tiles), and 1,000 'corners'. The digging of the clay and burning of the kilns was contracted for at 11*s*. the kiln, a thousand faggots were bought for fuel[4] at a cost of 45*s*., and another 10*s*. was spent on carriage of the clay and faggots. The total expenses were therefore £8 5*s*., and as plain tiles sold here for 2*s*. 6*d*. the thousand, festeux at three farthings each, and corners at 1*s*. 8*d*. the hundred, the value of the output was about £14 15*s*. In 1370, when thirteen kilns belonging to two tileries turned out 168,000 plain tiles, 650 festeux, and 900 corners, we have a more elaborate account. Wood was cut at the rate of 15*d*. for each kiln ; clay for the six kilns of one tilery was 'cast' at 14*d*. the kiln, and 'tempered' at the rate of 1*s*. 6*d*., but for the seven kilns of the other tilery payment was made in grain. The clay was carried to the six kilns for 4*s*., and prepared[5]

---

[1] Thorold Rogers, *Hist. of Agriculture and Prices*, i. 490.

[2] Mins. Accts., 899, 900.

[3] Possibly from the French, *fétu*=a straw, from their being moulded as hollow cylinders.

[4] Turf was evidently used by the Cambridgeshire tilers for fuel *Sacrist Rolls of Ely*, ii. 67, 93, 137.

[5] ' Pro luto tredando ad dictos vj furnos pro tegulis inde faciendis.' The meaning of *tredando* is uncertain, but as the process is

for moulding into tiles for 7s. ; the actual making and burning [1] of the tiles was paid for at 14s. the kiln, and an extra 12d. were given as gratuities to the tilers. Next year the output was considerably reduced, because in one tilery ' the upper course of the kilns (*cursus furni*) did not bake the tiles fully, nor will it bake them until extensive repairs are done ', and in the other tilery only four kilns were prepared, and one of these had to be left unburnt until the next year, owing to the lack of workmen. It was possibly for the defective kiln just mentioned that a ' new vault ' was made in 1373 at a cost of 6s. 8d.—with a further 8d. for obtaining loam (*limo*) for the work. Two years later repairs were done to the buildings of a tilery, which had been blown down by the wind. But the chief blow was struck to the industry here by the increasing difficulty of obtaining workmen. The work may have been unhealthy, for it is noteworthy that the Ringmer potters were on more than one occasion wiped out by pestilence : [2] the effects of the Black Death in 1350 on the Wye tilers are not recorded, but in 1366, as a result apparently of the second pestilence, two small tileries, one of three roods and the other of 1½ acres, which had been leased for 7d. and 14d. respectively, lost their tenants, and in 1375 mention is made of the scarcity of workmen, ' who died in the pestilence at the time of tile making '. In 1377

always mentioned after the clay had been carried to the kilns, it may have been the rolling of the clay to the right thickness for cutting tiles from : possibly it was usual to tread or trample the clay to the right consistency.

[1] The words used for burning, or baking, the tiles are *eleare* and *aneleare*, both connected with our word ' anneal '.

[2] *V. C. H. Sussex*, ii. 251.

Peter at Gate,[1] who for the past few years had hired
a number of kilns at 20s. apiece, only answered for four
kilns ' on account of hindrance to the workmen, who
had been assigned to guard the sea coast, and on account
of the great quantity of rain in the autumn, which did
not allow him to burn more kilns '. In the same year,
and also two years later, another tilery was unworked
for lack of labour.

The tileries at Wye belonged to the Abbot of Battle,
and there were tile kilns at Battle itself in the sixteenth
century [2] and probably much earlier, as in the adjoining
parish of Ashburnham in 1362 there was a ' building
called a Tylehous for baking (*siccandis*) tiles '.[3] Just
about the same time, in 1363, we find ' a piece of land
called Teghelerehelde ' in Hackington,[4] close to Canterbury, granted to Christian Belsire, in whose family it
remained for over a century, as in 1465 William Belsyre
leased to John Appys and Edmund Helere of Canterbury
' a tyleoste with a workhouse ' lying at Tylernehelde in
Hackington for two years for a rent of 26s 8d.[5] With
the ' tyleoste ' William Belsyre handed over 15,000 ' tyle
standardes '—worth 18d. the thousand, eighty ' palette
bordes and three long bordys for the kelle walles '.[6]
Various building accounts show that there were extensive tileries at Smithfield ; for Guildford Castle the tiles
came from Shalford, and for Windsor chiefly from ' la

---

[1] In 1373 Peter at Gate leased the pasturage of Nackholt, where
the tileries lay, at the low rent of 15s. on condition that he should
serve as ' the lord's workman for making tiles '.

[2] *V. C. H. Sussex*, ii. 252.   [3] De Banco, 407, m. 12.

[4] Harl. Ch., 76 D, 32.   [5] *Ibid.*, B. 50.

[6] Kelle = kiln : cf. Anct. D, A 4904, for a ' tylekelle ' at Woolwich in 1450.

Penne '. In the north tiles were made before the end of the thirteenth century at Hull, amongst other places, but one of the chief centres was Beverley. About 1385 the monks of Meaux complained that ' certain workmen of Beverley who were called tilers, makers and burners of the slabs (*laterum*) with which many houses in Beverley and elsewhere are covered ', had trespassed on the abbey's lands at Waghen and Sutton, taking away clay between the banks and the stream of the river Hull without leave, to convert into tiles. The monks seized their tools, their oars, and finally one of their boats, but the Provost of Beverley, on whose fee the tileries were, supported the tilers in their claim to dig clay in any place covered by the waters of the Hull at its highest.[1] Some thirty years earlier, in 1359, the list of customary town dues at Beverley included ' from every tiler's furnace fired ½*d*.[2] and in 1370 Thomas Whyt, tiler, took a lease of the tilery of Aldebek from the town authorities for four years, at a rent of 6,000 tiles.[3]

So far we have been dealing with roofing tiles, or ' thakketyles ', but from the middle of the fourteenth century onwards with increasing frequency we find mention of ' waltyles ' or bricks. For building a new chamber at Ely in 1335 some 18,000 wall tiles (*tegularum muralium*) were made at a cost of 12*d*. the thousand.[4] They seem to have been introduced from Flanders, and are frequently called ' Flaundrestiell ',[5] as, for instance, in 1357, when a thousand were bought for a fireplace at

[1] *Chron. de Melsa* (Rolls Ser.), iii. 179–80.
[2] *Hist. MSS. Com., Beverley MSS.*, 15.
[3] *Ibid.* 62.
[4] *Sacrist R. of Ely*, ii. 67.
[5] ' Flaunderistyle vocata Breke.'   Exch. K. R. Accts., 503, no. 12.

Westminster at 3*s*. 2*d*.[1] At Beverley, in 1391, three persons acquired from the gild of St. John the right to take earth at Groval Dyke, paying yearly therefore 3,000 ' waltyles ',[2] and in 1440 Robert Collard, tile-maker, took ' le Grovaldyke on the west side of le dem-myng' at a rent of 1,000 ' waltyl '.[3] It was pro-bably more particularly with regard to brick kilns than to ordinary tile kilns that the regulations drawn up in 1261 [4] ordered that, ' on account of the stench, fouling the air and destruc-tion of fruit trees, no one is to make a kiln to burn tile nearer the town than the kilns now are, under penalty of a fine of 100*s*.' The term ' brick ' does not seem to have come into common use much before

THE BRICKMAKER
16th cent.

1450, about which time the use of the material became general.

In addition to roof tiles and wall tiles, there were floor tiles. References to these occur in many building accounts. At Windsor, in 1368, ' paventyll ' cost 4*s*. the thousand, and a large variety 2*s*. the hundred, while

---

[1] *Ibid.*, 472, no. 4.
[2] *Hist. MSS. Com., Beverley MSS.*, 62. [3] *Ibid.*, 128.
[4] *Ibid.*, 47. These by-laws distinguish in one place between ' tilethakkers ' and ' tile wallers ', the latter being what we should call bricklayers.

plain roof tiles were 2s. 6d. the thousand.[1] These were probably plain red tiles, but at Westminster in 1278 we have mention of the purchase of ' a quarter and a half

CHERTSEY TILE : KING RICHARD I. 13th cent.

of yellow tiles ' for 7d.[2] Tiles with a plain yellow or green glazed surface are of common occurrence in mediaeval buildings, and in many churches and monastic ruins pavements of inlaid, so-called ' encaustic ', tiles remain more or less complete.[3] In the case of these

[1] Exch. K. R. Accts., 494, no. 4.
[2] *Ibid.*, 467, no. 6 (6).
[3] Such were, no doubt, the paving tiles of which 185,000 were

inlaid tiles the pattern was impressed or incised before baking, and then filled in with white slip, the whole being usually glazed. Some of the patterns thus pro-duced were of great beauty and elaboration, and it would seem that they were often designed, if not actually made, by members of monastic houses. The finest-known series are those discovered at Chertsey Abbey, and it is possible that the remarkable examples in the chapter-house of Westminster Abbey,[1] which date from *c.* 1255, are by the same artist. In the case of the Abbey of Dale in Derbyshire,[2] and the priories of Repton and Malvern,[3] the kilns used for making these inlaid tiles have been discovered, and similar kilns, not associated, so far as is known, with any religious estab-lishment, have also been found at Hastings.[4] The manu-facture of these inlaid tiles in England gradually died out towards the end of the fifteenth century, and has only been revived in recent years.

It is curious that although there is abundant circum-stantial evidence of GLASSMAKING in England during the mediaeval period, direct records of the manufacture are extremely scarce, and practically confined to a single district. From the early years of the thirteenth century, Chiddingfold and the neighbouring villages on the borders of Surrey and Sussex were turning out large quantities of glass. Laurence ' Vitrarius ' (the glassman) occurs as a landed proprietor in Chiddingford about

bought from Richard Gregory, in 1357, for Westminster Chapel at 6s. 8d. the hundred. *Ibid.*, 472, no. 4.

[1] Lethaby, *Westminster Abbey*, 48 ; *Arch. Journ.*, lxix. 36–73.

[2] *V. C. H. Derby*, ii. 375.

[3] *V. C. H. Worces.*, ii. 275.

[4] *Suss. Arch. Coll.*, xi. 230.

1225, and some fifty years later there is a casual reference to ' le Ovenhusfeld ', presumably the field in which was the oven or furnace house, of which the remains were uncovered some years since.[1] It is possible that in the case of glassmaking, as in the case of many other industries, improvements were introduced from abroad, for in 1352 we find John de Alemaygne [2] of Chiddingfold supplying large quantities of glass for St. Stephen's Chapel, Westminster.[3] In one batch he sent up three hundred and three weys (*pondera*) of glass, the wey being 5 lb., and the hundred consisting of twenty-four weys, being, that is to say, the ' long hundred ' of 120 lb. A little later he sent thirty-six weys, and soon after another sixty weys were bought at Chiddingfold, probably from the same maker. The price in each case was 6*d.* the wey, or 12*s.* the hundred, to which had to be added about 1*d.* the wey for carriage from the Weald to Westminster. In January 1355–6 four hundreds of glass were bought from the same maker for the windows of St. George's Chapel, Windsor, at 13*s.* 4*d.* the hundred.[4]

Towards the end of the fourteenth century the family of Sherterre, or Shorter, became prominent in the Chiddingfold district,[5] and on the death of John Sherterre in 1380 his widow engaged John Glasewryth, of Staffordshire, to work the glass-house for six years,

---

[1] *V. C. H. Surrey*, ii. 295.

[2] John of London, ' glasyere ', and John, son of John Alemayn of Chiddingfold, were acquitted on a charge of burglary at Turwick in 1342. Gaol Delivery R., 129, m. 12.

[3] Exch. K. R. Accts., 471, no. 6.

[4] *V. C. H. Surrey*, ii. 296.

[5] *Ibid.*

GLASS-MAKING.   15th cent.

receiving 20*d.* for every sheaf (*sheu*) [1] of ' brodeglass '
(i. e. window glass), and 6*d.* for every hundred of glass
vessels made. This is interesting as showing that glass
vessels were made here; the evidence of inventories,
however, seems to show that glass was as a whole very
little used for table purposes, though a few pieces of the
beautiful Italian glassware might be found in the houses
of the wealthy. The family of Shorter were succeeded
by the Ropleys, and they in turn by the Peytos, who
carried on the trade during the whole of the sixteenth
century, and as late as 1614, thus well overlapping the
modern period of glassmaking, which began with the
coming of the *gentilshommes verriers* from France early
in the reign of Elizabeth. [2]

Glass must have been made in many other districts
where fuel and sand, the chief requisites for the manufacture, were plentiful, but it is difficult to identify any
sites of the industry. One such, in the west of England,
is alluded to in 1309, when the Abbot of Vale Royal
complained that whereas Edward I had granted him a
quarry (presumably of sandstone) in the forest of Dela-
mere (Chester) with other easements for making glass,
he was now prevented from rebuilding a house in the
forest, used by him and his predecessors for the manufacture of glass, which had been burnt down. [3] Another
hint that the industry was carried on extensively in this
district is found in the fact that John de Brampton, the

---

[1] In 1404 the Sacrist of Durham had in store ' of new coloured
glass 2 *scheff*, of white glass and new 76 *cheffe* '. *Durham Acct. R.*
(Surtees Soc.), ii. 397.

[2] *V. C. H. Surrey*, ii. 297 ; *V. C. H. Sussex*, ii. 254.

[3] Pat. R., 2 Edw. II, pt. 1, m. 12 d ; cf. *Vale Royal Ledger-Book*,
24, 190.

king's glazier, was ordered in 1349 to buy glass in London and in the counties of Shropshire and Staffordshire.[1] In 1352 John Geddyng, glazier, was sent into Kent and Essex to get glass for St. Stephen's, Westminster,[2] but where he went and whether he was successful is not known. ' English glass ' is found in use at Durham in 1397,[3] and at York in 1471.[4] For York Minster sixteen sheets (*tabulae*) of English glass were bought from Edmund Bordale of Bramley buttes for 14s. 8d. in 1478,[5] and at an earlier date, in 1418, we find three seams, three weys of white glass bought from John Glasman of Ruglay (Rugeley) at 20s. the seam of twenty-four weys,[6] but whether these men were glass makers, or merely glass merchants, cannot be determined. That the industry, so far at least as real stained glass is concerned, was not flourishing in England in the fifteenth century is shown by the fact that Henry VI, in 1449, brought over from Flanders John Utynam to make glass of all colours for Eton College and the College of St. Mary and St. Nicholas (i. e. King's), Cambridge. He was empowered to obtain workmen and materials at the king's cost, and full protection was granted to him and his family. He was also allowed to sell such glass as he made at his own expense, and ' because the said art has never been used in England, and the said John is to instruct divers in many other arts never used in the realm ', the king granted him a monopoly, no one else being allowed to use such arts for twenty years without

[1] Pat. R., 23 Edw. III, pt. 2, m. 18.
[2] Exch. K. R. Accts., 471, no. 6.
[3] *Durham Acct. R.*, ii. 393.
[4] *Fabric R. York*, 76.
[5] *Ibid.*, 83. [6] *Ibid.*, 37.

his licence under a penalty of £200.[1] Most glass of which we have any account was bought through the glaziers of the larger towns ; but to what extent they made their own glass we cannot say. A certain amount, especially of coloured glass, was imported, and in 1447 we find the executors of the Earl of Warwick stipulating that no English glass should be used in the windows of his chapel at Warwick.[2] The York accounts show ' glass of various colours ' bought in 1457 from Peter Faudkent, ' Dochman ' (i. e. German), at Hull,[3] ' Rennysshe ' glass bought in 1530, Burgundy glass in 1536, and Normandy glass in 1537.[4] A complaint by the glaziers' craft in 1540 that Peter Nicholson, a foreign glazier, imports glass ready made, whereby our English men cannot be set in work,[5] suggests at first sight that there was an English glass-making industry, though it was suffering from foreign competition. I am inclined, however, to think that the expression ' ready made ' here means that the glass was brought in finished and made up ready for use in windows. This is borne out by the petition of the Glaziers' Company in 1542,[6] on the usual subjects of prices and foreign competition, in which there is no reference to English glass, the petitioners being wholly concerned about the relative wholesale and retail prices of Flemish, Burgundy, and Normandy glass.

[1] *Cat. of Pat.*, 1446–52, p. 255. The glorious windows now in King's College Chapel were made between 1515 and 1530 by four English and two Flemish glaziers, all of whom were resident in London. Atkinson and Clark, *Cambridge*, 361.

[2] Hartshorne, *Old Engl. Glass*, 129.

[3] *Fabric R. York*, 69.   [4] *Ibid.*, 104, 108, 109.

[5] *L. & P., Hen. VIII*, xv. 1029 (25).

[6] Ashdown, *Hist. of Co. of Glaziers*, 21 : the petition is unfortunately so badly transcribed that it is largely unintelligible.

GLASS-WORKS.   16th cent.

A full and elaborate account of the processes used in the making of glass and the composing of stained-glass windows was compiled by the monk Theophilus in the twelfth century.[1] The oven consisted essentially of a rectangular hearth, surrounded by thick walls of clay and stone, with an opening, for stoking the fire, at one end : this was covered in, at a height of about 4 feet, with a flat floor, in which were left a vent for the flames and smoke, and holes to take the crucibles. The whole was then covered in with an arched roof, windows being left in the front wall, through which the pots or crucibles could be put in and taken out. The furnace having been lit—dry wood being the fuel employed—the pots were filled with the frit, or mixture of two parts of wood-ashes (Theophilus says ashes of beech-wood, but other ashes, including those of bracken [2] seem to have been used) to one of clean sand, and were placed in the holes in the floor of the furnace. When the mixture had become thoroughly fused, the pot was withdrawn, a long hollow iron rod was dipped into the pot, twisted round and withdrawn with a mass of molten glass adhering to its end. The workman then blew down the rod until the glass assumed the shape of a bladder : the free end of this bladder was next melted in the flame and the opening widened out with a piece of wood to the width of the centre of the bladder ; the edges of the cylinder thus formed were then drawn together so that the opposite sides met at one point in the centre ; to this point

[1] Theophilus Rogerus, *De Diversis Artibus* (trans. by Robert Hendrie).

[2] In 1284 the Abbot of Vale Royal was allowed to take fern in Moltram Forest for glass-making. Close R., 12 Edw. I, m. 6.

the rod, detached from the other end, was applied, and
the other end of the bladder was treated in the same way.
The flattened cylinder was then taken to the cooling
oven, where it was allowed to cool down gradually.
Subsequently the cylinders were heated again, divided
down one edge with a hot iron and flattened out with
a piece of wood and stood on edge in the cooling oven.
When making coloured glass the process was the same
except that metallic
substances were
added to the frit—
copper for green,
lapis lazuli for blue,
and protoxide of
copper or of iron for
red.

Glass-furnace. 11th cent.

When the finished
glass was to be worked
up into a window, the
first step was to provide a flat wooden table, on
which the figures of the design were drawn in outline, the colours of the drapery being indicated by
letters. A piece of glass of the required colour was then
placed in position and the outline traced on it with
chalk ground in water. The iron dividing-rod was then
heated and drawn along the outline; the edges of the
piece thus cut out were smoothed and finished off with
the grozing-iron. The shading, faces, inscriptions, and
such other portions of the design as were not represented by pure pot-metal colour had to be painted
on and fixed by firing.[1] For this purpose a low arched

[1] In an account of work done at Guildford Castle in 1292 we have

furnace was constructed, across which ran three or four iron bars : on these bars rested an iron plate considerably smaller than the dimensions of the furnace. The painted glass was put on this iron slab, which was covered first with a layer of ashes or

THE GLAZIER. 16th cent.

lime, and the fire lit and gradually increased until the flames came up all round the iron slab and licked the glass ; the fire was then drawn and the furnace closed until the glass had cooled down. The glass was then brought back to the table and each piece laid in its place, surrounded by strips of lead and held in position by T-shaped nails. It only remained to solder the leads together at the necessary points, turn the window over and repeat the process.

In the accounts for the provision of windows for St. Stephen's Chapel, Westminster, in 1352,[1] we find John of Chester, John Lincoln, John Athelard, and three other master glaziers employed at a shilling a day drawings designs for the windows on ' white tables ', presumably flat wooden tablets, which were washed

evidently a reference to this : ' For making a furnace to burn glass, 8*d*.' Exch. K. R. Accts., 492, no. 10.

[1] *Ibid.*, 471, no. 6. Cf. Hope, *Windsor Castle*, 141.

with ale,[1] which served no doubt as a size or medium to prevent the colours running. About a dozen glaziers were employed at 7*d.* a day to paint the glass, and some fifteen, at 6*d.* a day, to cut or break the glass and join it.[2] To hold the glass, thus cut into shape, in place over the design 'clozyngnailles' were bought, and for the painting silver foil, gum arabick, jet (*geet*), and 'arnement' (a kind of ink) were provided. The stronger colours were supplied by the use of pieces of stained glass, purchases being made of ruby, azure, and sapphire glass.

[1] Ale is also said in one place to have been used ' pro congelacione vitri '.

[2] ' Frangentes et conjungentes vitrum super tabulas depictas.'

IX

CLOTHMAKING

IMPORTANT as was the wool trade, for centuries the main source of England's wealth, its history, pertaining to the realms of commerce rather than of industry, does not concern us here, and we may ignore the raw material to deal with the manufactured article. To treat at all adequately the vast and complicated history of cloth-making would require a volume as large as this book, even if the line be drawn at the introduction of the New Draperies by Protestant refugees in the time of Elizabeth, and all that is possible here is briefly to outline that history.

The weaving of cloth is of prehistoric antiquity, implements employed therein having been found in numbers in the ancient lake-village of Glastonbury, and on other earlier sites, but documentary evidence may be said to begin with the twelfth century. By the middle of that century the industry had so far developed in certain centres that the weavers of London, Winchester, Lincoln, Oxford, Huntingdon, and Nottingham, and the fullers of Winchester, had formed themselves into gilds, which were sufficiently wealthy to pay from 40s. to £12 yearly to the king for various privileges which practically amounted to the monopoly of cloth-working in their several districts.[1] If these were the principal they were by no means the only centres of the industry. Stamford,[2]

---

[1] Pipe R., 2 Hen. II.   [2] *V. C. H. Lincs.*, ii. 302.

on the borders of Lincolnshire and Northants, was another; also Gloucester;[1] while dyers are found at Worcester[2] in 1173, and at Darlington[3] ten years later. That the industry was organized and flourishing in Yorkshire is shown by Henry II granting a charter by which the manufacture of cloth, dyed or rayed (i. e. striped), in the county was restricted to the weavers of the city of York or of Beverley, Kirkby, Thirsk, Malton, and Scarborough and other demesne boroughs; for which modified monopoly the York weavers were to pay £10 a year.[4]

UPRIGHT LOOM and woman with distaff. 11th cent.

To the twelfth century also belong the remarkable ' laws of the weavers and fullers ' of Winchester, Marlborough, Oxford, and Beverley.[5] These, which all closely resemble one another and were intimately related to the regulations in force in London, show an antagonism towards the clothworkers and an endeavour to keep them in a state of subjection for

---

[1] See charter of Stephen, *Cal. Chart*, iii. 378.

[2] Pipe R., 19 Hen. II.

[3] Boldon Book. *V. C. H. Durham*, i. 338.

[4] Pat., 20 Edw. III, pt. 3, m. 19.

[5] Printed by Riley, *Liber Custumarum* (i. 130–1), and, from an earlier copy, by Leach, *Beverley Town Documents* (Selden Soc.), xliv.

which it is difficult to account. Briefly summarized, they lay down that no weaver or fuller may traffic in cloth or sell it to any one except to the merchants of the town, and that if any became prosperous and wished to become a freeman of the town, he must first abandon his trade and get rid of all the implements connected with it, and then satisfy the town officials of his ability to keep up his new position without working at his old trade. But the most singular provision, found in all these laws, was that no fuller or weaver could attaint or bear witness against a 'free man'.[1] Here it is clear that 'free man' is used not as opposed to a villain,[2] but as implying one possessing the full franchise of his town, in other words, a member of the governing merchant gild or equivalent body. It would seem as if the English cloth trade, which was very extensive during the twelfth century, was entirely in the hands of the capitalist merchant clothiers, at any rate so far as the great towns here in question were concerned, and they had combined to prevent members of the handicraft gilds of clothworkers from obtaining access to the merchant gilds. Generally, the merchant gilds were anxious to draw into their ranks members of all classes, being less afraid of sharing the privileges than desirous of sharing the financial responsibilities which were attached to their position. This exceptional treatment of the clothworkers may have been due less to a sense of their social inferiority than

---

[1] In 1200 the authorities at Lincoln asserted that fullers ' *non habent legem vel communiam cum liberis civibus* ' : Curia Regis 21, m. 5 d.

[2] The weavers were not villains ; had they been so, the leave of their lords would have been necessary before they could obtain the freedom of their town.

to a feeling of their dangerous power as an organized
body—the possession of a royal charter placing the
craft gild to some extent outside the control of the
merchant gild, which was otherwise the supreme authority. As the charter granted to the London weavers by
Henry II early in his reign confirms to them the rights
and privileges which they had in the time of Henry I,
and orders that no one shall dare to do them any injury
or despite,[1] it may be suggested that these restrictive
regulations were drawn up in the time of Stephen. For
the date at which they were collected, evidently as
precedents for use in London, we may hazard 1202, in
which year the citizens of London paid sixty marks to
King John to abolish the weavers' gilds.[2]

It is curious that most modern writers have assumed
the English cloth trade to have practically started with
the introduction of Flemish weavers by Edward III.
It is constantly asserted [3] that prior to this the cloth
made in England was of a very poor quality and entirely
for home consumption. Both statements are incorrect.
A very large proportion of the native cloth was certainly
coarse ' burel ', such as that of which 2,000 ells were
bought at Winchester in 1172 for the soldiers in Ireland,[4]
or the still coarser and cheaper Cornish burels which were
distributed to the poor by the royal almoner about this
time.[5] But at the other end of the scale were the scarlet
cloths for which Lincoln and Stamford early attained

---

[1] *Liber Custumarum*, i. 33.   [2] *Ibid.*, lxiii.

[2] e. g. Ashley, *Economic History*, i. 193 : ' No cloth was manufactured for export ; and a great part of the English demand for
cloth '—indeed the whole of the demand for the finer qualities—
' was met by importation '.   [4] Pipe R., 18 Hen. II.

[5] Pipe R., 27 Hen. II, and other years.

fame. Scarlet cloth, dyed if not actually made on the spot, was bought in Lincoln for the king in 1182 at the prodigious price of 6s. 8d. the ell, about £7 in modern money. At the same time ' blanket ' cloth and green say cost 3s. the ell, and grey say 1s. 8d.[1] Thirty years later the importance of the trade is indicated by the inclusion in Magna Carta of a section fixing the breadth of ' dyed cloths, russets, and halbergetts ' at two ells ' within the lists '.[2] Infringements of the ' assize of cloth ' were of constant occurrence, and were amongst the matters inquired into by the justices holding ' pleas of the Crown '; for instance, in Kent, in 1226, some thirty merchants and clothiers are presented as offenders in this respect.[3] Henry III at the beginning of his reign, in May 1218, had ordered that any cloths of less than two ells breadth exposed for sale should be forfeited,[4] but this order was not to take effect before Christmas so far as burels made by the men of London, Marlborough, and Bedwin (Wilts) were concerned, and in 1225 the citizens of London were exempted from keeping the assize, provided their burels were not made narrower than they used to be.[5] In 1246 the sheriff of London was ordered to buy one thousand ells of cheap burel to give to the poor ; [6] and in 1250 we find the king discharging an outstanding bill of £155 due to a number of London burellers, whose names are recorded ; [7] amongst them

[1] Pipe R., 28 Hen. II.
[2] The ' list ' is the strip of selvage at the edge of the cloth.
[3] Assize R., 358.   [4] Pat., 2 Hen. III, m. 4, 2.
[5] Pat., 9 Hen. III, m. 5.
[6] Lib. R., 30 Hen. III : some years earlier cloth to be distributed at Worcester had been bought at Oxford. Lib. R. 17 Hen. III.
[7] Lib. R., 35 Hen. III, m. 17.

was one Gerard le Flemeng, but otherwise they appear
to have been native workmen. Burels at this time seem
to have been made in lengths of 20 ells and sold at 8*d.*
the ell, while the better quality cloths—browns, plunkets,
blues, and greens—were nearly twice the length, and cost
about 22*d.* the ell.[1] The burellers seem to have been
drapers—members of the capitalist or at least of the
employer class—and to have already separated off from
the weavers ; they had certainly done so some time
before 1300, at which date disputes between the two
classes were common.[2]

Apart from the burels, which were probably very
similar wherever made, the cloths made at different
centres usually possessed distinctive characteristics.
Between 1233 and 1235 we find the king buying russets
of Oxford and of Leicester, burnets, ' powenacios '
(? plunkets), and blues of Beverley, and blankets and
haubergets of Stamford—which were to be dyed scarlet.[3]
In the list of customs paid at Venice on imported goods
in 1265,[4] we find mention of ' English Stamfords ', ' dyed
Stamfords ', and of ' Milanese Stamfords of Monza ',
showing that this particular class of English cloth was
sufficiently good to be copied abroad. It is rather a
noticeable feature of the cloth trade that so many of
the trade terms were taken from the names of the places
in which the particular wares originated. A prominent
instance of this occurs in the case of ' chalons ', which
derived their name from Chalons-sur-Marne, but were

---

[1] Exch. K. R. Accts., 350, no. 4.

[2] *Liber Custumarum*, i. 124.

[3] Close R., 16 Hen. III, m. 13 ; 20 Hen. III, m. 6 ; 19 Hen. III,
m. 14.

[4] *Cal. of S. P. Venice*, i. 3.

made in England from an early date. 'Chalons of Guildford' were bought for the king's use at Winchester Fair in 1252.[1] Winchester itself was an early centre of the manufacture of chalons, which were rugs used for coverlets or counterpanes, and in the consuetudinary of the city,[2] which dates back at least to the early years of the thirteenth century, the looms are divided into two classes, the 'great looms' used for burel weaving paying 5s. a year, and the 'little looms' for chalons paying 6d. or 12d., according to their size. The chalons were to be of fixed dimensions, those 4 ells long being 2 yards in breadth (*devant li tapener*), those of $3\frac{1}{2}$ yards $1\frac{3}{4}$ yards wide, and those of 3 ells long $1\frac{1}{2}$ ells wide. Coverlets formed also an important branch of the Norfolk worsted[3] industry; in this case the ancient measurements were said in 1327 to have been 6 ells by 5, 5 by 4, or 4 by 3.[4] At a later date, in 1442, we find worsted 'beddes' of much greater dimensions, the three 'assizes' being 14 yards by 4, 12 by 3, or 10 by $2\frac{1}{2}$,[5] but presumably these were complete sets of coverlet, tester, and curtains, such as those of which a number are valued at from 6s. 8d. to 20s. apiece in the inventory of the goods of the late King Henry V in 1423.[6] Besides bedclothes the worsted weavers made piece cloth, and amongst the exports from Boston in 1302 figure worsted cloths and worsted seys.[7] Boston, as we might expect from its nearness to Lincoln, exported a good deal of

---

[1] Lib. R., 36 Hen. III, m. 19.   [2] *Arch. Journ.*, ix. 70–1.

[3] The manufacture of this cloth must have originated in the village of Worsted, possibly with some settlement of Flemish weavers, but soon spread throughout the county.

[4] *Rec. of Norwich*, ii. 406.   [5] *Statutes*, 20 Hen. VI.

[6] *Rot. Parl.*, iv. 230, 236.   [7] Customs Accts., 5, no. 7.

scarlet cloth, while the amount of ' English cloth ' sent
out is proof of a demand for this material abroad : a
ship from Lubeck took ' English cloth ' worth £250 for
one merchant, Tideman de Lippe, and two other ships
carried cargoes of the same material worth more than
£200. ' Beverley cloths ' are also represented amongst
these exports, and coloured cloths of Lincoln and
Beverley are found about this time at Ipswich paying
the same tolls as foreign cloths.[1] At Ipswich also cloths
of Cogsall, Maldon, Colchester, and Sudbury are mentioned as typical ' clothes of Ynglond ' exported,[2] and
are classified as ' of doubele warke that men clepeth
tomannyshete ', and a smaller kind ' of long webbe that
they call omannesete ',[3] or ' oon mannys hete '. The
origin of these terms appears to be unknown, but they
appear to draw a distinction between cloth woven by
one man and that worked by two, and it is worth
noting that in the clothworkers' window at Samur two
weavers are shown sitting side by side at the loom.[4]
As the ' omannesetes ' were probably the narrow
cloths afterwards known as ' Essex straits ', there was
possibly some connexion with the narrow ' Osetes ' of
Bristol.[5]

So far as London is concerned, the skill of the weavers

[1] *Black Book of Admiralty* (Rolls Ser.), ii. 197. Blues of Beverley,
scarlets and greens of Lincoln, scarlets and blues of Stamford,
coverlets of Winchester and cloth of Totness occur in wardrobe
accounts of 1236. Pipe R., 19, 20 Hen. III.

[2] *Ibid.*, 187, 197.

[3] There was an ' omanseterowe ' in the Drapery at Norwich as
early as 1288. *Rec. of Norwich*, ii. 8.

[4] *Bristol and Glouc. Arch. Soc.*, xxxvi. 315.

[5] *Little Red Book of Bristol*, ii. 4, 40. Narrow ' Osetes ' were
also made at Salisbury. Exch. K. R. Accts., 344, no. 34.

at the end of the thirteenth century is shown by the variety of types of cloth which are referred to in the regulations of 1300.[1] Here we find mention of cloths called andly, porreye, menuet, virli, lumbard, marbled ground with vetch-blossom, hawes, bissets, &c. The variety and wide distribution of clothmaking in the country generally can be seen in the same way from the list of cloths of which the ulnager had the inspection. Thus in 1316 John Pecok was appointed inspector of canvas, linen, napery, wadmalles, heydok, mendeps, kerseyes, sayes of Louth, worsted of Norwich, Ireland, and Causton, serges, scarlets, and cloths of Lincoln, Essex, Norfolk, Suffolk, Kent, Stamford, Beverley, St. Osith's, Devon and Cornwall.[2] But, for all that, the English cloth industry was not in a flourishing condition. At Lincoln, where in 1157 there had been two hundred weavers, members of a wealthy and flourishing gild to whose annual rent of £6 all the weavers within 12 miles had had to contribute, the industry had so dwindled that by 1322 there were said to be no weavers and there certainly was no rent paid to the crown.[3] In the same year, 1322, the men of Leicester complained that, owing to the extortions of the late Earl Thomas of Lancaster, the cloth trade had been seriously injured— so much so that there was only one fuller in the town, and he was a poor man.[4] So also at Northampton the industry, which in the time of Henry III had employed three hundred men, had practically died out in 1334.[5]

---

[1] *Liber Custumarum*, i. 125 ; ii. 549.
[2] Pat., 9 Edw. II, pt. 1, m. 25.
[3] Pat., 22 Edw. III, pt. 2, m. 22.
[4] *Cal. Misc. Inq.*, ii. 548.   [5] *Rot. Parl.*, ii. 85.

Making all due allowance for the habitual exaggeration of the mediaeval tradesman, especially in the matter of pleading poverty, it is clear that something was wrong with the industry and if it was to be given new life something must be done. By a stroke of good fortune, foreign policy gave the key to the solution of the problem. The great clothworkers of Europe were the men of the Low Countries, and they, in their turn, depended largely on England for their raw material—wool. Edward I, during a dispute with Flanders, had prohibited the export of wool and the import of Flemish cloth, with the result that the Countess of Flanders had speedily come to terms. Relations between the two countries had now become more seriously strained : in 1326 Edward II withdrew the staple, or export market for wool and cloth, from Bruges, prohibited the export of dyes and other materials used for cloth-working, and forbade any one below the ranks of the nobility to wear cloth not made in England, Wales, or Ireland. Next year Edward III confirmed these measures and, in order to stimulate the home production of cloth, licensed the making of cloths of any length and breadth, at the same time proclaiming that he would grant suitable franchises to weavers, fullers, dyers, and other clothworkers whenever they asked for them.[1]

The primary object of these measures was to damage the trade of Flanders, as is shown by the fact that in 1337, when the export of wool was prohibited and the use of foreign cloth was restricted solely to members of

[1] Pat., 1 Edw. III, pt. 2, m. 24. The use of English cloth had been enjoined in 1258 by the Provisions of Oxford. Walter de Hemingburgh, *Chron.*, i. 306.

the royal family,[1] merchants of the friendly Duchy of Brabant were allowed to sell cloth in England and staples were set up within the Duchy at Brussels, Louvain, and Mechlin.[2] Incidentally this throws some light on the theoretical nature of many mediaeval laws and regulations, as it is obvious that if no one might wear cloth that was not of British make, the Brabantine merchants would have had small sale for their goods. Either in order to remedy the defects of the native cloths or with the deliberate intention of building up a clothmaking industry to compete with that of Flanders, Edward III now adopted the policy of encouraging foreign experts to settle in the country. As early as 1331 special protection had been granted to John Kempe of Flanders and any other clothworkers who wished to settle in England,[3] and in 1337 the king sent Thomas de Kenelyngworth to bring John Belle and other clothworkers to England.[4] Later in the year protection was granted to Nicholas Appelman, dyer, and other dyers and fullers who had come over with him and were exercising their trade at Winchester,[5] and similar protection was granted in 1343 to John de Bruyn, burgess of Ghent, making cloth at Abingdon,[6] while in 1352 proclamation was made that foreign clothmakers were not to be interfered with or compelled to join any gild ; in any town they might elect two of their mistery to oversee the work of

---

[1] Statutes, 11 Edw. III.
[2] A. H. Johnson, *Hist. of Co. of Drapers*, i. 67.
[3] Pat., 5 Edw. III, pt. 2, m. 25.
[4] Pat., 11 Edw. III, pt. 1, m. 6.
[5] *Ibid.*, pt. 2, m. 4.
[6] Pat., 17 Edw. III, pt. 2, m. 29.

the foreigners.[1] Such protection was necessary as, naturally, the newcomers were not very popular with the native weavers, and in 1340 the king had to send orders to the Mayor of Bristol to cease from interfering with Thomas Blanket and others who had set up machines for making cloth, and had brought over workmen.[2] The vexation against which Blanket had appealed seems to have been the regulation that every new weaving loom was to pay 5s. 1d. to the Mayor, and 40d. to the aldermen ; this rule was confirmed in 1346, but annulled in 1355.[3]

Before dealing with the various ordinances by which the manufacture of cloth was controlled, it may be as well to consider the processes through which the wool passed before it reached the market, for

> Cloth that cometh from the weaving is not comely
>   to wear
> Till it be fulled under foot or in fulling stocks ;
> Washen well with water, and with teasels cratched,
> Towked and teynted and under tailor's hands.[4]

Having dropped into verse, we may perhaps continue in that medium, and set out the various stages of the manufacture in a poem,[5] written in 1641, but equally applicable to earlier times.

---

[1] Pat., 26 Edw. III, pt. 1, m. 21.

[2] *Rot. Parl.*, ii. 449 ; Close 13 Edw. III, pt. 3, m. 11.

[3] *Little Red Book of Bristol*, ii. 3.

[4] Langland, *Piers Plowman*.

[5] ' A Concise Poem on . . . Shepton Mallet,' by Richd. Watts ; printed in *The Young Man's Looking Glass*, 1641. With this may be compared Deloney's ' Pleasant History of John Winchcombe (Jack of Newbury) ', written some fifty years earlier. *V. C. H. Berks.*, i. 388–9.

1. First the Parter, that doth neatly cull
   The finer from the courser sort of wool.[1]
2. The Dyer then in order next doth stand,
   With sweating brow and a laborious hand.
3. With oil they then asperge it, which being done,
4. The careful hand of Mixers round it runne.
5. The Stockcarder his arms doth hard imploy
   (Remembring Friday is our Market day).
6. The Knee-carder doth (without controule)
   Quickly convert it to a lesser roule.
7. Which done, the Spinster doth in hand it take
   And of two hundred roules one threed doth make.
8. The Weaver next doth warp and weave the chain,
   Whilst Puss his cat stands mewing for a skaine ;
   But he, laborious with his hands and heeles,
   Forgets his Cat and cries, Come boy with queles.[2]
9. Being fill'd, the Brayer doth it mundifie
   From oyle and dirt that in the same doth lie,
10. The Burler [3] then (yea, thousands in this place)
    The thick-set weed with nimble hand doth chase.
11. The Fuller then close by his stock doth stand,
    And will not once shake Morpheus by the hand.
12. The Rower next his armes lifts up on high,
13. And near him sings the Shearman merrily.
14. The Drawer last, that many faults doth hide
    (Whom merchant nor the weaver can abide)
    Yet is he one in most clothes stops more holes
    Than there be stairs to the top of Paul's.

[1]
       Then to another room came they
       Where children were, in poor array,
       And every one sat picking wool,
       The finest from the coarse to pull.

[2]
       Two hundred men, the truth is so,
       Wrought in their looms, all in a row ;
       By every one a pretty boy
       Sat making quills with mickle joy.

[3] The burler's business was to remove knots, loose ends, and other impurities.

The first process, then, was the sorting of the wool. The better quality was used for the ordinary cloths, and the worst was made up into coarse cloth known as cogware and Kendal cloth, three-quarters of a yard broad, and worth from 40*d.* to 5*s.* the piece.[1] The term cogware seems to have sprung from its being sold to cogmen, the crews of the ships called cogs ; but whether for their own use, or for export is not quite clear. The alternative name of Kendal cloths was derived from the district of Kendal in Westmorland, a seat of the industry, at least as early as 1256.[2] The mixing of different qualities of wool in one cloth was prohibited ; and as it was forbidden to mix English wool with Spanish,[3] so was the use of flocks, or refuse wool, in ordinary cloth,[4] except in the case of the cloth of Devonshire, in which, owing to the coarseness of the wool, an admixture of flock was necessary.[5] In the adjacent county of Cornwall the wool was of still poorer quality, and the cloth woven from it so inferior that it was exempted from paying customs prior to the sixteenth century. But by the time of Henry VIII the wool had greatly improved, and as good cloths were made there as elsewhere. On the other hand, the morals of the clothiers had not shown an equal improvement, and they were in the habit of using fine wool from other countries or even of bringing Tavistock and other white cloths into the country and then exporting them as ' course Cornysh cloths ', so

---

[1] The manufacture of these cloths was licensed in 1390, provided the quality was not improved. Statutes, 13 Rich. II.

[2] Assize R. 979, m. 2.

[3] *Liber Custumarum,* ii. 549. Spanish wool is prominent amongst the imports at Southampton in 1310. Customs Accts., 136, no. 8, n.

[4] Statutes, 4 Edw. IV.   [5] Statutes, 7 Edw. IV.

defrauding the revenue. It was therefore ordered that in future Cornish cloth should pay duty, and that merchants exporting it should swear that it was genuine coarse Cornish cloth.[1]

In dyeing two mediums are required, the colouring matter and the mordant which fixes the dye in the wool.

The mordant most in use in the Middle Ages was alum,[2] and at Bristol in 1346 we find that only 'Spyralym, Glasalym, and Bokkan' might be used, and that any one using 'Bitterwos' or 'Alym de Wyght', which must have derived its name from the Isle of Wight, or even found with any in his possession, was liable to be fined.[3] Far the commonest dye-stuff was the blue woad, of which enormous quantities were used. The plant (*Isatis tinctoria*) from which this was prepared is indigenous (the ancient Britons, indeed, wore the dye without the intervention of cloth), but practically all the woad used commercially in England was imported, Southampton

DYERS. 15th cent.

[1] S. P. Hen. VIII, cxiii. 132.

[2] An alkali, known as '*cineres*', possibly a kind of *barilla* or carbonate of soda (*Rec. of City of Norwich*, ii. 209) occurs fairly often : e. g. taxation of Colchester, *Rot. Parl.*, i. 244.

[3] *Little Red Book of Bristol*, ii. 6.

being one of the great centres of the trade.[1] Woad,
alum, potash, and teasels (used for raising the nap of
cloth) were among the articles on which toll was paid
at Torksey in 1228,[2] and at Berwick in 1303 teasels,
alum, and brasil (a red dye chiefly used for leather)
were exempt from import dues while, by an exceptional
regulation evidently made to encourage the dyeing
industry, woad paid an import duty of 22*d*. a frail but
paid 35*d*. if taken out of the port.[3] In 1286 the authorities at Norwich came to an agreement with the woad
merchants of Amiens and Corby as to the size of the
packages in which woad and weld, a yellow dye in much
demand, might be sold,[4] and at Bristol some sixty years
later elaborate regulations were drawn up for the preparation of the woad, of which two varieties are mentioned, that of Picardy and that of Toulouse.[5] The
woad was imported in casks in the form of dry balls ;
these had to be broken up small, moistened with water,
and then heaped up to ferment ; after a few days the
top layer became so hot that it could hardly be touched
with the hand ; the heap was then turned over to bring
the bottom to the top, and left till this in turn had
fermented ; a third turn usually sufficed to complete
the process.[6] In Bristol special ' porters ' were appointed
to undertake and supervise this seasoning and the subse-
quent storing of the woad, and a further regulation
compelled the merchant to sell his woad within forty

[1] e. g. Customs Accts., 136, nos. 4 and 12.
[2] Gras, *Early Engl. Customs System,* 156.
[3] *Ibid.,* 165.
[4] *Recs. of City of Norwich,* ii. 209.
[5] *Little Red Book of Bristol,* ii. 16–22.
[6] Lands. MS., 121, no. 21.

days after it had been stored and assayed.[1] The setting
of the woad, that is to say, its conversion into dye, was
also an art in itself, and it would seem that in Bristol
it was the custom for dyers to go to the houses of their
customers and prepare the woad-vats. Through their
undertaking more jobs than they could properly attend
to, much woad was spoilt, and in 1360 they were forbidden
to take charge of more than one lot of dye at one time.[2]
Further abuses arose through the ignorance and inca-
pacity of many of the itinerant dyers, and in 1407 it
was enacted that only those dyers who held a certificate
of competency should ply their trade in the town.[3] At
Coventry, another great centre of the trade, complaints
were made in 1415 that the dyers had not only raised
their prices, charging 6s. 8d. instead of 5s. for a cloth,
30s. instead of 20s. for 60 lb. of wool, and 6s. instead of
4s. for 12 lb. of the thread for which the town was
famous, but were in the habit of taking the best part
(*la floure*) of the woad [4] and madder for their own cloths,
and using only the weaker portion for their customers'
cloths.[5] A petition was therefore made that two drapers,
a woader and a dyer, should be elected annually to

[1] Cf. *Rec. Borough of Northampton*, i. 121 : the compiler has
mistaken ' wode ' for wood.

[2] *Little Red Book of Bristol*, ii. 39.

[3] *Ibid.*, ii. 81–90.

[4] The lighter less soluble part of the woad, that floated to the
top of the vat, was called indigo and used by painters. *Brit. Arch.
Ass. Journ.* (N.S.), ix. 101.

[5] In Lincoln, the chief seat of scarlet dyeing, in 1200 dyers were
not allowed to dye their own cloths, except in woad, ' because if
they did they would dye their own cloths in the first brew of dye
and the cloths of other men in the dregs (*drasca*).' Curia Regis, 21,
m. 5 d.

supervise the trade.[1]   Some fifty years later we have at
Coventry a notice of what appears to have been a
mediaeval instance of a quarrel between a ' trade union ',
the Dyers' Company, and ' blackleg ' firms.[2]   Thomas
de Fenby and ten other dyers of Coventry complained
against John Egynton and William Warde that they
had assembled the mem-
bers of their trade and
had compelled them to
swear to various things
contrary to the law and
their conscience, as that
no one should buy any
woad until it had been
viewed and appraised by
six men chosen for the
purpose by the said Egyn-
ton and Warde, and that
no dyer should make any
scarlet dye (*grene*) at less
than 6*s.* (the vat ?), or put
any cloth into woad for

THE DYER.   16th cent.

less than 4*d.* or 5*d.*   Warde and Egynton had also
adopted the mediaeval form of picketing, by hiring
Welshmen and Irishmen to waylay and kill the com-
plainants on their way to neighbouring markets.

A list of cloths made in York in 1395–6 [3] gives some
idea of the colours in general use.   For the first three
months, September–December, blue largely predomi-
nated, but for some unexplained reason—probably

---

[1] *Rot. Parl.*, iv. 75.   [2] Early Chanc. Proc., 7, no. 23.
[3] Exch. K. R. Accts., 345, no. 16.

because the supply of woad, which was harvested about midsummer, ran short or deteriorated—this colour almost disappeared from January to May, its place being taken by russet. Red, sangüine, murrey (or orange), plunket,[1] green, and motleys, white, blue, and green occur; also ' paly ', which was presumably some striped material, and in a very few cases black. By the regulations drawn up in London in 1298,[2] no dyer who dyed burnets blue [3] or other colours might dye ' blecche ' or tawny ; the reason does not appear, but this uncertain tint, ' blecche ', occurs again as reserved specially for Spanish wool.[4] For blue, as we have seen, woad was used, and for yellow weld, a combination of the two yielding green ; scarlet was derived from the grain (*greyne*),[5] and reds and russets from madder, which was imported in large quantities. Several varieties of lichen were probably included under the head of ' orchal ', and afforded shades of brown and red. Fancy shades were formed by double dyeing, and apparently were not always fast, as a statute [6] passed in 1533 ordered that none should dye woollen cloth ' as browne blewes, pewkes, tawnyes, or vyolettes ', unless they were ' perfectly boyled, greyned, or madered upon the

---

[1] Plunket appears to have been a pale blue, half the quantity of woad sufficing for plunkets than was used for azures, which in turn took half the amount required for blues. *V. C. H. Suffolk*, ii. 258.

[2] *Liber Custumarum*, i. 129.

[3] These were no doubt the ' browne blewes ' of later records : e. g. a Benenden clothier was fined in 1563 for ' a browne blewe, being a deceiptfull color '.—Memo. K. R., 7 Eliz., Hil., m. 330.

[4] *Liber Custumarum*, i. 125.

[5] Alkermes, an insect resembling cochineal.

[6] Statutes, 24 Hen. VIII ; cf. 4 Edw. IV.

WOMEN CARDING, SPINNING, AND WEAVING. 15th cent.

wode,[1] and shotte with good and sufficient corke or
orchall '. At this time brazil, or logwood, which was
used for dyeing leather red, was being adopted as a dye
for cloth, and its use was absolutely forbidden.

LOOM AND SPINNING-WHEEL. 15th cent.

Carding, or combing, and spinning are processes
which need not detain us long. They were both home
industries, and spinning,[2] in particular, was the staple

---

[1] Woad served the double purpose of a blue dye and a mordant—
colours applied to wool which had already been treated with woad
being more fast. *Brit. Arch. Ass. Journ.* (N.S.), ix. 103.

[2] The rock, or distaff, was used almost entirely for spinning, no
mention of a spinning-wheel apparently occurring before 1372,
when certain ' *filiatrices ad rotam* ' were presented at Halifax for
taking excessive wages. Heaton, *Yorks. Woollen Industry*, 24. A
spinning-wheel is mentioned, among goods unjustly detained, in

employment of the women, and accordingly regulations were not infrequently made to ensure a good supply of wool for their use. At Bristol, in 1346, no oiled wool ready for carding and spinning might be sent out of the town until the carders and spinners had had a chance of applying for it ; moreover, it might only be exposed for sale on a Friday, and no middleman might buy it.[1] Similarly at Norwich, in 1532, the butchers were ordered to bring their woolfells into the market and offer them for sale to the poor women who lived by spinning.[2] When the clothmaking trade got into the hands of the big capitalist clothiers, who gave out their wool to be carded and spun, it became necessary to pass laws [3] to ensure on the one hand that the workers should do their work faithfully, and not abstract any of the wool,[4] and on the other, that the masters should not defraud the carders and spinners by paying them in food or goods [5] instead of in money, or by the use of false weights, making women, for instance, comb $7\frac{1}{2}$ lb. of wool as a ' combing stone ', which should only contain 5 lb.[6]

Weaving was, of course, the most important of all the processes in clothmaking. Reduced to its simplest form, the weaver's loom consists of a horizontal [7] frame,

Kent in 1390. De Banco, 519, m. 499. Another is found at Norwich in 1401. *Recs. of Norwich*, ii. 22. They are represented in English MSS. of the fourteenth century ; e.g. the Luttrell Psalter and Roy. MS. 10 E. iv.

[1] *Little Red Book of Bristol*, ii. 8, 9.

[2] *Rec. of City of Norwich*, ii. 119.

[3] Statutes, 4 Edw. IV ; 3 Hen. VIII.

[4] *V. C. H. Essex*, ii. 255.   [5] *V. C. H. Worcs.*, ii. 286.

[6] *V. C. H. Essex*, ii. 383–4.

[7] The looms used in classical times were upright, and this primitive type is still used in the East and remained in use in Europe until

to the ends of which the warp threads, which run
longitudinally through the cloth, are fastened in such
manner that they can be raised and depressed by
heddles,[1] or looped threads, in alternate series, leaving
room between the two layers of warp for the passage
of the shuttle, charged with the woof.[2] The shuttle,
flying from side to side across the alternating warp

SPINNING AND WARPING.   13th cent.
stained glass

threads, covers them with woof, which is packed close
by a vertical frame of rods, the lay, slay, or batten,
swinging between the warp threads.   To weave tight

about the end of the eleventh century, when it was replaced by the
horizontal type.   The upright loom continued to be employed for
tapestry.

[1] The officials of the weavers' gild in London had to examine all
' heldes ' and ' slayes ' from time to time and point out any defects ;
if these were not remedied before the next visit the weaver was
fined.   *London Letter Book L,* 290.

[2] The use of the looser spun woof in place of warp was strictly
forbidden.   *Liber Custumarum,* i. 125 ;   *Little Red Book of Bristol,*
ii. 2.   At Worcester in 1497 any one bringing yarn to be woven into
cloth was to bring the warp and the woof separate.   *V. C. H. Worcs.,*
ii. 285.

and close required considerable strength, and at Norwich women were forbidden to weave worsteds because they were 'not of sufficient power' to work them properly.[1] On the other hand, at York the only restriction on women weaving was that they must, like the men, first serve their prenticeship.[2] There is plenty of evidence, literary and pictorial, that ladies of rank often passed their somewhat abundant leisure in weaving, and it would seem that such work was not beneath the dignity of a queen, as in 1290 a messenger was sent to Burgh and Aylsham to obtain certain weaving instruments for Queen Eleanor's use.[3] The probability, however, is that the looms used by

Man with yarn on frame and bobbins. 16th cent. stained glass

these noble amateurs were light, and that some of the material produced—like much produced in similar circumstances to-day—was more satisfactory from an artistic than from a technical standpoint. The cloth as it was woven was wound on a roll, bringing a fresh portion of the warp within the weaver's reach, but while its length was thus limited merely by custom or convenience, its breadth was obviously controlled by

[1] *Rec. of City of Norwich*, ii. 378.
[2] *York Memorandum Book* (Surtees Soc.). i. xxviii.
[3] Add. MS. 35294.

the width of the loom, and when Henry IV, in 1406, ordered that cloth of ray should be made six-quarters of a yard broad instead of five-quarters, as had always been the custom, the order had to be revoked, as it would have necessitated all the ray weavers obtaining new looms.[1] Similarly in 1536, when an Act[2] was passed fixing the breadth of ordinary cloth at seven-quarters of a yard, so much discontent was aroused, especially among the clothiers of Suffolk, that it was quite expected that the clothiers would join the Northern Rebellion.[3] A deputation of clothmakers interviewed the chancellor, Sir Thomas Audeley, and declared that if the Act was not at least postponed they would give up making cloths, as they could not keep the regulations as to breadth and the weavers were too poor to provide new ' lomes and slees '. The chancellor took up the correct official attitude of unyielding fixity of purpose, but dropped a private hint to Cromwell that it would be as well to extend the period of grace.[4] A year's extension, to give time for further inquiry,[5] was accordingly proclaimed, and the Act was eventually dropped.

For the right to use looms payments had often to be made to the authorities of the town. At Winchester in the thirteenth century, every burel loom paid 5s. yearly, the only exceptions being that the mayor, the hospital, and the town clerk might each work one loom free of charge.[6] Nottingham was another town where duties were paid on looms,[7] and at Bristol, as we have

---

[1] *Rot. Parl.*, iii. 618.　　　　[2] Statutes, 27 Hen. VIII, c. 12.

[3] *L. & P. Hen. VIII*, xi. 545, 576, 603, 635.

[4] *Ibid.*, xii. 737.　　　　[5] *Ibid.*, 863.

[6] *Arch. Journ.*, ix. 70 : cf. Assize R., 787, m. 86.

[7] *V. C. H. Notts.*, ii. 345. In 1220 the Prior of St. Neots paid to

seen, prior to 1355, the erection of a ' webanlam ' entailed payments of 8s. 5d. in all.

To guard against false working, it was the rule at Bristol that all looms must stand in shops and rooms adjoining the road, and in sight of the people, and the erection of a loom in a cellar or upstair room entailed a fine.[1] It was possibly for the same reason that weavers were forbidden to work at night,[2] though an exception was made at Winchester in favour of the period immediately preceding Christmas.[3] On the other hand, the London jurors in 1320 coupled this ordinance against working by candle light with the enforced holiday which the weavers' gild compelled its members to take between Christmas and the Purification (2nd February)[4] as measures prejudicial to the commonalty and intended to restrict the supply and so maintain the price of cloth.[5] A further device for the same purpose was the rule that no cloth of Candlewick Street was to be worked in less than four days, though they might easily be made in two or three days.[6] Thanks to these methods, and to the way in which admission to the gild was limited, the

the weavers' gild of Huntingdon 6d. for each loom in the township of St. Neots. Memo. R., K. R., 3, m. 8 d.

[1] *Little Red Book of Bristol,* ii. 4.

[2] *Liber Custumarum,* i. 134.   [3] *Arch. Journ.,* ix. 71.

[4] The suspension of worsted weaving for a month from 15 August was enforced in 1511 to avoid a shortage of agricultural labour during harvest. *Rec. of City of Norwich,* ii. 376.

[5] *Liber Custumarum,* i. 423.

[6] *Ibid.* Candlewick Street (now Cannon Street) was the centre of manufacture of a coarse cheap cloth used for horse trappings, and also bought in large quantities for the King's almoner from 1330 to 1380. Enrolled Wardrobe Accts., L. T. R., 2–4. It seems to have been practically the same as the earlier burel cloth, and to have died out about 1380.

looms in the city had been reduced in thirty years or so from 380 to 80, and the price of cloth had risen accordingly. The authorities throughout the country were constantly in the dilemma of having on the one hand to permit the restriction of the numbers of the weavers, with a consequent rise in the cost of their wares, or on

THE WEAVER.   16th cent.

the other hand running the risk of inferior workmanship, ' to the grete infamie and disclaundre of their worshipfull towne '. Not only were the unauthorized weavers often ignorant of their art, not having served their apprenticeship, but they used flock and other bad material, and bought stolen wool and ' thrummes '.[1] The latter were the unwoven warp threads left over at the end of the cloth, and as there was no export duty on thrums, the weavers contrived to cut them off as long as possible, and in this way much woollen yarn was sent out of the country without paying customs until the practice was made illegal by an Act of Parliament in 1430.[2]

The cloth on leaving the loom was in the condition known as ' raw ', and although not yet ready for use was marketable, and many of the smaller clothmakers preferred to dispose of their products at this stage rather

[1] *Little Red Book of Bristol*, ii. 40, 123.   [2] Statutes, 8 Hen. VI.

than incur the expense of the further processes. This seems to have been the case on the Welsh border, as Shrewsbury claimed to have had a market for ' *pannus crudus* ' from the time of King John.[1] Much raw cloth was also bought up by foreign merchants and sent out of the country to be finished ; and at the beginning of the sixteenth century, Parliament, with its usual terror of foreign trade, seeing only that the finishing processes would be carried out by foreign workmen instead of English, forbade the export of unfinished cloth. It had then to be pointed out that, as most of these cloths were bought to be dyed abroad, and as after dyeing all the finishing processes would have to be repeated, the cost of the cheaper varieties would be so raised that there would be no sale for them ; cloths below the value of five marks were therefore exempted.[2]

Raw cloth had next to be fulled, that is to say, scoured, cleansed, and thickened by beating it in water. Originally this was always done by men trampling upon it in a trough, and the process was known as ' walking ', the fuller being called a ' walker ' (whence the common surname), but during the thirteenth century an instrument came into general use called ' the stocks ', consisting of an upright, to which was hinged the ' perch ' or wooden bar with which the cloth was beaten. The perch was often worked by water power, and fulling, or walking, mills soon became common.[3] In 1274 there was a pretty quarrel between the people of St. Albans

---

[1] *V. C. H. Shrops.*, i. 428.   [2] Statutes, 3 & 5 Hen. VIII.

[3] Fulling mills are mentioned in 1256 at opposite ends of England —at Appleby in Westmorland (Assize R. 979, m. 13) and at Dunster in Somerset (Maxwell Lyte, *Hist. of Dunster*, 297).

and the Abbot, the people claiming the right to full their coarse and common cloths where they pleased and the Abbot trying to force them to use his fulling mill. The monastery officials went to the house of Henry atte Gate in Fullerstrete and seized a russet cloth because he had put up a perch (*truncum*) for fulling cloth in his house. The townsmen made a general levy to raise money for fighting the question, and took advantage of a visit of the popular Queen Eleanor to the Abbey to appeal to her, the women, ' whose attack was to be feared, since it is hard satisfactorily to calm the anger of women,' taking a leading part in the appeal. The monks retorted by organizing prayers and processions and by the even more effective invocation of the law, which decided in their favour.[1] By the regulations of the fullers' gild of Lincoln recorded in 1389,[2] no fuller was to ' work in the trough ', that is to say, to walk the cloth, and a further rule forbade any man to work at the perch with a woman, unless she were the wife of a master or her handmaid. Probably the intention of this last rule was to put a stop to the employment of cheap female labour, ' by the whiche many . . . likkely men to do the Kyng servis in his warris and in the defence of this his lond, and sufficiently lorned in the seid crafte, gothe vagaraunt and unoccupied and may not have thar labour to ther levyng '.[3] On the other hand, we find John Graunt paying 8*d.* maltote at Hythe in 1414 for the craft of a ' tokehere ' (tucker, or fuller) exercised by

[1] *Gesta Abbatum*, i. 410.

[2] Toulmin Smith, *Engl. Gilds*, 179. The gild was founded in 1297, but this regulation was probably of later date.

[3] *Little Red Book of Bristol*, ii. 127.

his wife for sixteen weeks,[1] and in 1449 the wife of
John Howedelowe fulled the cloth which had been
specially woven for the use of the servants at St. Rade-
gund's, Cambridge.[2] About 1297 a number of London
fullers took to sending cloths to be fulled at certain mills
in Stratford, and as this was found to result in much
loss to the owners of the cloths, orders were given to
stop all cloths on their way to the mills, and only allow
them to be sent on at the express desire of the owners.[3]
This seems to point to mill fulling being inferior to manual
labour, while possibly the fulling being conducted outside the control of the city may have tended to bad work.
At Bristol in 1346, one of the rules for the fullers forbids
any one to send ' rauclothe ' to the mill, and afterwards
receive it back to be finished,[4] and in 1406 the town
fullers were forbidden to make good the defects in
cloths fulled by country workmen.[5]

In one particular trade, fulling by mills was strictly
forbidden : this was the manufacture of caps and
' hures ' (shaggy felt hats). Not only did the ' hures '
damage cloths if they were fulled together,[6] but they
could not be properly fulled in a mill, or even by walking,
but must be fulled by hand.[7] Accordingly we find
Roger Laurence, ' hurer,' in 1427 forfeiting eleven dozen
' nightcappes ' and one long cap, which he had fulled
in a mill.[8]

For cleansing the cloth, use was made of the peculiar
absorbent earth known as Fuller's earth, or ' walker-

[1] *Hist. MSS. Com. Rep.*, iv. 435.   [2] *Ibid.*, ii. 120.
[3] *Liber Custumarum*, i. 128–9.
[4] *Little Red Book of Bristol*, ii. 13.   [5] *Ibid.*, 79.
[6] Riley, *Mems. of London*, 401.   [7] *Ibid.*, 403, 559.
[8] *London Letter Book K*, 59.

herth ',[1] as it was sometimes called. Fuller's earth is only found in a few places, the largest deposits being round Nutfield and Reigate,[2] and on account of its rarity and importance its export was forbidden.

The cloth, having been fulled, had to be stretched on tenters to dry, and references to the lease of tenter grounds are common in mediaeval town records.[3] A certain amount of stretching was legitimate and even necessary,[4] but where the cloth belonged to the fuller—and it was a common practice for fullers to buy the raw cloth—there was a temptation to ' stretch him out with ropes and rack him till the sinews stretch again ' [5] so as to gain several yards. As a result of this practice, which greatly impaired the strength of the cloth, ' Guildford cloths,' made in Surrey, Sussex, and Hampshire, lost their reputation, and in 1391 measures had to be taken to restore their good name by forbidding fullers, or other persons, to buy the cloth in an unfinished state.[6] In 1482 the possession of private tenters was forbidden in London under a heavy penalty, and all those existing were ordered to be destroyed except ten—five at the Fullers' Hall and five at Leadenhall.[7] Several Acts were passed dealing with this offence, and during the sixteenth century ordinances were issued against the use of powerful racks with levers, winches, and ropes.

---

[1] *V. C. H. Notts.*, ii. 346. Urine was occasionally used instead of Fuller's earth, but this was forbidden in 1376. Riley, *Mems. of London*, 401.

[2] *V. C. H. Surrey*, ii. 279.

[3] e. g. at Nottingham ; *V. C. H. Notts.*, ii. 346.

[4] *V. C. H. Warwick*, ii. 252.   [5] *Ibid.*

[6] Statutes, 15 Rich. II.

[7] *London Letter Book L*, 197.

Infringements of these Acts were numerous,[1] and as an example of the extent to which cloths were stretched we may quote a return from Reading in 1597, which mentions one cloth of thirty yards stretched with ' a gyn and a leaver with a vice and a roape ' to thirty-five yards, and another stretched with a rope ' to the quantitye of three barrs length—every barr contayneth about $2\frac{1}{2}$ yards '.[2]

On leaving the fuller the cloth passed into the hands of the rower, whose business it was to draw up from the body of the cloth all the loose fibres with teazles. Teazles, the dried heads of the ' fuller's thistle ', are mentioned amongst the goods of some of the Col-chester cloth-workers in 1301,[4] were used from the earliest times, and have never been entirely supplanted even in these days of machinery. Several unsuccessful attempts have been made to invent substitutes, and in 1474 the use of iron cards, or combs, instead of teazles, had to be forbidden.[5] The loose portions of the cloth thus raised by the teazles were next cut off by the shear-man, upon whose dexterity the cloth depended for the finish of its surface. Occasionally that dexterity was

CLOTH-SHEARER[3]

---

[1] e. g. *V. C. H. Surrey*, ii. 344 : *V. C. H. Sussex*, ii. 257.

[2] Exch. Dep. by Com., 41 Eliz., East. 1.

[3] One of the panels in the ' clothworkers' window ' at Samur, 14th century.

[4] *Rot. Parl*, i. 243. [5] Statutes, 4 Edw. IV.

displayed in the wrong way, for when the shearmen had damaged cloths by shearing too low and too close to the thread they would ' powdre theym with flokkes ' and so conceal the injury.[1] But, assuming that the shearman had done his work satisfactorily, after the drawer had skilfully repaired any small blemishes, the cloth was ready for sale.

In view of the multiplicity of processes involved, it is obvious that the manufacture of cloth must have afforded employment to an immense number of persons. An account written in Suffolk just over the borders of our mediaeval period, in 1618, reckons that the clothier who made twenty broad cloths in a week would employ in one way and another five hundred persons.[2] But even at that time, when the capitalist clothier was firmly established, there were not very many with so large an output as twenty cloths a week, and in earlier times there were very few approaching such a total. The ulnager's accounts [3] of the duties paid on cloths exist for most counties for the last few years of Richard II, and throw considerable light on the state of the trade. In the case of Suffolk for the year 1395, we have 733 broad cloths made by about one hundred and twenty persons, of whom only seven or eight return as many as twenty cloths ; the chief output, however, was narrow cloth, made in dozens (pieces of 12 yards, a ' whole cloth ' being 24 yards) ; of these, 300 makers turned out about 9,200, fifteen of their number making from 120 to 160 dozens each. In the case of Essex there is more evidence

---

[1] *London Letter Book L*, 196.
[2] *V. C. H. Suffolk*, ii. 262.
[3] Exch. K. R. Accts., bdles. 339–45.

for the capitalist clothier, as at Coggeshall the 1,200 narrow cloths are assigned to only nine makers (the largest items being 400, 250, and 200 dozens), while Braintree, with 2,400 dozens, had only eight makers, of whom two pay subsidy on 600 dozens each and one on 480. The great clothiers, however, at this time are found in the west, at Barnstaple, where John Parman paid on 1,080 dozens, and Richard Burnard on 1,005, other nine clothiers dividing some 1,600 dozens between them. For the rest of Devonshire, sixty-five makers account for 3,565 dozens, or rather over fifty a piece. If Devon stood at one end of the scale, its next door neighbour was at the other, for Cornwall's total output was only ninety cloths, attributed to thirteen makers. At Salisbury the year's output of 6,600 whole cloths was divided between 158 persons, only seven of whom accounted for more than 150 each, while at Winchester, where over 3,000 cloths are returned, only three clothiers exceeded the hundred, and men of such local prominence as Robert Hall and ' Markays le Fayre ' [1] had only eighty and forty to their respective accounts. Throughout Yorkshire the average does not seem to have been above ten cloths, and in Kent, a stronghold of the broad cloth manufacture, only one clothier exceeded fifty dozens, and only three others passed twenty-five. The whole evidence seems to limit the spheres of influence of the capitalist clothiers to a few definite towns prior to the beginning of the fifteenth century. But the latter half of the fifteenth century saw the rise of the great

---

[1] Marcus le Fair of Winchester was the only clothier not a Londoner from whom cloth was bought for the royal household in 1408. Exch. K. R. Accts., 405, no. 22.

clothiers such as John Winchcombe,[1] the famous ' Jack of Newbury ', and the Springs of Lavenham,[2] employers of labour on a scale which soon swamped the small independent clothworkers, and drew them into a position of dependence.

Skill and industry in the cloth trade had always been assured of a good return, and when combined with enterprise had often led to wealth ; but there have in all times and all places been men who would try the short cut to fortune through fraud ; and the openings for fraud in the cloth trade were particularly numerous.

' Certayne townes in England . . . were wonte to make theyre clothes of certayne bredth and length and to sette theyre seales to the same ; while they kept the rate trulye strangers dyd but looke over the seale and receyve theyre wares, wherebye these townes had greate vente of theyre clothes and consequently prospered verye welle. Afterwards some in those townes, not content with reasonable gaynes but contyntually desyrynge more, devysed clothes of lesse length, bredthe and goodnes thanne they were wonte to be, and yet by the comendacioun of the seale to have as myche monye for the same as they had before for good clothes. And for a tyme they gate myche and so abused the credythe of theyr predecessours to theyre singulere lukere, whiche was recompensede with the losse of theyre posterytye. For these clothes were founde fawltye for alle theyre seale, they were not onelye never the better trustede but myche lesse for theyre seale, yea although theyre clothes were well made. For whanne theyr untruth and falshed was espyede than no manne wolde buye theyre clothes untylle they were enforsede and unfoldede, regardynge nothynge the seale.' [3]

---

[1] *V. C. H. Berks.*, i. 388.   [2] *V. C. H. Suffolk*, ii. 256.
[3] *Hist. MSS. Com. Rep.*, viii. 93.

This complaint, written in the time of Henry VIII, is borne out in every detail by the records of Parliament and of municipalities. Regulations were constantly laid down for ensuring uniformity, and officials called ulnagers [1] were appointed to see that they were obeyed, no cloth being allowed to be sold unless it bore the ulnager's seal. The assize of cloth issued in 1328 [2] fixed the measurements of cloth of ray at 28 yards by 6 quarters, and those of coloured cloths at 26 yards by $6\frac{1}{2}$ quarters, in the raw state, each being 24 yards when shrunk. The penalty for infringement of the assize was forfeiture. [3] This assize, which was confirmed in 1406, repealed next year, but reaffirmed in 1410, [4] applied only to broad cloths, but in 1432 it was laid down [5] that narrow cloths called 'streits' should be 12 yards by 1 yard, when shrunk ; if smaller they were not forfeited, but the ulnager cut the list off one end, to show that it was not a whole cloth, and it was sold as a 'remnant' according to its actual measure. In the case of the worsteds or serges of Norfolk, four different assizes were said in 1327 to have been used from time immemorial, namely, 50, 40, 30, and 24 ells in length ; [6] but as early as 1315 merchants complained that the cloths of Worsted and Aylesham did not keep their assize, 20 ells being sold as 24, 25 ells as 30, and so on. [7] In the western counties, Somerset, Gloucester, and Dorset, fraudulent

---

[1] Vlnage, or aulnage, from *aulne* = an ell.

[2] Statutes, 2 Edw. III.

[3] The penalty of forfeiture was withdrawn in 1354 as injurious to trade, deficient cloths being marked with their actual size. *Ibid.*, 27 Edw. III.

[4] Statutes, 7, 8, 10 Hen. IV. [5] Statutes, 11 Hen. VI.

[6] *Rec. of City of Norwich*, ii. 407. [7] *Rot. Parl.*, i. 292.

makers were in the habit of so tacking and folding their cloths that defects in length or quality could not be seen, with the result that merchants who bought them in good faith and took them to foreign countries were beaten, imprisoned, and even slain by their angry customers, 'to the great dishonour of the realm'. It was, therefore, ordered in 1390 that no cloth should be sold tacked and folded, but open.[1] The frauds in connexion with stretching Guildford cloths have already been referred to, and in 1410 we find that worsteds which had formerly been in great demand abroad were now so deceitfully made that the Flemish merchants were talking of searching, or examining, all the worsted cloths at the ports of entry. To remedy this 'great slander of the country', the mayor and his deputies were given the power to search and seal all worsteds brought to the worsted 'seld', or cloth market, and regulations were made as to the size of 'thretty elnys streites' (30 ells by 2 quarters), 'thretty elyns brodes' (30 ells by 3 quarters), 'mantelles, sengles, doubles, et demy doubles, si bien les motles, paules, chekeres, raies, flores, pleynes, monkes-clothes et autres mantelles' (from 6 to 10 ells by $1\frac{1}{4}$ ell), and 'chanonclothes, sengles, demy doubles et doubles' (5 ells by $1\frac{3}{4}$), the variety of trade terms showing the extent of the industry.[2] A similar complaint of the decay in the foreign demand for worsteds owing to the malpractices of the makers was met in 1442 by causing the worsted weavers of Norwich to elect annually four wardens for the city and two for the county to oversee the trade.[3] Half a century later,

---

[1] Statutes, 13 Rich. II ; 11 Hen. IV.
[2] *Rot. Parl.*, iii. 637.   [3] Statutes, 20 Hen. VI.

in 1473, English cloth in general had fallen into disrepute abroad, and even at home, much foreign cloth being imported : to remedy this, general orders were issued for the proper working of cloth, the maintenance of the old assize, and the indication of defects, a seal being attached to the lower edge of any cloth where there was any ' raw, skaw, cokel or fagge '.[1]

The last-mentioned statute of 1473 gives the measurements of the cloths as by the ' yard and inch '. Originally it would seem to have been customary when measuring cloth to mark the end of each yard by placing the thumb on the cloth at the end of the clothyard, and starting again on the other side of the thumb. Readers of George Eliot will remember that the pedlar, Bob Salt, made ingenious use of his broad thumb in measuring, to the detriment of his customers ; and the London drapers in the fifteenth century claimed to buy by the ' yard and a hand ', marking the yards with the hand instead of with the thumb, and thereby scoring two yards in every twenty-four.[2] Although this was forbidden in 1440, the use being ordered of a measuring line of silk, 12 yards and 12 inches long, the end of each yard being marked an inch, it evidently continued in practice, as the ' yarde and handfull ' was known as London measure at the end of the sixteenth century.[3]

From one cause and another the English clothing industry encountered a period of depression from about the middle of the fifteenth century. The towns in particular were affected, as the jealous rigidity with which they maintained the rules and privileges of their

---

[1] Statutes, 4 Edw. IV.
[2] Statutes, 18 Hen. VI.   [3] Exch. Dep. by Com., 41 Eliz.

gilds led the more enterprising clothiers to establish themselves in the country districts, where they were less harassed by obsolete regulations, and where, in some cases, they were better able to exploit cheap labour. At Bury St. Edmunds in 1477 the craft, at which large numbers of men, women, and children were employed, was reported to be much decayed ; which was attributed to the ' deceyvable and untrewe werkyng and wewyng ' of some members.[1]   At Canterbury in 1506, where the same state of affairs prevailed, an attempt was made to stimulate the industry by forbidding the sale of wool out of the city and by an agreement that the mayor and each of his brethren should have two whole cloths woven during the next year, the members of the council and others of similar standing commissioning one cloth each.[2] The foreign trade was large, 300,000 ducats worth of cloth being shipped at London in 1514 by Venetian merchants for export to Constantinople and Scio alone,[3] and many Venetians and ' Araguseys ' (merchants of Ragusa) making fortunes by trading in English kerseys to Turkey ; [4] but in spite of that we find the clothiers of Stoke and of Kent complaining in 1528 that they have no sale for their cloth in London,[5] and will have to give up their business if some remedy is not found.[6]   The social and economic revolution brought about by the dissolution of the monasteries had a considerable effect upon the cloth industry.   On the one hand, the estates and buildings of the religious houses, often including

---

[1] *Hist. MSS. Com. Rep.*, xiv (8), 133.   [2] *Ibid.*, ix. 174.

[3] *Cal. S. P. Venice.*   [4] *L. & P. Hen. VIII*, xiv (1), 910.

[5] Bartholomew Fair was one of the chief places at which cloth was bought for export.   *Ibid.*, xiii (1), 1453.   [6] *Ibid.*, iv (2), 4239.

fulling mills and other workshops kept for the supply of
the monastic households, came into the market and were
purchased by capitalist clothiers. On the other hand,
a large amount of cheap labour became available in the
persons of the innumerable dependents of the monasteries who were thrown out of work, or out of alms. In
1538 Abingdon was said to be likely to decay unless the
people were put to work to ' drape cloth ', and Tuckar,
a cloth-maker of Burford, offered to spend 100 marks a
week in wages if he could have the use of two fulling
mills and other property belonging to the dissolved
abbey,[1] while at Oxford it was suggested that if the
friaries were granted to the corporation the town could
become a clothing centre, as there were good sites for
fulling mills at both the Black and the Grey Friars.[2]
Some years later William Stumpe, the great clothier
who had bought Malmesbury Abbey, offered to take
over Oseney Abbey and convert it into a cloth factory
for the Oxford district, undertaking to employ 2,000
persons, if so many could be found ' that wyll do their
worke well continually in clothemakyng '.[3]

Attempts to deal with the growing problem of poverty
and unemployment during Elizabeth's reign by the local
encouragement of clothmaking were numerous. At
Leicester in 1572 the corporation made a loan of 100
marks to Thomas Bradgate to enable him to set up
clothing in the town and provide work for the poor.[4]
This device had been employed at Lincoln as early as
1516, when a contribution was got up to start cloth-

[1] *L. & P. Hen. VIII*, xiii (1), 332.   [2] *Ibid.*, 1342.
[3] W. H. Turner, *Rec. of Oxford*, 185.
[4] *Hist. MSS. Com. Rep.*, viii. 427.

making in the town—so far had Lincoln fallen from the days of her famous scarlets and greens—the mayor obtained a clothier to superintend the work, and the freedom of the city and other boons were offered to all clothworkers who would settle there.[1] The scheme had not had any lasting effect ; Lincoln continued to decay, and in 1551 another attempt to encourage the industry was made. Tolls on wool, woad, madder, oil, alum, or other things used for clothmaking brought into the city, and on cloth brought there, were suspended for seven years. All young people or others who were idle were to be taken by the clothiers for eight or nine years, receiving meat, drink, clothes, and necessaries, those who refused to work being given a month's notice to leave the town. Also the disused church of the Holy Rood was handed over to the clothiers, to convert into a walk-mill and dyehouse, rent free, provided they made at least 20 broad cloths yearly.[2] One other instance may be given as showing the struggle between a free trade corporation and a protectionist gild. In 1575 the need for finding employment for the poor in Chester led the corporation to form a scheme to introduce the manufacture of ' cottons friezes russets baies &c.' as made in Shrewsbury ; this was strenuously opposed by the Weavers' Company, who tried to drive the new-comers out of the city. The mayor and corporation, however, took up a firm position and granted freedom to outside workers to practise the making of cloths of the Shropshire or Welsh type, and also allowed George Sherington of Preston to introduce the making of Kentish cloth and to employ 20 persons thereon. At the same

[1] *Hist. MSS. Com. Rep.*, xiv (8), 26.   [2] *Ibid.*, 44.

time a ' House of Correction ', or workhouse, to use the
more familiar name, was set up to employ 40 people in
cloth making.[1] The maximum wages at Chester at this
time were : spinning and hand-carding a ' waight ' of
wool, 6*d.* ; stock-carding a stone (of 4 ' waights ') of wool,
6*d.* ; dyeing a stone, 16*d.* ; weaving a piece of cloth
of 22 yards, 12*d.* ; walking the same, 8*d.* ; shearman
for dressing the same, 10*d.*[2]

The last years of the mediaeval period of the woollen
industry, which we take as terminating with the introduction of the ' New Draperies ' by foreign refugees
early in the reign of Elizabeth, are chiefly concerned
with the endeavours of the town clothiers to suppress
the country cloth workers, assisted by Acts which
restricted, or at least aimed at restricting, the industry
to corporate boroughs and market towns, and prohibited
any from setting up in trade without having passed
a seven years' apprenticeship.[3] Infringements of these
laws were frequent, and thanks to the system of granting
a portion of the fines inflicted to the informer, accusa-
tions were constantly levelled against clothiers for
breaking the various regulations with which the trade
was hedged about.[4] Many of the charges fell through,
and in some cases they look like blackmail, but that
offences were sufficiently plentiful is clear. For the one
year, 1562, as many as sixty clothiers from Kent
alone, mostly from the neighbourhood of Cranbrook
and Benenden, were fined for sending up to London
for sale cloths deficient in size, weight, quality, or

[1] Morris, *Chester,* 390, 408.
[2] *Ibid.,* 409.
[3] Statutes, 5 Edw. VI ; 1 Mary, &c.
[4] See Memoranda Rolls, K. R., *passim.*

colour.[1] An absolute fulfilment of all the regulations was, perhaps, no easy thing, for although cloths which had been sealed by the ulnager in the district where they were made were not supposed to pay ulnage in London, the makers preferred as a rule to pay a halfpenny on each cloth to the London searchers rather than risk the results of too close a scrutiny.[2]

During the reign of Edward VI there appears to have been a rapid rise in the price of cloth, mainly due, no doubt, to the fall in the purchasing value of money, which had been caused by the lowering of the standard of the silver coinage. A list drawn up in 1551 showing the prices at that time and four years earlier is of interest, not only for its statistics but also as giving the names of the chief varieties of cloths : [3]

Welsh cottons had risen from	8*d*. the ' goyde ' in 1547 to							13*d*.
Cheshire	,,	,,	,,	,,	£7 the pack	,,	,,	£14, or £14 10*s*.
Northern kerseys		,,	,,	£24	,,	,,	,,	£40.
Hampshire	,,	,,	,,	£29	,,	,,	,,	£50, or £52.
Devonshire dossens	,,	,,	£26	,,	,,	,,	,,	£50.
Northern	,,	,,	,,	£23	,,	,,	,,	£38.
Welsh fryses	,,	,,	,,	23*s*. the piece	,,	,,	46*s*.8*d*.
Bristol	,,	,,	,,	,,	24*s*. ,,	,,	,,	44*s*.
Penyston whites	,,	,,	15*s*.	,,	,,	,,	,,	30*s*.
Suffolk sorting cloth	,,	,,	£3 6*s*. 8*d*.	,,	,,	,,	£7.
Kentish cloths	,,	,,	,,	£6	,,	,,	,,	£10, or £11.
,,	,,	(fine)	,,	,,	£10, £12	,,	,,	£19, or £20.

---

[1] Memo. R., K. R., Hil. 7 Eliz., m. 329. As an earlier instance, sixteen drapers in Coventry, thirteen in York, and seven in Lincoln, besides others elsewhere, were fined in the first quarter of 1390 for cloths of ray, not of assize. *Ibid.*, Hil. 13 Rich. II.

[2] Exch. Dep. by Com., 30 Eliz., Hil., 8.

[3] A. H. Johnson, *Hist. of Co. of Drapers*, ii. 395.

Of the many local varieties of cloth made in England, that which derived its name from the village of Worsted in Norfolk was, on the whole, the most important. We have seen that by the end of the thirteenth century worsted weaving was well established in Norfolk, and particularly in Norwich, and that worsted serges and says were articles of export, while a century later the forms in which these cloths were made up were very varied. Norwich continued to hold the monopoly of searching and sealing worsteds, wherever made, until 1523, when the industry had grown to such an extent in Yarmouth that the weavers of that town were licensed to elect a

The Weaver's panel at Spaxton Church. 16th cent.

warden of their own to seal their cloth; the same privilege was granted to Lynn, provided there were at least ten householders exercising the trade there; but in all cases the cloths were to be shorn, dyed, coloured, and calendered in Norwich.[1] When the art of

[1] Statutes, 14–15 Hen. VIII.

calendering worsteds, that is to say, giving them a smooth finish by pressing, was introduced in Norwich is uncertain, but in the second half of the fifteenth century the 'fete and misterie of calendryng of worstedes' in London was known only to certain Frenchmen. An enterprising merchant, William Halingbury, brought over from Paris one Toisaunts Burges, to teach the art to English workers, and, in revenge, one of the London French calenders endeavoured to have Halingbury arrested on his next visit to Paris.[1] At the beginning of the sixteenth century a process of dry calendering with 'gommes, oyles and presses' was introduced, by which inferior worsteds were made to look like the best quality, but if touched with wet they at once spotted and spoiled. The process was therefore prohibited in 1514, and at the same time the practice of wet calendering was confined to those who had served seven years' apprenticeship, and had been admitted to the craft by the mayor of Norwich or the wardens of the craft in the county of Norfolk.[2]

In 1315 cloths of Aylsham (in Norfolk) are coupled with those of Worsted as not conforming to the old assize,[3] and at the coronation of Edward III some 3,500 ells of 'Ayllesham' was used for lining armour, covering cushions, and making 1,860 pennons with the arms of St. George.[4] But as Buckram and Aylsham are constantly bracketed together,[5] being used, for instance, in 1333 for making hobby horses (*hobihors*) for the king's

---

[1] Early Chanc. Proc., 141, no. 4.

[2] Statutes, 5 Hen. VIII.   [3] *Rot. Parl.*, i. 292.

[4] The same material was used in 1323 for the pillows of the king's new beds. Enr. Ward. Accts., 3, m. 2.

[5] *Ibid.*, m. 10.

games,[1] presumably at Christmas, it would seem that
Aylshams were linen and not woollen, especially as
' lynge teille de Eylesham ' was famous in the fourteenth
century.[2]

Very little appears to be ascertainable about the
history of linen-weaving in England. That it was carried
on fairly extensively is evident from casual references.
Thus, in the list of purchases for the king's wardrobe in
1336, as much as 9,693 ells of English linen are entered,
against 237 ells from Paris and 1,125 ells from Rennes
(a great centre of the manufacture).[3] Similar purchases
a few years earlier show 1,380 ells of English linen and
313 of linen of Paris and of Wilton together.[4] From
other entries it is clear that Wilton was in early times
the seat of the finest if not the most prolific manufacture
of linen in this country. As early as 1232 we find the
sheriff of Wiltshire ordered to buy at Wilton 500 ells of
linen to make tablecloths for the royal household for
Christmas, at 3*d*. or 3½*d*. an ell.[5] Twenty years later
1,000 ells of beautiful and delicate linen were ordered
through the same sheriff.[6] An extensive purchase of
linen in Herefordshire is mentioned in 1180,[7] and at the
opposite side of the country a linen market existed in
Norwich at the end of the reign of Henry III.[8] Generally
speaking, no sharp line was drawn between the weaving
of linen and of woollen cloth ; at Bury St. Edmunds in
1477 ordinances were drawn up for the weavers of ' all

---

[1] Enr. Ward. Accts., 2, m. 11.
[2] *Engl. Hist. Rev.*, xvi. 289.
[3] Enrolled Accts. of Wardrobe, ii. 5.   [4] *Ibid.*, iii. 10.
[5] Liberate R., 17 Hen. III, m. 10.
[6] *Ibid.*, 37 Hen. III, m. 4.   [7] Pipe R., 27 Hen. II.
[8] *Ibid.*, 56 Hen. III.

maner of wuluene and lynene cloethe ',[1] and in London, where the question had been raised in 1440 whether the ' lynnewebbes ' were included in the weavers' gild founded in the twelfth century,[2] the bailiffs of the weavers in 1492 were to be one a woollen weaver and the other a linen weaver, and it was stipulated that no linen weaver should take any woollen yarn to weave unless he could work it himself and had the necessary gear,[3] evidently implying that some did work both materials, just as at Hythe in 1412 we find a man paying dues for 800 ells of woollen cloth and 500 of linen woven that year.[4] As with woollen cloth, so the linen industry appears to have decayed in the sixteenth century ; the prevalent unemployment was largely ascribed in 1532 to the excessive imports of foreign linen, and to remedy this farmers were ordered to sow at least a quarter of an acre of flax for every acre of arable that they cultivated,[5] and seven years later an Act was drafted to set idle people (i. e. the unemployed poor) to work on making linen cloth.[6]

In Suffolk the village of Kersey was an early centre of clothmaking, and gave its name to a type of cloth which was afterwards made in a great number of districts. The kerseys of Suffolk and Essex were exempted in 1376, with other narrow cloths, from keeping the assize of coloured cloths,[7] and just a century later the measure-

---

[1] *Hist. MSS. Com. Rep.*, xiv (8), 133.
[2] Pat., 18 Hen. VI, pt. 3, m. 19d. ; cf. Chanc. Proc., 45, no. 30.
[3] *London Letter Book L*, 290.
[4] *Hist. MSS. Com. Rep.*, iv. 434.
[5] Statutes, 24 Hen. VIII, c. 4.
[6] *L. & P. Hen. VIII*, xiv (1), 872.
[7] *Rot. Parl.*, ii. 347.

ment for kerseys was set out as 18 yards by 1 yard.[1]
Curiously enough the chief trouble with the assize of
kerseys, at least in the sixteenth century, was not short
measure, but over long, the explanation being that
kerseys paid export duty by the whole cloth, and it was
therefore to the merchant's advantage to pay duty on
a piece of 25 yards rather than to pay the same duty on
18 yards.[2] Kerseys were largely made for export, and
a petition against restrictions tending to hamper foreign
trade was presented, about 1537, by the kersey weavers
of Berks., Oxon., Hants, Surrey, Sussex, and Yorkshire.[3]
These counties were the chief centres of the manufacture,
though Devonshire kersies were also made ; in Berk-
shire, Newbury was then the great seat of the industry,
and the kerseys of John Winchcombe (' Jack of Newbury ') in particular had a more than local fame. Hampshire kerseys was the generic name applied to these made
in Hampshire, Sussex, and Surrey, but in earlier times
the Isle of Wight had almost a monopoly of the manufacture in the district. The ulnage accounts for Hampshire in 1394–5 give ninety names of clothiers for the
Isle of Wight,[4] who made 600 kerseys, and no other kind
of cloth, and about a century later we find a draper
complaining that when he had bargained with a London
merchant for a certain number of ' kersys of Wyght '
worth £6 he had been put off with Welsh kerseys worth
only £4 13s. 4d.[5]

---

[1] Statutes, 4 Edw. IV.   [2] *V. C. H. Surrey*, ii. 343.
[3] *Ibid.*, 343.
[4] Exch. K. R. Accts., 344, no. 10. The output from Berks. for
the same period was 1,747 kerseys, of which Steventon accounted
for 574 and East and West Hendred for 520. *Ibid.*, 343, no. 24.
[5] Early Chanc. Proc., 140, no. 54.

Suffolk did a considerable trade in a cheap coarse variety of cloth known as ' Vesses or set cloths ' for export to the East ; and as it was the recognized custom to stretch these to the utmost, and they were bought as unshrunk, this class of cloth was exempted in 1523 from the regulations as to stretching cloth.[1] Possibly these Vesses were connected with the ' Western Blankett of Vyse (Wilts.) and Bekinton '.[2] Blanket is found in 1395 as made at Maldon, and, on the other side of England, at Hereford, while at an earlier date, in 1360, Guildford blanket was bought for the royal household.[3] As Norwich had its ' monk's cloth ' and ' canon cloth ', presumably so called from its suitability for monastic and canonical habits, unlike the fine cloth of Worcester, which, we are told, was forbidden to Benedictines,[4] so we find that the newly made knight of the Bath had to vest himself in ' hermit's array ' of Colchester russet.[5] Most of the cloths made in Essex were ' streits ' or narrow cloths, of rather a poor quality, being often coupled with the inferior cloths such as cogware and Kendal cloth. Of the latter a writer of the time of Henry VIII says, ' I knowe when a servynge manne was content to goo in a Kendall cote in sommer and a frysecote in winter, and with playne white hose made meete for his bodye. . . . Now he will looke to have at the leaste for Somere a cote of finest clothe that may be gotten for money and his hosen of the finest kerseye, and that of some straunge dye, as Flaunders dye or Frenche puke, that a prynce or

---

[1] Statutes, 14–15 Hen. VIII.
[2] *Rot. Parl.*, iv. 361.
[3] Enr. Ward. Accts., 4, m. 3.
[4] *V. C. H. Worcs.*, ii. 284.
[5] *V. C. H. Essex*, ii. 384.

a greate lorde canne were no better if he were [wear] clothe '.[1]

By the sumptuary law of 1363, farm labourers and others having less than 40s. in goods were to wear blanket and russet costing not more than 12d. the ell.[2] In a list of purchases of cloth in 1409, narrow russet figures at 12d. the ell, while of the other cheap varieties short blanket, short coloured cloth, rays, motleys, and friezes varied from 2s. to 2s. 4d. the ell.[3] Of friezes the two chief types in use were those of Coventry and Irish friezes, which might either be made in Ireland or of Irish wool : these seem to have come into use about the middle of the fourteenth century, as in 1376 Irish ' Frysseware ' was exempted from ulnage,[4] and about the same time purchases of Irish frieze for the royal household become more common, as much as nearly 3,000 ells of this material being bought in 1399.[5]

With such local varieties as Manchester cottons, Tauntons, Tavistocks, Barnstaple whites, Mendips, ' Stoke Gomers alias thromme clothes,' [6] and so forth, space does not permit of our dealing, while by the limitation which we have set ourselves the ' new draperies ' are excluded, and we may thankfully leave on one side ' arras, bays, bewpers, boulters, boratoes, buffins, bustyans, bombacyes, blankets, callimancoes, carrells, chambletts, cruell, dornicks, duraunce, damask, frisadoes,

---

[1] *Hist. MSS. Com. Rep.*, viii. 93.

[2] *Rot. Parl.*, ii. 278. [3] Exch. K. R. Accts., 405, no. 22.

[4] *Rot. Parl.*, ii. 372. The assize of coloured cloths did not apply to ' Dudderiware ', ' Faldyngware ', and other cloths of Ireland. Pat., 48 Edw. III, pt. 2, m. 11.

[5] Enr. Ward. Accts., 5.

[6] Memo. R., K. R., 21 Eliz., East., m. 106.

fringe, fustyans, felts, flanells, grograines, garterings, girdlings, linsey woolseyes, mockadoes, minikins, moun-taines, makerells, oliotts, pomettes, plumettes, per-petuanas, perpicuanas, rashes, rugges, russells, sattins, serges, syettes, sayes, stamells, stamines, scallops, tukes, tamettes, tobines, and valures '.[1]

[1] *Rep. Dep. Keeper of Recs.*, xxxviii. 444 ; suit *re* draperies at Norwich, 1601.

X

LEATHER WORKING

THE dressing of skins and preparation of leather must have been one of the most widely diffused industries in mediaeval times.[1] Two different processes were employed, ox, cow, and calf hides being tanned by immersion in a decoction of oak bark, while the skins of deer, sheep, and horses were tawed with alum and oil, and the two trades were from early times kept quite separate, tanners and tawyers being forbidden to work skins appropriated to each other's trade. A certain concentration of the industry must have been brought about in 1184, when orders were issued that no tanner or tawyer should practise his trade within the bounds of a forest except in a borough or market town,[2] the object being to prevent the poaching of deer for the sake of their skins. Market towns had the further advantage of being well supplied with the raw material, as butchers were compelled to bring the hides of their beasts into market with the meat, and the tanners had the sole right of purchase, no regrater or middle-man being allowed to intervene, while on the other hand the tanners were not allowed to buy the hides outside the open market.[3] Towards the end of the sixteenth century it

---

[1] Thorold Rogers, *Six Centuries of Work and Wages*, 46.

[2] The suggestion that this law caused the trade to be established in Norwich (*Recs. of Norwich*, II. xii) can hardly be correct, as there was no forest in Norfolk.

[3] For instances of the infringement of these and other regulations, see *V. C. H. Surrey*, ii. 331–5 ; *V. C. H. Sussex*, ii. 259.

was said [1] that ' in most villages of the realm there is some one dresser or worker of leather, and . . . in most of the market towns three, four, or five, and many great towns 10 or 20, and in London and the suburbs . . . to the number of 200 or very near '. Casting back, we find at Oxford in 1380 there were twelve tanners, twenty

skinners, twelve cordwainers, or shoemakers, and four saddlers,[2] while in 1300 there were at Colchester forty householders employed in the various branches of the leather trade.[3]

Originally, no doubt, the leather dresser worked up his own leather, and as late as 1323 it would seem that at Shrewsbury cordwainers were allowed to tan leather,[4] but in 1351 the tanners and

THE SKINNER. 16th cent.

shoemakers were definitely forbidden to intermeddle with each other's craft, and a series of regulations, parliamentary and municipal, served to separate the tanners, the curriers, who dressed and ' suppled ' the rough tanned hides, the tawyers, and the various branches of leather-workers. At Chester the tanners in 1362 obtained from the Black Prince a charter forbidding the cordwainers to meddle with their trade.

[1] Lansd. MS., 74, 55.　　　　[2] *V. C. H. Oxon.*, ii. 254.
[3] *V. C. H. Essex*, ii. 459.　　[4] *V. C. H. Shrops.*, i. 433.

This was revoked in 1370 as contrary to the interests
of the city, and a joint charter was granted to the skinners, shoemakers, and tanners, but the three crafts
eventually separated again.[1]

The stock in trade of the tanner was simple. The
inventories of the goods of half a dozen tanners at
Colchester in 1300 are identical in kind though varying
in value ;[2] each consists of hides, oak bark, and a
number of vats and tubs. In the case of the tannery at
Meaux Abbey[3] (the larger monastic houses usually
maintained their own tanneries) in 1396 rather more
details are given. There were in store cow and calf
leather, ‘ sole peces, sclepe, clowthedys, and wambes ’
to the value of £14 10s. 4d., 15 tubs and various tools,
such as 3 ‘ schapyng-knyfes ’ and 4 knives for the
tan ; 400 tan turves (blocks of bark from which the tan
had been extracted), and ‘ the tan from all the oaks
barked this year ’. The raw hides had first to be soaked,
then treated with lime to remove the hair, and then
washed again before being placed in the tan vat. Consequently leather dressers settled ‘ where they may have
water in brooks and rivers to dress their leather ;
without great store of running water they cannot dress
the same ’.[4] In 1461 William Frankwell, when making
a grant of a meadow at Lewes, reserved the right to use
the ditch on the south side of the meadow for his hides,[5]
and complaints of the fouling of town water supplies
by leather-workers were not unusual.[6] The process of

---

[1] Morris, *Chester*, 410.
[2] *Rot. Parl.*, i. 243–65.   [3] Cott. MS. Vitell., C. vi, f. 239.
[4] Lansd. MS., 74, f. 52.   [5] Add. Chart, 30687.
[6] e. g. at Colchester in 1425. *V. C. H. Essex*, ii. 459 : and at
Richmond in 1280. Assize R., 1064, m. 32. In London the tanners

tanning was, and for the best leather still is, extremely slow ; the hides were supposed to lie in the ' wooses ' (ooze, or liquor) for a whole year, and stringent regulations were issued to prevent the hastening of the process, to the detriment of the leather. The bark from which the tan was obtained, and which was so important a feature of the process that ' barker ' was an alternative name for tanner, had to be only of oak, the use of ash bark being forbidden ; nor might lime or hot liquor be used, the embedding of the vats in hot beds of old tan being prohibited.

Hides, both raw and tanned, ranked with cloth as a leading article of trade, both home and foreign ; [1] and, like cloth, tanned leather was early subject to examination by searchers, appointed either by the craft gild or by the town authorities. As a rule the searcher's seal was affixed in the market, or at the particular ' seld ' or hall where alone leather might be sold. This was the case in London, where the hides were inspected at Leadenhall by a joint committee of cordwainers, girdlers, and curriers, and stamped with a special seal to show whether they were good or bad,[2] but at Bristol in 1415 the searchers were empowered to examine the hides at the curriers' houses before they were curried.[3] The curriers, whose business it was to dress the ' red ' hides with tallow,[4] rendering them smooth and supple, were

were held partly responsible for blocking the course of the Fleet in 1306. *Rot. Parl.*, i. 200.

[1] Customs Accts., *passim* : e. g. those quoted in *V. C. H. Dorset*, ii. 327.

[2] W. H. Black, *Hist. of Leather-sellers' Co.*, 25.

[3] *Little Red Book of Bristol*, ii. 114.

[4] The use of train oil instead of tallow was forbidden.

not allowed to dress badly tanned hides.[1] Several grades
of tanning were recognized, the most lengthy and
thorough workmanship being required for leather intended for the soles of boots and rather less for the
uppers. When forty-seven hides belonging to Nicholas
Burle, of London, were seized in 1378 as not well tanned,
he admitted that they were not fit for shoe leather, but
urged that he intended to sell them to saddlers, girdlers,
and makers of leather bottles : a mixed jury of these
various trades, however, condemned the hides as unfit
for any purpose, and they were forfeited.[2]

Although there was thus an efficient control exercised
over tanned leather, the tawed soft leathers used by
glovers, pointmakers, pursemakers, saddlers, girdlers,
coffermakers, budgetmakers, stationers, &c., seem for
the most part to have escaped supervision, with the
result that at the end of the sixteenth century the
markets were flooded with counterfeit leathers.[3]

| ' All Tawed leather is dressed with | Oil, as | Buff } of the first and Shamys } best sort. |
| | or with Alum and Oker as the hides of | Bull, Ox, Steer, Cow, Horse, Stag, Hind, Buck, Doe, Calf, Dog, Seal, Sheep, Lamb, Kid. |

' The leather dressed with oil is made more supple,
soft and spongey, and is wrought with a rough cotton,
as bayes and fresadoes are, the cotton being raised in
the fulling mill where cloth is fulled, and serveth for the
more beauty and pleasure to the wearer.

' The leather dressed with alum and oker is more
tough and " thight ", serving better for the use of the
poor artificer, husbandman, and labourer, and a more

[1] *V. C. H. Northants,* ii. 311.
[2] Riley, *Mems. of London,* 421.　　　[3] Lansd. MS., 74, f. 48.

easy price by half, and is wrought smooth or with cotton which is raised by hand with a card or other like tool, and as the alum giveth strength and toughness, the oker giveth it colour, like as the oil doth give colour to Buff and Shamoys.

' And this diversity of dressing, with oil or alum, is to be discerned both by smell and by a dust which ariseth from the alum leather. . . .

' All Shamoys leather is made of goat skins brought for the most part out of Barbury, from the " Est countries ", Scotland, Ireland, and other foreign parts, unwrought, and is transported again being wrought. And there is much thereof made from skins from Wales and other parts within the realm. . . . Being dressed with oil it beareth the name Shamoys, but being dressed with alum and oker, it beareth not the name or price of Shamoys, but of Goat skins.'

' Shamoys [1] is made of goat, buck, doe, hind, sore, sorrell, and sheepskins. The true way of dressing is in " trayne oyle ", the counterfeit is with alum and is worth about half. . . . Shamoys dressed in train oil can be dressed again three or four times, and seem as good as new, but dressed in alum it will hardly dress twice and will soon be spied. And when Shamoys dressed in alum cometh to the rain or any water they will be hard like tanned leather, and Shamoys in oil make the cheapest and most lasting apparel, which the " low countrie man and the highe Almayn " doth use.'

Frauds in the preparation and sale of leather were of frequent occurrence, and in 1372 the mayor and aldermen of London ordained penalties for the sale of dyed sheep and calf leather scraped and prepared so as to look like roe leather. At the same time the leather dyers were forbidden to dye such counterfeit leathers, and also to use the brasil or other dye provided or selected by one

[1] Lansd. MS., 74, f. 53.

customer for the goods of another.[1] With the same
object of preventing frauds, the tawyers who worked for
furriers were not allowed to cut the heads off the skins
which they dressed, and were also liable to imprisonment
if they worked old furs up into leather.[2] Further
penalties for false and deceitful work, especially in the
making of leather ' points and lanyers ', or laces and
thongs, were enacted in 1398.[3] By these ordinances
such laces might only be made of ' wild ware ' (i. e.
' Herte, Hynde, Bukke, Doo, Roo, Goote and Kydde ')
and not of sheep and calf skins, which did not wear so
well. But in 1467 the leather-sellers declared that these
regulations were out of date: when they were passed
there was a good supply of wild-ware from Norway,
Spain, Guienne, and Scotland, but now the supply had
fallen off—partly because the leather-workers had so
increased in numbers that many had set up outside the
city, even in Scotland, so that little came now from there.
Also, the provincial workers had flooded the market
with cheap laces of sheep, lamb, and calf leather, so
that people would not buy the more expensive kind.
Moreover, sheep and calf leather was much better
worked now : so the use of any kind of leather was
licensed—provided that its nature was specified, and
with the exception that ' armyng poyntes ', or laces for
fastening armour, must still be made of wild-ware.[4] In
the same way in 1434 the girdlers had obtained a revision
of their ordinances of 1344 on the ground that they were
out of date, many of the trade terms having become

[1] Riley, *Mems. of London*, 364–5.
[2] *Ibid.*, 331.   [3] *Ibid.*, 546–7.
[4] W. H. Black, *Hist. of Leather-sellers' Co.*, 33.

unintelligible and fashions having changed so that ox-leather, the use of which was enjoined by the regulations, was no longer much used.[1]

With the growth of capitalism during the reign of Elizabeth, the control exercised by the Leather-sellers' Company became almost nominal, some half a dozen wealthy members of the company getting the whole trade into their own hands. By buying up the leather all over the country, they forced up prices ; having, moreover, a practical monopoly of tawed leathers, they were able to make the glovers and other leather-workers take the dressed skins in packets of a dozen, which contained three or four small ' linings ' or worthless skins.[2] They also undertook the dressing of the skins, and cut out the good workmen by scamping their work and employing men who had only served half their seven years' apprenticeship.[3] They also caused dogskins, ' fishe skynnes of zeale,' calf, and other skins to be so dressed as to resemble ' right Civill [i. e. Seville] and Spannish skynnes ', worth twice as much. These skins were dressed ' with the powder of date stones and of gaule and with French shomake that is nothinge like the Spannish shomake, to give them a pretie sweete savor but nothinge like to the civile skynnes, and the powder of theise is of veary smale price and the powder of right Spannish shomake grounded in a mill is wourth xxx^s the c^{lb} weight, which shomake is a kynd of brush, shrubb, or heath in Spayne and groweth low by the ground and is swete like Gale [4] in Cambridgshire and is cutt twise

---

[1] *London Letter Book K*, 199.
[2] Lansd. MS., 74, f. 49.
[3] *Ibid.*, 60. [4] i. e. bog-myrtle.

a yeare and soe dried and grounded into powder by milles and dresseth all the Civile and Spannish skynnes brought hither.' [1] To remedy these frauds there was a general demand that tawed leather should be searched and sealed in the same way as tanned, and in 1593 Edmund Darcy turned this to his own advantage by obtaining a royal grant of the right to carry out such searching and sealing. This was opposed by the leather-sellers, on the grounds that it would interfere with the sale and purchase in country districts if buyer and seller had to wait till the searcher could attend, and that the proposed fees for sealing were exorbitant, amounting to something between a ninth and a half of the value of the skins. They also said that if a seal were put on, it would almost always be pared away, washed out, or ' extincte by dying ' before the leather reached the consumer.[2] Upon examination the suggested fees were found to be too large, and a table of the different kinds of leather and their values was drawn up, and fees fixed accordingly : [3]

White tawed.	Value.	Fee.
Sheep skins . .	7s.—3s. the doz. . .	2d., 1d.
Kid and fawn .	4s. 6d.—1s. 8d. the doz.	2d., 1d.
Lambs . .	4s. 4d.—1s. 8d. ,,	2d., 1d.
Horse [4] .	5s.—2s. 6d. each .	2d.
Dogs . . .	4s.—1s. 6d. the doz.	2d., 1d.
Bucks . .	4s.—3s. 4d. each .	8d. the doz.
Does . .	2s. 4d.—1s. 8d. each .	8d. ,,
Calf . .	12s.—4s. the doz. .	6d., 3d.
Goat . . .	2s. 6d. each—3s. 6d. the doz.	6d., 2d. each.

[1] Lansd. MS., 74, f. 53.   [2] *Ibid.*, f. 48.

[3] *Ibid.*, f. 58.

[4] At Colchester in 1425 the charge for tawing a horse hide was 14d., a buckskin 8d., doe 5d., and calf 2d.   *V. C. H. Essex*, ii. 459.

Oil dressed.				*Value.*		*Fee.*
Right Buffe [1]	.	.	.	33s. 4d.—15s. each	.	7d.
Counterfeit Buffe	.	.	.	13s. 4d.—7s. ,,	.	7d.
Right Shamoise	.	.	.	30s. the doz.	.	7d.
Counterfeit ,,	.	.	.	14s. ,,	.	7d.
Sheep ,,	.	.	.	8s. ,,	.	3½d.
Lamb ,,	.	.	.	6s. ,,	.	3½d.
Right Spannish skins [2]	.	.	.	30s. ,,	.	7d.
Counterfeit Spannish skins of goat and buck	.		.	3li. ,,	.	7d.
Counterfeit Spannish sheep skins	.		.	12s. ,,	.	3½d.
Right Cordovan skins	.	.	.	40s. ,,	.	12d.
Seal skins dressed	.	.	.	40s. ,,	.	7d.
Stagge skins,[3] English, Scottish, as big as buffyn, dressed like buffe	.		.	12s. each	.	6d.
Stag skins, Irish, dressed like buffe	.		.	3li. the doz.	.	12d.
Buck and doe, dressed like buffe	.		.	40s. ,,	.	12d.
Calf skins, in like sort	.	.	.	16s. ,,	.	7d.

A number of trades, such as glovers, saddlers, purse-makers, girdlers, and bottlemakers, used leather, but the most important class were the shoemakers. They in turn were divided into a number of branches, at the head of which stood the cordwainers, who derived their name from having originally been workers of Cordovan leather, but were in actual practice makers of the better class of shoes.[4] At the other end were the cobblers, or menders of old shoes. Elaborate regulations were made in London in 1409 to prevent these two classes trespassing on one another's preserves.[5] The cobbler might

[1] Right Buffe were made from ' Elke Skynnes or Iland hides brought out of Muscovia or from by Est '; the counterfeits were of horse, ox, and stag skins. Lansd. MS., 74, f. 53.

[2] The price given for Spanish skins is probably an error; possibly the values of the ' right ' and ' counterfeit ' are reversed.

[3] In 1347 the London white tawyers charged 6s. 8d. for working a ' dyker [a packet of ten] of Scottes stagges or Irysshe ', and 10s. for the ' dyker of Spanysshe stagges '. Riley, *Mems. of London*, 234.

[4] Corveiser was a still more common name for a shoemaker.

[5] Riley, *Mems. of London*, 572–3.

clout an old sole with new leather or patch the uppers, but if the boot required an entirely new sole, or if a new shoe were burnt or broken and required a fresh piece put in, then the work must be given to the cordwainer. A distinction was also drawn at a much earlier date, in 1271,[1] between two classes of cordwainers, the *allutarii* and the *basanarii*, the latter being those who used 'basan' or 'bazan', an inferior leather made from sheepskin. Neither was to use the other's craft, though the *allutarius* might make the uppers (*quissellos*) of his shoes of bazan: to prevent any confusion the two classes were to occupy separate positions in the fairs and markets. In

SHOEMAKERS. 16th cent.

1320 we find eighty pairs of shoes seized from twenty different persons, thirty-one pairs being taken from Roger Brown of Norwich, and forfeited for being made of bazan and cordwain mixed.[2] Fifty years later, in 1375, a heavy fine was ordained for any one selling shoes of bazan as being cordwain,[3] and a similar ordinance was in force at Bristol in 1408.[4] By the London rules of 1271, no cordwainer was to keep more than eight journeymen (*servientes*), and at Bristol in 1364 the

[1] *Liber Albus*, ii. 441–5.
[2] Riley, *Mems. of London*, 136.　　　[3] *Ibid.*, 391.
[4] *Little Red Book of Bristol*, ii. 108.

shoemakers were restricted to a single ' covenant-hynd ', who was to be paid 18*d.* a week and allowed eight pairs of shoes yearly.[1] In the case of Bristol, however, no limit is stated for the number of journeymen, who were paid by piecework, the rates being, in 1364, 3*d.* a dozen for sewing, and 3*d.* for ' yarking ' ; 3*d.* for making a pair of boots entirely, that is to say, 1*d.* for cutting and 2*d.* for sewing and yarking ; 2*d.* for cutting

a dozen pairs of shoes, namely, 1*d.* for the over-leathers and 1*d.* for the soles, and a further 1*d.* for lasting the dozen shoes. The rates of pay were still the same in 1408, though there are additional entries of 12*d.* for sewing, yarking, and

Shoemaker. 15th cent.

finishing a dozen boots and shoes called ' quarter-schone ', and 7*d.* for sewing and yarking, with an extra 1½*d.* for finishing a dozen shoes called ' course ware '.[2] Very similar rates were prevalent at York in 1430.[3]

The sale of the finished articles was also an object of regulations : in London in 1271, shoes might only be hawked in the district between Corveiserstrete and Soperes Lane, and there only in the morning on ordinary days, though on the eves of feasts they might be sold in the afternoon.[4] Leather laces also might not be sold

---

[1] *Little Red Book of Bristol*, ii. 43.

[2] *Ibid.*, ii. 105.

[3] *York Memorandum Book* (Surtees Soc.), i. 193–4—a list of rates of payment for piece-work, of much interest for its numerous trade terms : cf. piece-work rates of the curriers, *ibid.*, 65–6.

[4] *Liber Albus*, ii. 445.

at the ' eve chepings '.[1] Possibly it was considered that
bad leather might be more easily passed off in a bad
light, but the idea may simply have been to prevent the
competition of the pedlars and hawkers with the shopkeepers. At Northampton, in 1452, the two classes of
tradesmen were separated, those who had shops not
being allowed to sell also in the market.[2] Northampton had not at this date begun to acquire the
fame which it earned during the seventeenth century
as the centre of the
English boot trade, but
regulations for the ' cory-
vsers crafte' there had
been drawn up in 1402,[3]
and much earlier, in 1266,
we find Henry III order-
ing the bailiffs of Northampton to provide a
hundred and fifty pairs

Shoemaker.   15th cent.

of shoes, half at 5*d*. and half at 4*d*. the pair.[4] These were
for distribution to the poor ; and similar orders in other
years were usually executed in either London or Winchester : no particular importance can be attached to this
single order being given to Northampton, as presumably
any large town could have carried out the order.   So far
as any town can be placed at the head of the shoemaking
industry, the distinction must be given to Oxford, where
the cordwainers' gild was in existence early in the twelfth
century, it being reconstituted in 1131,[5] and its monopoly
confirmed by Henry II.[6]

[1] Riley, *Mems. of London*, 547.   [2] *V. C. H. Northants.*, ii. 318.
[3] *Ibid.*   [4] Liberate R., 50 Hen. III, m. 11.   [5] Pipe R., 31 Hen. I.
[6] *Cal. Chart*. R., ii. 34.

XI

FISHING

F<small>ISHING</small> is an industry for which it is difficult to draw a line between the mediaeval and modern periods. Short of the introduction of steam trawlers it is hard to find any change in the methods employed. The bulk of commercial fishing has always been carried on with nets,[1] and may be divided into the pursuit of fish with moveable nets and their ensnaring by means of stationary nets and traps such as eel-pots. Both kinds of fishing are referred to in the Domesday

Primitive fishing with rod and line.
11th cent.

Survey. Of the many river fisheries mentioned in that record, it is not always possible to say whether the word *piscaria* means the general right to take fish or the actual possession of a weir, a contrivance of stakes and wattles by which the fish were directed into fixed nets or wicker traps. In the case of the sea-coast manors, however, where a fishery is entered it can hardly be anything but a stationary kiddle or stake net, a ' sea hedge ' (*heia maris*)

---

[1] Certain fish, such as cod, were caught with line and hook, but there is very little documentary reference to line fishing.

as it is well called at Southwold.[1] These kiddles, or kettle-nets, which were at one time very common along the shelving shores of the south and east coast and are still in use, resemble the river weirs; they consist of a more or less semicircular hedge of stakes and wattles and nets, the whole of which is covered by the sea at high tide ; as the water recedes the fish which have swum in over the top or round the ends of the fence are cut off and impounded.[2] This type of net has often been condemned as very destructive to the fry and small fish, and the use of kiddles anywhere except along the coast was forbidden by Magna Carta and many later statutes, partly because of their destructiveness and partly from their interference with navigation when used in rivers.[3]

The existence of flourishing deep-sea fisheries in the eleventh century is indicated by the entries in Domesday of herring rents, chiefly in Suffolk and Sussex. Renders of 4,000 herrings at Brighton, 16,000 at Itford, and 38,500 at Southease, on the estuary of the Sussex Ouse, occur ; [4] while in Suffolk, besides a number of small quantities, Blythburgh rendered 10,000, Southwold 2,000, and Beccles and Dunwich 60,000 each.[5] In the case of Kessingland the 22,000 herrings paid are said to be two lasts and two barrels, and the value of salted herrings is given as 38s. the last.[6] The last was ten thousand, but as the ' long hundred ' of six score was used the actual number would be 12,000.[7] It is curious that Domesday

---

[1] *V. C. H. Essex,* i. 425.   [2] *Ibid.*

[3] *Rot. Parl.,* i. 475.

[4] *V. C. H. Sussex,* i. 366.   [5] *V. C. H. Suffolk,* ii. 289–90.

[6] *V. C. H. Suffolk,* ii. 289–90.

[7] The long hundred is still used in some parts of England for reckoning herring.

should give no indication of the importance of Yarmouth as a centre of the herring fishery. Yet there can be little doubt that Yarmouth practically owed its existence to the herring, and there seems good reason to believe that the confederation of the Cinque Ports, whose fleet formed the nucleus of our ancient navy, arose from the assemblage of the ships of the Kent and Sussex ports off the Yarmouth coast during the herring season. Hastings, the head of the Cinque Ports, was the first to acquire the

Man packing herrings in a barrel. 16th cent.

special privileges of ' dene and strand '—the right to use the shore for drying nets—at Yarmouth, which were afterwards extended to the other ports. As Yarmouth increased in importance, the control exercised by the bailiffs of the Ports over her great herring fair was a source of increasing irritation and led to the great ' herring war ' of the thirteenth and fourteenth centuries,[1] in which hundreds of lives were lost and many thousands of pounds damage done to the rival fleets. The importance of the Yarmouth herring fishery may be gauged by the fact that at the end of the thirteenth century the Sussex ports were spending over £2,000 yearly on fitting out ships to take part in it.[2]

It is an interesting mark of the importance attached to the herring fishery on the east coast that the city of Norwich rendered annually to the king twenty-four pies of the first fresh herrings of the season, each pie

[1] *V. C. H. Sussex*, ii. 132–3.   [2] *Ibid.*, 267.

containing five herrings, flavoured with ginger, pepper, cinnamon, cloves, and other spices.[1] Land in East Carleton was held by the service of carrying these pies to the king, and the carrier had a pie for himself and on his arrival at court was entitled to a liberal allowance of food and drink. Of this east-coast fishery Yarmouth had a virtual monopoly ; no herrings might be sold or cured within seven leagues of the town.[2] This monopoly resulted in a manipulation of prices, until herring reached the exorbitant price of two a penny ; [3] the general outcry then compelled the king in 1376 to cancel his charter and withdraw the monopoly.[4] The men of Yarmouth, with the assistance of the London fish-mongers, succeeded in getting their charter back in 1378,[5] only to have it revoked in 1382 [6] but again restored in 1385 on a representation that without such a monopoly Yarmouth would be ruined and even deserted.[7]

North of what we may call the herring belt lay the cod fisheries, of which the great centres were Scarborough and Grimsby. Regulations for the fishmarket at Grimsby were drawn up in 1258,[8] but are mainly concerned with the prevention of forestalling. With the ' haraunge de

---

[1] *Norwich Recs.*, ii. 209.

[2] Statutes, 31 Edw. III.

[3] The opposite extreme of cheapness had been reached in 1238, when, owing to a Tartar invasion, the men of Gothland and Friesland did not come to buy at Yarmouth. Herrings were so plentiful that they sold, even inland, at 40 or 50 for a penny. Matt. Paris, *Chron.*, iii. 488.

[4] *Chron. Anglie* (Rolls Ser.), 94.

[5] Pat., 1 Ric. II, pt. 5, m. 18.

[6] Pat., 5 Ric. II, pt. 2, m. 23.

[7] Pat., 8 Ric. II, pt. 2, m. 25.   [8] *Cal. Chart.* R., ii. 14–15.

Gernemue ' and the ' morue de Grymsby ' in the early fourteenth-century list of towns and their specialities [1] went ' loches de Wexebrugge ', which seem to be stock-fish of ' Weybridge ' on the east coast (Weybourn, about 5 miles E. of Blakeney). At any rate, in 1357 when rules were laid down for the great fish fair at Blakeney, [2] on the north coast of Norfolk, ' lochefisshe ' were divided into the three classes of lob, ling, and cod, from which it would seem that they were the kinds of fish which when dried were known as stockfish ; if the lob may be identi-fied with the mulvell, or green cod, these three classes would correspond to the ' Lengestokfisshe and mulvel-stokfisshe ' which sold in London in 1298 at a penny and three farthings respectively, and ' croplenge ', which sold at three a penny. [3] The Blakeney regulations contain another uncertain term : ' If any orgeys, namely fish larger than lob, be found in a lodeship the master and mariner shall have twenty orgeys for every long hundred of lob, ling, and cod ; if there be less they shall have all that there are, but if more then the surplus shall be given to the purchaser with his other fish.'

Whatever ' loches ' may have been there can be no doubt about the ' playz de Winchelsee ' and the ' merlyng de Rye ' that occur in the same list, and we find Rye and Winchelsea supplying large quantities of whiting and plaice for the king's court from 1237 onwards. [4] But however favoured by any particular fish a part of the coast might be, the local fishermen did not confine themselves to their own district. To

---

[1] *Engl. Hist. Rev.*, xvi. 289. [2] Statutes, 31 Edw. III.
[3] *Liber Custumarum*, i. 118. [4] *V. C. H. Sussex*. ii. 266.

Yarmouth they came from Kent and Sussex and even from Cornwall, to Scarborough in the same way, and still farther afield they went, to Iceland. During the fifteenth and sixteenth centuries the ' Iceland fare ' of the fishing boats from the east coast was of great importance,[1] though in 1430 the Government found it necessary to stop it temporarily, forbidding Englishmen to go to Iceland or Denmark owing to the frequent quarrels brought about by the provocative behaviour of our fishermen,[2] who were a hardy set of ruffians, always ready for a fight, as Sir Robert Logan, admiral of the Scots, found to his cost in 1400 when he tried to seize the Lynn fishing fleet on its way to Aberdeen and was badly beaten by them.[3]

Little is known about the way in which fish brought from a distance was kept fresh ; the use of ice was unknown ; apparently there was some kind of a well in the hold of the ships in which the fish were kept alive. For land carriage the fish were probably packed in salt, which was made all round the coast by evaporating sea-water. This same coarse salt was used in great quantities for salting herrings and other fish.

The documentary history of fishing as an industry is concerned with (1) rights or privileges of fishing, (2) regulation of methods, and (3) restriction of sale. So far as fishing rights are concerned, there is clearly a distinct difference between sea- and fresh-water fisheries. ' In rivers, and to some extent in estuaries, the riparian owner usually claimed—and in most cases obtained—

---

[1] e. g. in 1451 Walberswick sent 13 boats to Iceland : *V. C. H. Suffolk*, ii. 290.

[2] *Ibid.* 211.   [3] Walsingham, *Hist. Angl.*, 246.

a monopoly of fishing rights,[1] but no such interference
was possible in the case of the deep seas. There were,
of course, foreshore rights, to which I shall revert later,
and there were also restrictions with regard to special
fish, using the word loosely. The sturgeon, whale, and
porpoise were regarded as royal fish, belonging to the
Crown wherever caught, unless subject to a special
grant. Such grants were not infrequent, especially as
regards porpoises ; William the Conqueror, for instance,
granted to Battle Abbey all porpoises that should come
ashore in Dengemarsh, and further granted that if any
came to land on their adjacent property the monks
should have two-thirds of the porpoise, with its tongue.[2]
The tongue was evidently considered a delicacy, as when
Henry I, the tradition of whose death from a surfeit of
lampreys stamps him as an epicure where fish were
concerned, gave to the Bishop of London the right to
all porpoises taken on his lands, he expressly added
' except the tongue, which I have retained for myself '.[3]
A partial grant was made to Christchurch (Hants) by
William de Redvers, Earl of Devon, who, when bestowing
upon that monastery the tithe of ' wreck ' from his
lands, excepted porpoises (*craspeis*), of which the monks
were to have only the left breast.[4] In the case of Filey

[1] It seems clear that many ' several fisheries ' were really usurped.

[2] Dugdale, *Monastion*, iii. 243.

[3] *Cal. Chart. R.*, iii. 292.

[4] *Ibid.*, 230. The Crown's right to sea beasts was sometimes
confused by private rights of ' wreck ', which extended to whales, &c.,
cast up by the sea (e. g. *Chron. Abb. Ramsey*, 267). In 1255 the
Bishop of Norwich's claim to a ' great monstrous fish ' as wreck was
disputed on the ground that it was taken at sea, six boats being
sunk in the attempt (Memo. K. R., 39 Hen. III, m. 9). This was
the sea monster referred to by Matthew Paris (*Hist. Minor*, iii. 343).

harbour a similar partial ownership existed where
whales were concerned ; when one of these came into
the harbour the king had the head and tail, while the
remainder was divided between Gilbert de Gaunt and

CATCHING AND CUTTING UP WHALES.   16th cent.

Richard Malebiche.[1]   At what date whale and porpoise
went out of fashion as articles of diet I am not sure, but
throughout the mediaeval period they figured constantly
on bills of fare.   At the end of the thirteenth century
whale ' of this year's salting ' fetched 2d. a pound, or
16s. the hundredweight, in London, while if more than

[1] *Quo Warranto*, 189.

a year old (*superannuata*) it was only half the price.[1]
At the same time ' sea pig ',[2] or porpoise, was half a
mark (presumably for a hundredweight). Some fifty
years earlier Henry III ordered the sheriff of London to
send to Winchester 100 slices of best whale (*karvellos
optime balene*), 25 pieces of sturgeon, and 2 porpoises.[3]
Nine years later, in 1254, the same king ordered a whale
which had come ashore at Milton in Kent to be sent up
to Westminster and handed over to his larderer.[4] As
late as the reign of Henry VIII porpoise was still in
demand ; the Justices of the Peace for Devon at that
time complained [5] that while all along their coasts there
was ' yerely grete resorte of the fysche called Porpes,
whereof yf any by chaunce happyn to be takyn thofficers
of the Admiraltie compel the pore men fyschers of the
same to pay and delyvere them of every of the seid
fysch the tone half ', as a result no one will catch them,
whereas if they were not interfered with enough would
be caught to supply all the shires from Devon to London.
The Justices hazarded the opinion that the king's prerogative extended only to whales and sturgeon, but in
that they were clearly wrong. Still later, in 1569,
when ' grampasses to the nombre of xvii verye huge and
grete ' were taken in Orwell haven and brought into
Ipswich, one was sent to the queen, one to the Council,
and the rest disposed of by the advice of ' expert men,
maryners and bochers '.[6]

---

[1] *Liber Cust.* (Rolls Ser.), 118.
[2] ' Porcus maris ' : *ibid.* ' Mereswyne ', *Liber Albus*, 375.
[3] Liberate R. (K. R.), 30 Hen. III, m. 17.
[4] *Ibid.*, 39 Hen. III, m. 13.
[5] Star Chamb. Proc., Hen. VIII, file 12, no. 212.
[6] *Hist. MSS. Rep.*, ix. 249, 252.

At Stokenham in Devon in 1310 the lord of the manor had all porpoises and salmon which his men caught and also one-third of the mullet ; he had further the right to buy his fish at a special rate, eight plaice or bream for a penny, a ray for a penny, and so forth.[1] At the other end of England an Elizabethan survey [2] shows that while the lord of Burgh on Sands had a right to the ' royal and principal fishes, namely whales, sturgeons, porpoises, thirlepolles, seals, turbots, and such like ', he did not—at that date—exercise his right without compensation, but gave his tenants 3s. 4d. for sturgeon, 20d. for thirlepolle, and 12d. for turbot. In practice, no doubt, some such system of rewards was general, or the prerogative fish would never have been taken. A somewhat similar case of accommodation is recorded in 1214 ; [3] the abbot of Fountains had a fishery in ' Codric ' and no one might fish in his lake without his licence, and when he wished to fish himself he caused a horn to be blown so that his neighbours might come and help ; for their help the fishers had half the fish [4] taken, but if any big pike of 4 or 5 feet fell to their share the abbot might buy it from them for 6d.[5]

Besides the reservation of specific fish to the Crown or other overlord, the mediaeval fisherman had often to consider rights of foreshore. The privilege of using the shore for drying and mending nets seems to have been

---

[1] *Cal. Inq. p. m.*, v. 213.   [2] *V. C. H. Cumb.*, ii. 334.

[3] *Plac. Abbrev.*, 90.

[4] At Stafford when the king netted his fishery outside the east-gate he kept all the pike and bream, and the keeper of the fishery had all the other fish. *Cal. Inq. p.m.*, ii. 13.

[5] At the end of the same century a pike of 3 ft. fetched 6s. 8d. in London. *Liber Cust.* (Rolls Ser.), 118.

known on the east coast as ' denage ', and the grant of
rights of ' dene and strand ' at Yarmouth to Hastings,[1]
and afterwards to the other Cinque Ports, was as strenuously enforced by the portsmen as it was resisted by the
local fisheries, who on one occasion early in the thirteenth

MEN FISHING : hauling in a net.   15th cent.

century set fire to the timbers on which the Hastings
men had stretched their nets.[2]   At Lowestoft ' denage '
was paid to the lord of Lothingland, the rate in the
sixteenth century being 4*d.* for a small boat, 8*d.* for an
English ship, and 18*d.* for a foreign ship.[3]   William
Skeftling gave to the northern abbey of Holmcultram
a fishery in the sea at the mouth of the Ellen (? Eden)

---

[1] *Cal. of Charter R.,* iii. 222.   [2] *Plac. Abbrev.,* 75.
[3] *V. C. H. Suffolk,* ii. 293.

with one fishing boat,[1] and a toft on shore to dry their
nets.[2] The other way in which foreshore rights were of
value to their possessors was the exaction of payments
for permission to set kiddles or other standing-nets.
Such payments are common entries in the accounts of
manors upon the coast. To quote a single example, in
1450 Reynold Manfeld leased at 12*d.* a year a lagoon

Water-mill with eel-traps.   14th cent.

called Cotemanware at Appledram near Chichester
in which to set up a kiddle.[3] Still more common and
more profitable were the fish traps of various types set
up in rivers. The Domesday Survey is full of entries of
' fisheries ' yielding in many cases hundreds and in
some instances thousands of eels yearly, and all these
fisheries—if not all the Domesday *piscariae*—were of the
nature of weirs (*gurgites*) with ' weels ', ' boraches ' or

[1] Cf. grant by Randall Earl of Chester to the nuns of St. Mary's
of a boat on the water of Chester to fish with ' hetun (? hecon = a
heak net), dreynett, flodnett, and stalnett '.—*Cal. Chart. R.*, i. 320.

[2] *V. C. H. Cumb.*, ii. 334.

[3] Court R. (P. R. O.), bdle. 205, no. 46.

bottle-shaped traps of wickerwork, and stakenets. Similar to these were the *leirae lampronum* at Christchurch (Hants), where lampreys were caught with baskets (*alvei*) fastened to stakes, payment being made to the lord of the manor according to the number of stakes leased.[1]

As already mentioned, these kiddles and similar nets were destructive of small fish and obstructive of navigation, and orders were constantly made for their restriction or removal. Thus the salmon weirs in the Eden, Esk, and Derwent might not be carried completely across the stream, but must leave a free passage in midstream, the size of the passage being stated in 1278, and again in 1293, as wide enough for a sow and her five little pigs to pass through ; [2] this picturesque but inconvenient measurement had been changed by 1372 for a fixed breadth of 24 feet. So far as the Thames was concerned, special justices were appointed at least as early as the thirteenth century to control the river, but they appear to have neglected their duties, so that the journey from Oxford to London was rendered hazardous by the number of dangerous weirs, while the fish were destroyed by the use of illegal nets.[3] To prevent the destruction of the fry and small fish, constant supervision of the nets in use was necessary, all nets of which the meshes were too small being destroyed. At the end of the

---

[1] Mins. Accts., bdle. 984, nos. 19–21.

[2] *V. C. H. Cumb.*, ii. 335. In a Scottish statute of 1177 the midstream was to be free to the extent that a 3-year old sow, well fed, could not touch either side with its head or tail. The connexion of pigs and salmon is not obvious, but I believe it is still a superstition that you should not mention pigs when you are fishing for salmon.   [3] *Rot. Parl.*, i. 475.

thirteenth century the mesh for salmon nets in the northern counties was 4 inches from knot to knot,[1] that for the great nets in the Thames 2 inches, and for the ' trinks ', or fixed nets, in the same river $1\frac{1}{2}$ inches.[2] In 1329 eight fishermen were brought up at the Guildhall

SEINE NETS. 16th cent.

for fishing in the Thames with ' tromekeresnets ', a variety of trinks, of which the ' mascles ' or meshes were only half an inch, by which the fry and small fish were caught ; the nets were destroyed and the fishermen committed to Newgate.[3] Twenty years later in a similar case, which had a similar ending, the offenders

[1] *V. C. H. Cumb.*, ii. 335. [2] *Liber Cust.*, 118.
[3] Riley, *Mems. of London*, 72.

were found to have in their nets three bushels of small fish, ' which fish by reason of their smallness could be of no use to any one.' [1] In the same way in 1376 and 1402 complaints were made that salmon and other fish in the Thames were being destroyed by certain contrivances which took in all the fry and small fish, which were of no use to any one and were only used to feed the pigs.[2] In the same year, 1376, it was stated that during the last seven years some fishermen had introduced an instrument which they called a ' Wondyrchoun ' made like an oyster drag, of excessive length, attached to which was a net so close that no kind of fish could get through. When this was used along the coast its heavy long iron destroyed the mud, seaweed, and the spat of oysters and mussels, and so deprived the fish of their food and drove them away.[3]

Besides regulating the implements of the industry, some control in the way of constituting close times was exercised over the periods at which it might be carried on. In 1278, in view of the great destruction of spawning salmon in the Derwent and neighbouring rivers, a close time, from 29 September to 30 November and again from 1 May to 24 June, was instituted, and a few years later, in 1285, an Act was passed by which a close time was appointed for salmon from 8 September to 11 November.[4] In London in 1298 great nets of 2-inch mesh might be used west of London Bridge all the year round, and ' peteresnet ' all the year except during the smelt season.[5] East of London Bridge, in the Thames

---

[1] Riley, *Mems. of London,* 244.
[2] *Rot. Parl.,* ii. 331 ; iii. 499.
[3] *Ibid.,* ii. 369.
[4] *Ibid.*
[5] *Liber Cust.,* 117.

estuary, codnets—nets with a cod or purse in which a stone [1] was placed—went from 2 February to 25 March, and during the same time the great nets employed for smelts might be used ' with their bosom ', but from 25 March to Midsummer they were to go without this ' bosum ',[2] the nature of which is not obvious. ' Pridnets ', which might only be used from 22 September to 11 November, were presumably nets for catching the pride or lampern, which enjoyed a close time from Easter till a little before Michaelmas. At Norwich, in 1382, no nets might be used in the river for the last two weeks of April and the first two weeks of May, with the excep-

FISHERMAN. 16th cent.

tion of ' draglamms ', and seynes might only be used during August and September.[3] Fishing on Sundays and feast days was, of course, forbidden like all other work, and in some cases night fishing was also prohibited, the real reason being no doubt to prevent the fishermen evading the laws, and not, as alleged at Rye, because

[1] Similar to the ' capston ', which was not to weigh more than 2 pounds. *Norwich Recs.*, i. 85.

[2] *Liber Cust.*, 116. ' Bose nettys ' occur at Rye in 1448 and are later called ' bosmys ', which suggests a connexion with ' boom ', a balk of timber. *Hist. MSS. Rep.*, v. 490.

[3] *Norwich Records*, ii. 85.

the fish, being thereby ' disquieted and wanting natural rest, doe become both leane, unserviceable, and not so well bayted as in former tymes '.[1]

So far as the fishermen's own customs and regulations are concerned, there is not a great deal to be said. They do not appear to have formed any trade gilds, and it is hard to say in the case of many seaport towns whether such fishing customs as are found were originated by the fishermen themselves or imposed upon them by the town authorities. It may, however, be assumed that the custom of ' shares '[2] prevalent in the Sussex ports and probably elsewhere from the twelfth century onwards was instituted by the men themselves. By this custom the fish caught by each boat were divided between the men employed, the owners of the boat and nets, and the rector of the parish ; the lord of the manor also sometimes claimed shares, as at Rye in the twelfth century, where the abbot of Fécamp received from ships of 26 oars two and a half shares, from those of 22 or 20 oars two, of 18 or 16 one and a half, and from all smaller boats one share, except in the case of boats called *heccheres*, which if they had crews of from 8 to 12 rowers paid one share, but if fewer only half.[3] The rector's or church's share was often called ' Christ share ', as for instance at Eastbourne, where, in 1353, the vicar was bound in return for it to celebrate three days a week in the chapel of St. Gregory.[4] It would seem that the ' Christ share ' was additional to and not in lieu of

[1] *Hist. MSS. Com. Rep.*, xiii (4), 124.

[2] *V. C. H. Sussex*, ii. 265.

[3] *Cal. Docs. France*, 43.

[4] Assize R., 941, m. 11.

tithe, to which the harvest of the sea was liable as much as the harvest of the land.[1]

After satisfying the demands of the church and the manorial lord, the fisherman was still not completely free to dispose of his catch. Many of the coast towns had monopolies or exclusive rights of landing and selling fish. The most notable example of this was at Yarmouth, to which reference has already been made. Blakeney, again, was the sole port of discharge for its own district,[2] and Dunwich had such distinct rights that in 1230 its burgesses were able to make the men of Blythburgh and Walberswick pay 5s. yearly for every fishing boat of twelve or more oars, the smaller boats not being interfered with.[3] Naturally the fishing ports took toll from the boats which came in with fish. At Scarborough, for instance, the town received one fish in every hundred herring,[4] and a similar toll was claimed in the middle of the fourteenth century by the bailiff at Lynn, who also demanded two salmon from ships carrying thirty-two or more salmon and other similar dues, even attempting to take money from boats laden with saltfish and stockfish which were passing through the port on their way to Cambridgeshire, Northants, or elsewhere.[5] In London there was an elaborate system of renders ;[6]

---

[1] *V. C. H. Sussex*, ii. 265 ; *Rot. Parl.*, ii. 87. Richard I gave the tithes of all the Yorkshire coast fisheries to Scarborough church, which belonged to the Abbey of Citeaux. *Cal. Chart. R.*, iii. 222.

[2] Statutes, 31 Edw. III.

[3] Just a century later the burgesses complained that Sir Edmund Clavering had thrown up a great mole (*britaske*) at Walberswick, at the mouth of their harbour, and intercepted the fishing boats. *Rot. Parl.*, ii. 44 ; *Curia Regis*, 104, m. 8.

[4] *Rot. Parl.*, ii. 221.

[5] Coram Rege, 415, m. 10 rex.   [6] *Liber Albus*, 374–6.

boats with whiting, haddock, mackerel, or dabs paid 26 fish ; in the case of herrings the first boat in from Yarmouth paid 200 herrings, and later boats, which presumably did not get such a good price for their fish, 100. Almost equivalent, also, to a toll was the right of the king's purveyor to select fish for the royal household before it was exposed for sale. When the ships returned from Iceland to Yarmouth, the purveyor went on board and threw out 400 cod or ling, and then picked out from them 200 for the king's use,[1] and, if we may accept the statements of the Blakeney fishers in the thirteenth century, the purveyors did not pay market prices, but often 30 per cent. less.[2]

Prices, it may be observed, were not left to the automatic action of supply and demand in this any more than in other industries ; or at least, if supply and demand did play a larger part in the regulation of prices in this case, where supplies were essentially variable, they were by no means uncontrolled agents. The part played by fish in the diet of the nation when fresh meat was unobtainable for a large part of the year and fast days were numerous was far greater than at the present, and the authorities, parliamentary and local, did their best to keep the prices down. Measures were constantly enacted against engrossers and regraters who bought up fish before they came to shore and resold them for a profit,[3] thus infringing the great mediaeval principle that

[1] Swinden, *Hist. of Yarmouth*, 116. In 1526 this custom was confined to boats carrying 10 weys of salt ; smaller boats gave half the number.

[2] Exch. K. R. Accts., bdle. 403, no. 29.

[3] e. g. at Grimsby in 1258 ; *Cal. Chart. R.*, ii. 14. And at Yarmouth in 1357 ; Statutes, 31 Edw. III.

profit should not accrue without cause and that goods should not be sold unaltered for a higher price than they had cost. With the same object of preventing the cornering of fish supplies, fish had to be sold publicly in the appointed fish market unless they were sold actually on the boat. All secret dealing in fish was prohibited; fish might not be landed between sunset and sunrise or sold inside shops.[1] At Grimsby fishermen were not allowed to keep their fish for special customers, but must sell to any burgess who wished to buy; and if any merchant made a private bargain by which he was to have all the fish on a boat, the fish were seized and sold by the town officers, the merchant being made to fulfil his bargain towards the fishers but receiving only 12d. for a last of herring or a hundred cod.[2] A complication in the sale of fish is introduced by the existence of 'hosts', whose exact position is not quite clear; they appear to have been intermediaries between the fishers and the public, practically fish vendors though not on the scale of the fish merchants proper, to whom they were often tied down.[3] In origin these 'hosts', 'ostes', or 'hostelers', seem to have been the owners of booths at which they allowed the fishermen to sell their catches. By the regulations made for the Yarmouth herring fair in 1357 [4] they were to receive 40d. for every last of herrings sold through them, and in return for this pay-

---

[1] *Liber Albus*, 382. [2] *Cal. Chart.*, ii. 15.

[3] William de Rookhage in 1382 left to his wife 'quatuor hospites meos piscatores . . . ad piscandum dicte Cristiane ad terminum vite sue, capiendo de dictis hospitibus catalla que mihi debentur'. Swinden, *Hist. of Great Yarmouth*, 77. Here 'hospes' seems to be used for an actual fisherman.

[4] Statutes, 31 Edw. III.

ment they were responsible for due payment being made by the buyer. They were not to interfere with the sale of fish, nor were they to buy up all herrings by offering high prices, above 40s. the last.[1] In spite of this last regulation, the fishmongers and their hosts persisted in regrating herring, cornering the market, and forcing prices up.[2] In the inquiry that followed it was shown that 30 fishmongers had each five or more hosts in their employ, while about the same number had four or fewer.[3] At Rye, at a later date, the term 'oast' was applied to the royal purveyor[4] and to the agents of the Fishmongers' Company who bought for the London market, to which the fish were carried by 'ripiers'[5] with pack horses, the fish being usually packed in 'dorsers'[6] or paniers.

It has been already stated that the sale of fish was only allowed in towns, on board ship, or in the fish market, and the market itself was in many instances subdivided; in London, for instance, fresh-water fish might be sold only in Bridge Street and Old Fish Street,[7]

[1] This price seems absurd in view of the fact that herring were fetching next year at Yarmouth as much as £6 the last : Assize R. 609. On the other hand, 40s. the last was the price fixed for herring in London in 1298 : *Liber Cust.*, 118.

[2] Cf. complaint against the 'mestres hostes' in 1376 : *Rot. Parl.*, ii. 353.

[3] Assize R., 609.   [4] *V. C. H. Sussex*, ii. 266.

[5] *Ibid.* These ripiers no doubt acted as general carriers on their return journeys to the coast. One of them brought an antiphonary from London to Lydd at the time of the Romanist Revival under Mary. *Recs. of Lydd*, 412.

[6] Each dorser was supposed to hold one bushel (Riley, *Mems. of London*, 116) and the fish were to be as good at the bottom as at the top (*Liber Albus*, 382).

[7] *Liber Albus*, 689.

and lampreys at the wall of St. Margaret's in Old Fish Street.[1] An exception, however, was made in the case of hawkers who sold fish from street to street, their chief customers being workmen who could not leave their work to buy at the shops.[2] These hucksters or birlesters were not allowed to take up their stand at any point, but must keep on the move.[3] An interesting case concerned with these hucksters occurred in 1382, when Thomas Welford, a fishmonger whose ship was lying at Queenhithe laden with salted herrings, declared that he could not let the 'hukke-steres' have them cheaper than five a penny, which meant that they could only sell them at four a penny.

Selling fish at a stall.   13th cent.

This was so dear that the mayor and aldermen expostulated, and at last Thomas agreed to sell six herrings for a penny, so that the hucksters could retail them at five a penny. It then appeared that although Thomas had sworn that he could not sell cheaper without loss, he had actually sold 600 at ten a penny to William Botild to be taken out of London, and it was therefore enacted that he and all other fishmongers with herring for sale should sell at nine for a

---

[1] *Ibid.*, 382.   [2] *Rot. Parl.*, i. 370.
[3] *Liber Albus*, 689 ; Riley, *Mems. of London*, 508.

penny.[1] This price, it may ·be noted, was double what
had been fixed a century earlier, in 1298,[2] when red
herring were to be sold at twenty for a penny or 40s.
the last ; fresh herring at the same time were six a penny
before Michaelmas and half that price after. Fresh
herring were (naturally) móre expensive in London than
salted, and in the same way whiting were four fresh or
twelve pickled (*pouderati*) for a penny, but at Yarmouth,
where the question of carriage and preservation did not
come in, the reverse was naturally the case ; here in
1357 the rule was that when fresh herring cost 40d. the
last or less, the extra charge on a last of dried herring
should not be more than half a mark.[3] This amount
extra might be charged whether the last were of full or
of shotten [4] herring, although the shotten fetched only
half the price of the full when fresh, because the cost
of curing a last was equal for either kind.

Amongst the fish of which the prices were regulated
for the London market in 1298 [5] were conger at 12d.,
turbot 6d., dorey 5d., gurnard 1d., mackerel 1d. each
in Lent and two a penny afterwards, plaice 1d., soles
four a penny. Fresh salmon, between Christmas and
Easter 5s., and after Easter 3s. ; this price evidently
went up during the next century, as in 1376, when certain
regulations for preserving the young salmon in the
Thames and elsewhere were suggested, it was represented
that in this way in three years people would be able to
buy for 2s. as good a salmon as then cost 10s. ; [6] even
the lower price should be sufficient, when the relative

---

[1] Riley, *Mems. of London,* 467.
[2] *Liber Cust.,* 118.
[3] Statutes, 31 Edw. III.
[4] i. e. spawned.
[5] *Liber Cust.,* 118.
[6] *Rot. Parl.,* ii. 331.

value of money is considered, to dispose of the popular
legend that salmon was so plentiful in the Middle Ages
that the London apprentices protested against being
fed upon it. Of fresh-water fish a pike of 3 ft. cost
half a mark but one of 2 ft. only 2s., a roach sold for
a penny or a half-penny according to size, and eels were
sold by the ' stick ' of twenty-five for 2d. At a later
date, in 1412, eels were graded in three sizes and sold
by weight, the large ' stobele ' at 2d. the pound, the
middle-sized ' shastele ' at 1½d., and the small ' pymper-
nele ' at 1d.[1] The little Thames lamperns were about
twelve a penny, but their big brethren the lampreys, in
comparison with which Henry III considered all other
fish insipid,[2] fetched high prices—those from the Severn,
their chief source,[3] being 4s. each before Mid-Lent and
afterwards 2s., while the imported lampreys from Nantes
were 16d. when they first came in, falling to 8d. after a
month and 6d. after Easter.

So far no mention has been made of shellfish. Yet it
is obvious that Hamlet without the Prince of Denmark
would be less incomplete than an account of English
fisheries which ignored the oyster, for whose sake some
say that Caesar conquered Britain. Certain it is that
the Romans appreciated the British oyster, Sallust
considering it the only good thing that came out of
Britain, while Juvenal makes it the mark of the true
epicure to appreciate the oysters of Rutupiae (Rich-
borough). During the Middle Ages, however, the oyster

[1] Riley, *Mems. of London*, 581.

[2] ' Omnes pisces a lampredis videntur regi et regine insipidi.'
Cal. Close R., 21 Hen. III, m. 16.

[3] e. g. Close R., 17 Hen. III, m. 10.

suffered a temporary eclipse. Our ancestors certainly ate oysters—as they ate everything else that the sea produced, from shrimps [1] to whales—but they do not seem to have regarded them as superior to the now despised mussel and whelk. All three kinds of shellfish were classed together in the thirteenth century at London, where they might only be sold by the fishermen themselves, unless they were not disposed of by noon, in which case they might be sold in gross and put on sale in the shops. [2] From a whelk-boat bringing five ' tandles ' or more of whelks the king received one tandle, [3]— possibly because, as mediaeval cookery books show, whelks were usually served with that royal fish the sturgeon—but no such levy was made on the ' oystre-botes '. At Lincoln in 1540 oysters were to be sold at 4*d*. the ' wasche ' (=10 bushels), [4] and persons who refused to sell them at that price were not allowed to sell whelks or mussels, of which the price was the same ; from which we may perhaps gather that oysters were beginning to become more appreciated by the richer classes, and therefore to fetch a higher price, while the other kinds of shellfish were in more general demand.

Such references as we have to oysters before the seventeenth century are mostly incidental. Thus in 1303 Isabel de Stopham is found in possession of a rent of 3,000 oysters from a tenement in North Mundham,

---

[1] About 1380 Daniel Rowe of Romney was dealing in fish, including shrimps and oysters, which he sent to London, St. Albans, Hertford, Cambridge, and elsewhere. *Hist. MSS. Rep.*, vi. 545. In 1460 a ' shrympe net ' is mentioned with herring nets, sport nets, and keddelle nets seized for distraint. *Ibid.*, 542.

[2] *Liber Albus*, 381. [3] *Ibid.*

[4] *Hist. MSS. Rep.*, xiv (8), 36.

Sussex.[1] So also in 1285 a quarrel is recorded to have arisen between sailors of Sandwich and Yarmouth over a purchase of oysters at Colchester,[2] which was one of the great centres of the fishery, the ' accustomyd trade of trayling oysters . . . in the water of Colne ' being alluded to in 1566.[3] Another great centre was Faversham, where Walter le Oysterman occurs in 1305,[4] though the existence of ' a company of free dredgers ' in the time of Henry II and the grant by King John to the abbey of the right of dredging [5] appear to have been evolved out of more general references to fishing rights, in which dredging for oysters is not specifically mentioned. However, in the fifteenth century there was a complaint [6] by the mayor and commonalty of London that the abbot of Faversham had newly imposed a charge upon all fishers and draggers for ' draggure des oystres, muskles, crabbes, creuers (crayfish or lobsters), welkys, et autr pessons esshelez ' taken in the neighbourhood of Faversham, and by 1595 a large part of the inhabitants were supported by the oyster fisheries.[7] The rule that oysters are not to be eaten in the months which ' are void of the letter R ' was already known when Harrison published his *Description of England* [8] in 1577, and in that same year the dredging of oysters in the Medway estuary was forbidden between Easter and Lammas (the beginning of August).[9]

---

[1] Assize R. 1330, m. 17.   [2] *Cal. Misc. Inq.*, i. 2272.

[3] *V. C. H. Essex*, ii. 431.   [4] Coram Rege, 184, m. 50.

[5] Jacob, *Hist. of Faversham*, 78.

[6] Early Chanc. Proc., 6, 241.

[7] Jacob, *loc. cit.* ; cf. Exch. Dep. by Com., Easter, 42 Eliz., no. 10 ; Trin., 42 Eliz., no. 7.

[8] *Op. cit.*, book iii, c. 10.   [9] *Hist. MSS. Rep.*, ix. 289

Another excellent shellfish, peculiarly localized, was the Selsey cockle, which had already become famous in 1539, when the Earl of Southampton sent some to Thomas Cromwell, adding a note to the effect that they were not quite so good as they would be at the full of the moon.[1] When sending another parcel of cockles he adds : ' no doubt you are daily supplied with them by the Bishop of Chichester—if not, he does not deserve to eat any himself.'[2]

[1] *L. & P. Hen., VIII*, xiv (1), 573.   [2] *Ibid.*, xiii (1), 500.

XII

BREWING—ALE, BEER, CIDER, WINE

MALT liquors have been from time immemorial the national drink of England, but the ale of mediaeval times was quite different from the liquor which now passes indifferently under the names ale or beer. It was more of a sweet wort, of about the consistency of barley water. Andrew Borde,[1] writing in the first half of the sixteenth century, says : ' Ale is made of malte and water ; and they the which do put any other thynge to ale than is rehersed, except yest, barme or godesgood, doth sofysticat theyr ale. Ale for an Englysshe man is a naturall drynke. Ale must have these propertyes : it muste be fresshe and cleare, it muste not be ropy nor smoky, nor must it have no weft nor tayle. Ale should not be dronke under v dayes olde. Newe ale is unholsome for all men. And sowre ale, and dead ale the which doth stand a tylt, is good for no man. Barly malte maketh better ale then oten malte or any other corne doth : it doth ingendre grose humoures ; but yette it maketh a man stronge.'

The supremacy of English ale was already established by the middle of the twelfth century, that of Canterbury being particularly famous,[2] and casks of ale were amongst

---

[1] *A Dyetary of Helth* (E.E. T. S.), 256.

[2] *Giraldus Cambs.* (Rolls Ser.), iv. 41. Ely—which at the present day strikes a casual visitor as composed entirely of public-houses and a cathedral—was also famous in early days for beer. *Engl. Hist. Rev.,* xvi. 501.

the presents taken by Becket to the French Court on the
occasion of his embassy in 1157.[1] At this time it really
deserved the title of ' the people's food in liquid form ' ;
the consumption per head of population must have been
enormous, the ordinary monastic corrody, or allowance
of food, stipulating for a gallon of good ale a day, with
very often a second gallon of weak ale. It must be borne
in mind that it was drunk at all times, taking the place
not only of such modern inventions as tea and coffee,
but also of water, insomuch that a thirteenth-century
writer describing the extreme poverty of the Franciscans
when they first settled in London (A. D. 1224) exclaims,
' I have seen the brothers drink ale so sour that some
would have preferred to drink water.' [2] Such was the
importance attached to ale that it was coupled with
bread for purposes of legal supervision, and the right to
hold the ' assize of bread and ale ' was one of the earliest
justicial privileges asserted by municipal and other
local courts. The Assize of Ale as recorded on the
Statute Rolls in the time of Henry III fixed the maximum price of ale throughout the kingdom on the basis
of the price of malt, or rather of the corn from which
malt was made.[3] When wheat stood at 3s. or 3s. 4d.
the quarter, barley at 20d. to 2s., and oats at 16d., then
brewers in towns were to sell two gallons of ale for
a penny, and outside towns three or four gallons. And
when three gallons were sold for a penny in a town, then
four gallons should be sold for a penny in the country.
If corn rose a shilling the quarter, the price of ale might

[1] *Mat. for Hist. of T. Becket* (Rolls Ser.), iii. 30.
[2] *Mon. Franc.* (Rolls Ser.), ii. 8.
[3] Statutes, temp. Hen. III.

be raised a farthing the gallon.[1] A later ordinance, issued in 1283, set the price of the better quality of ale at $1\frac{1}{2}d.$ and that of the weaker at $1d.$; and the commonalty of Bristol, fearing that they might be punished if the brewers of the town broke this regulation, issued stringent orders for its observance, infringement entailing the forfeiture of the offender's brewery.[2]

A very casual examination of court rolls and other local records is sufficient to convince the student that brewing was universal, every village supplying its own wants, and that infringements of the regulations by which the trade was supposed to be controlled were almost equally universal. The same names are found, where any series of rolls exists, presented at court after court for breaking the assize in one way or another, and it is clear that a strict observance of the laws was difficult, it being more profitable to break them and pay the small fines extorted practically as licensing dues. At Shoreham in the thirteenth century, the brewers, whose trade was particularly active because of the numbers of foreigners who visited the port, paid $2\frac{1}{2}$ marks yearly to escape the vexations of the manorial court,[3] and in the same way the hundred of Shoyswell (in Sussex) paid a yearly fine in order that the ale-wives (the trade was largely in the hands of women) might be excused attendance at the law-days.[4] In neither case, however, can we suppose that the manorial control over the brewing

---

[1] ' [A Brewer's assise] is xij^d. highing and xij^d. lowing in the price of a quarter Malte, and evermore shilling to q^a ' (= farthing). *Coventry Leet Bk.* (E. E. T. S.), 397. In other words, ale was as many farthings a gallon as malt was shillings a quarter.

[2] *Little Red Book of Bristol,* 223.

[3] Assize R., 912, m. 49.   [4] *Hundred R.,* ii. 216.

trade was appreciably relaxed, but rather that personal attendance at the court, with its interruption of business, was dispensed with. Besides these monetary payments, there were often payments in kind due to the lord of the manor or borough. At Marlborough every public brewery had to pay to the constable of the castle from each brew a measure known as ' tolsester ' prior to 1232, when this render of ale was granted to the canons of St. Margaret's.[1] ' Tolsester ' was also paid in Newark and Fiskerton,[2] and Chester—where it was defined as the payment of a ' costrum ' of ale, containing 16 gallons of new ale measured under the ' shakesyf ', for leave to brew.[3] The ' sester ' (*sextarius*) or ' cestron ' was, in Coventry at any rate, 13 or 14 gallons.[4] Ale was always supposed to be sold, whether in gross or retail, in measures of which the capacity had been certified by the seal or stamp of the official appointed for the purpose.[5] The list of standard measures kept at Beverley in 1423 shows a potell, quart, pint, and gill of pewter, panyers, hopir, modius, firthindal, piece, and halfpiece of wood, and a gallon, potell, third, and quart, also of wood.[6] Court Rolls, however, show that the use of unstamped measures and the retailing of ale in pitchers and jugs (*per ciphos et discos*) was of constant occurrence,[7] mainly, no doubt, for the convenience of customers who brought

[1] *Cal. Chart. R.*, i. 168.   [2] *V. C. H. Notts*, ii. 364.

[3] Morris, *Chester*, 426.

[4] *Coventry Leet Bk.* (E. E. T. S.), 25, 678, 710.

[5] *Ibid.*, 772.

[6] *Beverley Town Docts.* (Selden Soc.), liv. In 1413, 260 barrels (30 gallons) and firkins (7½ gallons) made for Richard Bartlot of unseasoned wood and under size were burnt. Riley, *Mems. of London*, 597.

[7] e. g. *V. C. H. Sussex*, ii. 261.

their own jugs, but also occasionally with intent to deceive, as in the case of Alice Causton,[1] who in 1364 filled up the bottom of a quart measure with pitch and cunningly sprinkled it with sprigs of rosemary,[2] for which she had to ' play bo pepe thorowe a pillery '. It is interesting to notice that at Torksey in 1345, if a woman was accused of selling ale ' against the assize ', she might clear herself by the oaths of two other women, preferably her next-door neighbours.[3]

When a public brewer had made a fresh brew he had to send for the official ' ale-conner ' or ' taster ', or to signify that his services were required by putting out in front of his house an ' ale stake ', a pole with a branch or bush at the end : this was also used as the universal sign of a tavern ; and some of the London taverners, possibly recognizing that their liquor was not sufficiently good to ' need no bush ', made their ale-stakes so long as to be dangerous to persons riding in the street.[4] At Chester when the ale had settled and was ' clensed and of a nyght and a daie old ' the brewer had to put out ' the signe of a hande made of woode hangynge at thend of a wand '.[5] No ale might be sold until it had been approved by the ale-conner. If the latter found the ale fit for consumption but not of full quality, he might fix the price at which it might be sold.[6] At Salisbury[7] there were four tasters, one for each ward ;

---

[1] Riley, *Mems. of London*, 319.
[2] From this it would seem that it was customary to put herbs into ale.
[3] *Borough Customs* (Selden Soc.), i. 185.
[4] Riley, *Mems. of London*, 386.
[5] Morris, *Chester*, 428.　　　　[6] *Liber Albus*, i. 360.
[7] *Hist. MSS. Com. Rep.—Various*, iv. 205.

they had to taste the ale in every taverner's house while it was in the vessel called ' the kyse ' ; if it was defective in soundness, strength, or flavour, the tavern lost its licence and was suppressed—or, at least, might be. In Worcester the instructions to the ale-conner were, ' You shall resort to every brewer's house within this

BEER-BREWER.
16th cent.

city on their tunning day and there to taste their ale, whether it be good and wholesome for man's body, and whether they make it from time to time according to the prices fixed. So help you God.' [1] There seems reason for the pious ejaculation when we find that in Coventry in 1520 there were in a total population of 6,600 men, women, and children, 60 public brewers,[2] while in the small town of Faversham in 1327, out of 252 traders who contributed to a tallage, or assessment, no fewer than 84 were ale-wives.[3] When the ale was good the task must have had its compensations, but when it was bad the taster must often have wished to make the punishment fit

---

[1] *V. C. H. Worcs.*, ii. 256.

[2] *Coventry Leet Bk.* (E. E. T. S.), 675. There were at least thirty brewers in Oxford in 1380. *V. C. H. Oxon*, ii. 159.

[3] *Hist. MSS. Com. Rep.*, vi. 505.

the crime, as was done in the case of a Londoner who
sold bad wine, the offender being compelled to drink
a draught of the wine, the rest of which was then poured
over his head.[1] Our sympathy may in particular be
extended to the ale-tasters of Cornwall, where ' ale is
starke nought, lokinge whyte and thycke, as pygges had
wrasteled in it '.[2] Oddly enough we find mention in
Domesday Book of forty-three *cervisiarii* at Helstone in
Cornwall ; they are usually supposed to be tenants who
paid dues of ale, but the term is clearly used in the
description of Bury St. Edmunds for brewers. In the
sixteenth century, however, Borde [3] in an unflattering
dialect poem makes the Cornishman say :

> Iche cam a Cornyshe man, ale che can brew ;
>   It wyll make one to kacke, also to spew ;
> It is dycke and smoky, and also it is dyn ;
>   It is lyke wash as pygges had wrestled dryn.

To ensure the purity of the ale not only was the
finished product examined, but some care was taken to
prevent the use of impure water, regulations to prevent
the contamination of water used by brewers, or the use
by them of water so contaminated, being common.[4]
On the other hand, owing to the large quantities of water
required for their business, they were forbidden in
London,[5] Bristol,[6] and Coventry [7] to use the public
conduits. For the actual brewing, rules were also laid

---

[1] Riley, *Mems. of London*, 318.
[2] Andrew Borde, *Introduction* (E. E. T. S.), 123.
[3] *Op. cit.*, 122.   [4] e. g. *V. C. H. Sussex*, ii. 262.
[5] Riley, *Mems. of London*, 225.
[6] *Little Red Book of Bristol*, ii. 229.
[7] *Coventry Leet Bk.* (E. E. T. S.), 584.

down. The malt used was to be ' clene swete and drye and wele made, not capped in the sakkes, nor raw dried malte, dank or wete malte or made of mowe brent barley (barley burnt or overheated in the mow or stack), belyed (i. e. swollen) malte, edgrove (i. e. germinating) malte, acrespired (i. e. sprouting at both ends) malte, wyvell eten (weavil eaten) malt or medled '.[1] The necessity for this regulation is evident when we find Thomas Sharp in 1432 selling to the Abbot of Colwick malt so ' raw, recked and damaged with weevils ' that it killed the hogs, hens, and capons to which it was given.[2] In Oxford in 1449, in which year nine brewers were said to brew weak and unwholesome ale, not properly prepared, and not worth its price, but of little or no value, the brewers were made to swear that they would brew in wholesome manner so that they would continue to heat the water over the fire so long as it emitted froth, and would skim the froth off, and that after skimming the new ale should stand long enough for the dregs to settle before they sent it out, Richard Benet in particular undertaking that his ale should stand for at least twelve hours before he sent it to any hall or college.[3] In London also casks when filled in the brewery were to stand for a day and a night to work, so that when taken away the ale should be clear and good.[4] This explains the regulation at Coventry in 1421 that ale ' new under the here syve [hair sieve] ' was to sell for 1¼d. the gallon, and that ' good and stale ' for 1½d [5] At

---

[1] *London Letter Book L*, 202. For lists of the contents of a fifteenth-century brewhouse see *ibid.*, 232, and *Cal. of Anct. Deeds*, A. 11565.

[2] *V. C. H. Notts.*, ii. 364.

[3] *V. C. H. Oxon.*, ii. 260.   [4] *Liber Albus*, i. 358.

[5] *Coventry Leet Bk.* (E. E. T. S.), 25.

Seaford there was a third state, ' in the hoffe ', or ' huff ',
which sold for 2*d*.[1] Further gradations in the quality
of the ale are referred to in regulations made at Chester
in 1540 : a crock of best ale, containing 4 gallons, under
the ' shaksciv ' was to be sold for 1½*d*., a gallon of best
ale, stale, for 2*d*., of second ale 1*d*., and of third ale
4 gallons for a penny.[2]

So far were the brewers regarded as the servants of
the people that not only was their brewing strictly
regulated, but they were compelled to brew even when
they considered that new ordinances [3] or a rise in the
price of malt would make their trade unprofitable ; [4]
and in 1434 the brewers of Oxford were summoned to
St. Mary's Church and there ordered to provide malt,
and to see to it that two or three brewers brewed twice
or thrice every week, and sent out their ale ; [5] moreover,
if a brewer refused to brew when malt was dear and then
when it became cheap again resumed his trade, he had
to pay such fine as the gild might fix.[6] The needs of the
poorer classes were considered at Leicester, where it
was ordered that ' alle brwers that brwythe to selle
shalle make good ale and holsome for mans bodye,
neyther rowred nor roppie but that yt be clene brwyed
according to the statute, and to sell according to thassysz
that Mr. Mayer shall gyve, and to make good holsome
smalle drynk for the poore peopylle after ob. (=a half-
penny) a gallon '.[7] This charitable consideration was

---

[1] *Suss. Arch. Coll.*, vii. 96.   [2] Morris, *Chester*, 426.

[3] *Liber Albus*, i. 359.

[4] *Coventry Leet Bk.* (E. E. T. S.), 637.

[5] *V. C. H. Oxon.*, ii. 260.   [6] W. H. Turner, *Recs. of Oxford*, 10.

[7] *Hist. MSS. Com. Rep.*, viii. 426.

carried still farther at Gloucester,[1] in the sixteenth century, the brewers being expected to give some kind of weak wort, possibly the scum or dregs of their brew, to the poor to make up into a kind of very small beer, which must have been something like the ' second washing of the tuns ', which formed the perquisite of the under brewers at Rochester Priory.[2] At Norwich, barm or yeast was a similar subject of charity, and in 1468 it was set forth that ' wheras berme otherwise clepid goddisgood, without tyme of mynde hath frely be yoven or delyvered for brede whete malte egges or othir honest rewarde to the value only of a farthyng at the uttermost and noon warned [i. e. denied], because it cometh of the grete grace of God ; certeyn . . . comon brewers . . . for ther singler lucre and avayle have nowe newely begonne to take monye for their seid goddisgood ', charging a halfpenny or a penny for the least amount, therefore the brewers were to swear that ' for the time ye or your wife exercise comon brewing ye shall graunte and delyver to any person axyng berme called goddis- good takyng for as moche goddisgood as shall be sufficient for the brewe of a quarter malte a ferthyng at the moost ', provided that they have enough for their own use, and that this do not apply to any ' old custom ' between the brewers and bakers.[3]

About the end of the fourteenth century a new variety of malt liquor, BEER, was introduced from Flanders. It seems to have been imported into Win-

[1] Exch. Dep. by Com., Mich., 18–19 Eliz., no. 10.
[2] Cott. MS. Vesp., A. 22, f. 115.
[3] *Recs. of Norwich*, ii. 98.

chelsea as early as 1400,[1] but for the best part of a century its use was mainly, and its manufacture entirely, confined to foreigners. Andrew Borde,[2] who disapproved of it, says, ' Bere is made of malte, of hoppes and water : it is a naturall drynke for a Dutche man. And nowe of late dayes it is moche used in Englande to the detryment of many Englysshe men ; specyally it kylleth them the which be troubled with the colycke and the stone and the strangulion ; for the drynke is a cold drynke ; yet it doth make a man fat, and doth inflate the bely, as it dothe appeare by the Dutche mens faces and belyes. If the bere be well served and be fyned and not new it doth qualify the heat of the lyver '. Libellous attacks on this excellent liquor were authoritatively repelled in 1436, when a writ was addressed to the sheriffs of London to proclaim that all brewers of beer shall continue their art in spite of malevolent attempts made to prevent natives of Holland and Zeeland and others from making beer, on the ground that it was poisonous and not fit to drink and caused drunkenness, whereas it is a wholesome drink, especially in summer.[3] That, thanks to the large foreign settlement in London, beer brewing soon attained considerable dimensions in the city is evident from the fact that in 1418, when provisions were sent to Henry V at the siege of Rouen, 300 tuns of ' ber ' were sent from London, and only 200 tuns of ale, but the beer was valued at only 13*s.* 4*d.* the tun, while the ale was 20*s.*[4] About the middle of the fifteenth century large quantities of hops were being imported at

[1] *V. C. H. Sussex*, ii. 261. [2] *Dyetary* (E. E. T. S.), 256.
[3] *London Letter Book K*, 205.
[4] Riley, *Mems. of London*, 666.

Rye and Winchelsea, and in the church of the neighbouring village of Playden may still be seen the grave of
Cornelius Zoetmann, ornamented with two beer barrels
and a crossed mash-stick and fork.[1] A little later we
find beer being exported from the Sussex ports and also
from Poole,[2] which had long done a large trade in ale to
the Channel Islands.

In 1441, attention having been called to the fact that
the beer brewers were not inspected or controlled, the
king appointed Richard Lounde and William Veysy for
life to have the survey and correction of all the beer
brewers of England.[3] Neither of these men was an
expert—Veysy, in fact, was a brick-maker—and inquiries
had to be made as to the rules in force abroad. The
resulting report was that both the malt and the hops
whereof beer is made must be perfect, sound and sweet,
the malt of good sound corn, to wit, of pure barley and
oats or of barley and wheat, not too dry nor rotten nor
full of worms called ' wifles ', and the hops not rotten
or old. The beer may not leave the brewery for eight
days after brewing, when the officials test it to see that
it is sufficiently boiled, contains enough hops, and is not
sweet. When malt was 3s. 4d. the quarter, a barrel of
' double coyt ' (twice cooked) beer, containing 36 gallons,
should be sold for 2s. 8d., and the price should vary—as
in the case of ale—by a farthing the gallon to each
shilling on the quarter of malt. Barrels of ' syngle coyt '
beer, however, should always be sold for 2s. This assize
was therefore adopted for England, and Lounde and

[1] *V. C. H. Sussex*, ii. 261.
[2] *V. C. H. Dorset*, ii. 367.
[3] Pat., 19 Hen. VI, pt. 1, m. 10.

Veysy were empowered to take a halfpenny on every barrel that they, or their deputies, passed as good.[1] Just twenty years later the good men of the mistery of ' berebruers ' in London petitioned for leave to elect two men annually to act as searchers, pointing out that theirs was the only trade without authorized rules, and that ' the common people for lacke of experience can not knowe the perfitnesse of bere as wele as of ale '.[2] In 1493 they became a definite craft, or gild, with wardens and other officers.[3]

Such beer brewers as occur during the fifteenth century almost all bear foreign names. For instance, in 1473, Thomas Seyntleger and John Goryng of Southwark recovered heavy damages for theft against John Doys of St. Botolph's-outside-Aldgate and Gerard Sconeburgh of Southwark, ' berebruers ', whose sureties were Godfrey Speryng and Edward Dewysse, also ' berebruers '.[4] Probably in this case the ' theft ' was an illegal seizure in distraint of goods for a debt for beer supplied, as although most of the goods said to be stolen were armour and objects of value, such as a book of Gower's poems and an illuminated *Sege of Troye*, there were also ten barrels of ' sengilbere ', thirty-five barrels of ' dowble-bere ', ten lastys of barrels and kilderkins, and two great sacks for ' hoppys '. There was still a prejudice against beer, and in 1471, at Norwich, the use of hops and ' gawle ' in brewing was forbidden,[5] while in 1519 the authorities at Shrewsbury prohibited the employment of the ' wicked and pernicious weed, hops '.[6] In London

[1] Pat., 21 Hen. VI, pt. 2, m. 20.
[2] *London Letter Book L*, 52.   [3] *Ibid.*, 296.
[4] Coram Rege 852, m. 23.
[5] *Recs. of Norwich*, ii. 100.   [6] *V. C. H. Shrops.*, ii. 422.

the brewers were forbidden in 1484 to ' put in any ale
or licour wherof ale shalbe made or in the wirkyng and
bruyng of any maner of ale any hoppes, herbes or other
like thing but onely licour malt and yeste '.[1] The
wording of the prohibition suggests that it was aimed
rather at maintaining the standard of the old English
ale than at preventing all brewing of beer. This is the
more probable as it was only six years since the council
had declared that the action of the brewers in raising
the price of beer was ' against the common weal ',[2] and
only five years before the beer brewers, as we have seen,
became a recognized gild. This would also explain the
apparent contradiction that while, in 1531, the royal
brewer was forbidden to use hops or brimstone, an Act
of Parliament passed in the same year bore testimony
to the establishment of the industry by exempting alien
brewers from the penal statutes against foreigners
practising their trades in England, and also by allowing
beer brewers to employ two coopers while ale brewers
might only employ one.[3] At the same time the barrel
of beer was fixed at thirty-six gallons, and that of ale
at thirty-two, the kilderkin and firkin being respectively
half and quarter of those amounts.

From this time the brewing of beer steadily prospered,
the Leakes of Southwark [4] and other alien brewers
amassing great riches, English brewers following in their
footsteps, and the taste for beer spreading through the

---

[1] *London Letter Book L*, 211.

[2] *Ibid.*, 155. At Norwich in 1498 (*Recs. of Norwich,* ii. 155)
complaints were made that the price of beer had gone up but ' the
same bere is nowe thinner and wers drynk '. History sometimes
repeats itself.

[3] *V. C. H. Surrey,* ii. 382.   [4] *Ibid.,* ii. 382–4.

country so rapidly that in 1577 Harrison in his *Description of England*—in which he describes with loving profusion of detail the way in which his wife brewed beer—could speak contemptuously of the old ale as thick and fulsome, ' an old and sick man's drink,' [1] and no longer popular except with a few.

William Harrison also says : ' In some places of England there is a kind of drinke made of apples, which they call CIDER or pomage, but that of peares is named pirrie, and both are ground and pressed in presses made for the nonce. Certes, these two are verie common in Sussex, Kent, Worcester, and other steads where these sorts of fruits do abound, howbeit they are not their onelie drinke at all times, but referred unto the delicate sorts of drinke '. A generation earlier Andrew Borde,[2] whom we have already quoted for ale and beer, wrote :

' Cyder is made of the juce of peeres, or of the juce of apples ; and other whyle cyder is made of both ; but the best cyder is made of cleane peeres, the which be dulcet ; but the beste is not praysed in physycke, for cyder is colde of operacyon, and is full of ventosyte, wherfore it doth ingendre evyll humours and doth swage to moche the naturall heate of man and doth let dygestyon and doth hurte the stomacke ; but they the whych be used to it, yf it be dronken in harvyst it doth lytell harme.'

Andrew Borde makes no distinction between cider and perry. We find mention of the latter in 1505, when

---

[1] Cf. a purchase of ale in 1541 ' for Ser Jhon Beren becawse he cowd drencke no bere '. *Hist. MSS. Com., Belvoir,* iv. 317.

[2] *Dyetary* (E. E. T. S.), 256.

a foreign ship entered Poole with a cargo of apples, pears, &c., and ' 3 poncheons de pery ', valued at 10s.,[1] but references to perry are not numerous. Cider, on the other hand, we find in constant demand from the middle of the twelfth century onwards. It figures on the Pipe Rolls of Henry II,[2] and the contemporary historian and journalist, Gerald de Barri, alleged its use by the monks of Canterbury instead of Kentish ale as an instance of their luxury.[3] A little later, in 1212, the sale of cider is one of the numerous sources of the income of the Abbey of Battle ; [4] part of this cider may have come from its estates at Wye, which produced a good deal of cider during the fourteenth century.[5]

Possibly the industry was introduced from Normandy, from which district large quantities of cider were imported into Winchelsea about 1270,[6] and this might account for the hold which it took upon Sussex. In the western part of the county, at Pagham, we find mention of an apple mill and press having been wrongfully seized by the escheator's officer in 1275,[7] and at the same place in 1313 the farmer of the archbishop's estates accounted for 12s. spent on buying four casks in which to put cider, on repairing a cider press, and on the wages of men hired to make cider.[8] It is, however, in the Nonae Rolls of 1341 that the extent of the cider industry in Sussex is most noticeable.[9] In no fewer than eighty

---

[1] *V. C. H. Dorset*, ii. 369.
[2] Pipe R., 6 Hen. II, Essex ; 13 Hen. II, Windsor.
[3] *Giraldus Cambr.* (Rolls Ser.), iv. 41.
[4] Pipe R., 13 John.
[5] Mins. Accts., bdle. 899.
[6] *V. C. H. Sussex*, ii. 263.
[7] *Ibid.*
[8] Mins. Accts., 1128, no. 4.
[9] *V. C. H. Sussex*, ii. 263.

parishes, of which seventy-four were in West Sussex, the tithes of cider are mentioned as part of the endowment of the church, and in another twenty-eight cases the tithes of apples are entered. Moreover, the value of these tithes was very considerable, reaching 100s. in Easebourne, and as much as 10 marks (£6 13s. 4d.) at Wisborough. In the last-named parish in 1385, William Threle granted to John Pakenham and his wife certain gardens and orchards, reserving to himself half the trees bearing fruit either for eating or for cider (*mangable et ciserable*), in return for which they were to render yearly a pipe of cider and a quarter of store apples (*hordapplen*) ; he also retained the right of access to the 'wringehouse', or building containing the press, and the right to use their cider press for his fruit.[1] Sometimes the wild crab-apples appear to have been used for cider ; as at Wakefield in 1296 Simon de Monte was fined for not collecting 'wood apples' (*poma bosci*) faithfully, so that the lord of the manor lost two hogsheads of cider.[2]

Beyond an abundance of casual references to cider presses and to the purchases and sale of cider, there is little to record of the industry in mediaeval times ; nor need we devote much attention to the manufacture of WINE in England. Domesday Book shows us that the great Norman lords in many cases planted vines near their chief seats, and not many years later William of Malmesbury spoke of the Vale of Gloucester as planted more thickly with vineyards than any other part of England, and producing the best grapes, from which a wine little inferior to those of France was made.

[1] Memo., K. R., 17 Ric. II, Hil.
[2] *Wakefield Court Rolls* (Yorks. Rec. Soc.), i. 252.

Vines continued to be grown by the great lords [1] and monasteries [2] till the end of the fourteenth century. Under Edward III and his grandson the vineyards at Windsor, [3] in which gardeners from the wine districts of

SETTING, PRUNING, AND TRAINING VINES. 15th cent.

[1] The Bishop of Ely had vineyards in Holborn in 1290, and the Bishop of Hereford one at Ledbury, which yielded 7 pipes of white wine in 1289 and was still in existence in 1539. *London and Middlesex Arch. Soc.*, iii. 408–9.

[2] In 1238 a tun of English wine was bought for the king's household from Tewkesbury. *Cal. Liberate R.*, i. 311.

[3] C. Roach Smith, *Collect. Antiq.*, vi. 96–101.

Gascony were occasionally employed, were well cared for and proved productive. The wine produced there in 1393 brought in over £20, the red wine selling at from 18*s.* to 30*s.* a pipe, and the white at from 10*s.* to 18*s.* These vineyards were certainly kept up as late as 1433, and those of the Bishop of Rochester at Snodland down at least to the time of Edward IV.[1] About 1500 an Italian visitor speaks of having eaten English grapes, and adds, ' wine might be made in the southern parts, but it would be harsh,'[2] from which we may judge that English wine-making was practically at an end by the sixteenth century, though a little continued to be made in different places for another 250 years.

[1] *Ibid.*, 103 ; the suggestion is made that blackberries were here mixed with the grapes, as both occur in the same record.

[2] *A Venetian Relation of the Island of England* (Camden Soc.), 9.

MARKET-HALL WITH STALLS. 15th cent.

XIII

THE CONTROL OF INDUSTRY

THE control of industry is a subject for the treatment of which there are materials sufficient for more than one large volume. I do not, however, regret that I can devote comparatively small space to the subject, as its principles are simple and admit of broad treatment. There is, moreover, in the case of the student who is not a specialist, a danger of obscuring the outlines with a multiplicity of detail. And there is also the danger of selecting some puzzling and obscure incident or enactment, due to local causes of which we are ignorant, and using it as a basis for ingenious generalizations. Broadly speaking, the Control of Industry may be said to be either External, by parliamentary or municipal legislation, or Internal, by means of craft gilds. These two sections again admit of subdivision according as their objects are the protection of the consumer, the employer, or the workman. Nor can we entirely ignore legislation for purposes of revenue—subsidies, customs, and *octroi* dues.

Of industrial legislation by the King's Council, the predecessor of Parliament, we find very little trace. The royal charters of the twelfth century confirming or licensing craft gilds may be more justly regarded as revenue enactments, their object being rather to secure a certain annual return from the craft to which the royal protection was granted than to exercise any control over the craft. The proclamation in the early thirteenth century of the Assize of Cloth and of the Assize of Bread and Ale may be considered to mark the beginning of a national control of industry, though in each case existing regulations were formally adopted rather than new rules imposed. The growth of the towns and the rise of a wealthy merchant class during the reign of Henry III brought about the birth of Parliament, and naturally led to a certain amount of trade legislation. But with trade—the distribution of finished products by persons other than the producers—we are not concerned. Edward III, thanks perhaps to his queen, Philippa, from the cloth land of Hainault, realized the possibilities of the English cloth manufacture, and endeavoured to foster it by a series of statutes to which reference has been made above. During his reign, in 1349, the Black Death, that great landmark in mediaeval history, by reducing the numbers of the craftsmen, increased the market value of the survivors, who at once demanded and obtained higher wages. Parliament retorted by passing the Statute of Labourers,[1] according to which no smith, carpenter, mason, tiler, shipwright, leather-worker, tailor, or other artificer was to take higher wages than he had received three years earlier, before the pestilence. Though this was legislation in favour of the employer, it was not exactly a case of favouring the wealthy, for by imposing a penalty on the giver of excessive wages as well as upon the receiver, an attempt was made to prevent the small employer being deprived of his workmen by richer rivals. The Act was, so far as we can judge, inspired partly by fear that the capitalist might control the sources of labour, and partly

[1] Statutes, 23 Edw. III.

by fear that those sources might get beyond control. Whatever its origin, the statute failed in its expressed intention, and wages remained, as Thorold Rogers has shown,[1] permanently higher. This was not due to any laxity in applying the Act ; for many years after it was passed justices were appointed in every part of England to enforce it,[2] but the records of their proceedings, as, for instance, in Somerset in 1360,[3] where many hundreds of offenders are named, show that the workmen had no hesitation in demanding, and found no difficulty in getting, wages higher than the law allowed. Wholesale imprisonment as a remedy for scarcity of labour was scarcely satisfactory, and the small fines which were inflicted proved no deterrent.

As the position of the artificer had improved after the Black Death, so the crafts in general were assuming a greater importance in public estimation, and from about 1380 onwards the regulation of industries occupies an increasing amount of space on the Statute Rolls. With their growing influence most of the crafts began to make their voices heard crying out for protection, which was usually given them with a liberal hand. But, although the pernicious effects of protective measures (deterioration of quality and rise of price) were to a large extent checked by the control kept over quality and prices by the national and municipal authorities, the consumer was sometimes roused to action. One of the best instances of the struggle between public and private interests is the case of the Yarmouth herring fishery, already mentioned. Edward III had granted to Yar-

---

[1] *Six Centuries of Work and Wages,* 233.
[2] *Engl. Hist. Rev.,* xxi. 517.   [3] Assize R., 773.

mouth the monopoly of the sale of herrings on the east coast during the season of the fishery. As a consequence the price of herrings had risen enormously, and the king was driven to cancel the privilege : the men of Yarmouth at once began to pull the strings, and in 1378 recovered their monopoly, with the same result as before. Once more the consumer made his voice heard, and in 1382 the Yarmouth charter was revoked, only to be restored in 1385 on the ground that without protection of this kind Yarmouth would be ruined. Other instances, less complicated and more strictly local, might be given. For example, in 1362, when the tanners of Chester obtained a charter from the Black Prince forbidding the cordwainers to meddle with the art of tanning, the corporation, unawed by the act of their lord, caused the charter to be revoked as against the interests of the city.[1] At Chester also, in 1558, when the joiners and carvers were found to be selling their goods to Ireland and other places over sea at high prices, so that they became rich, but the citizens were left unserved, the practice was forbidden.[2] A similar insistence on the craftsman's position as the servant of the commonalty is seen in the orders issued at Lydd that the brewers shall see that there is no lack of beer, and chandlers that there is no lack of candles at any time, on pain of amercement.[3]

If a large number of parliamentary enactments were protective of the producer, as for instance the prohibition in 1463 of the import of a vast variety of goods, from silk ribbons to dripping-pans, and from razors to tennis balls, including such incompatibles as playing cards and

[1] Morris, *Chester,* 410.   [2] *Ibid.,* 405.
[3] *Hist. MSS. Com. Rep.,* v. 531.

sacring bells,[1] yet still more were protective of the consumer. For one thing, of course, a single Act prohibiting certain imports might protect a dozen classes of manufactures, while the denunciation of one particular species of fraud would probably lead ingenious swindlers to invent a succession of others, each requiring a separate Act for its suppression. Sentimental admirers of the past are apt to imagine that the mediaeval workman loved a piece of good work for its own sake and never scamped a job. Nothing could be farther from the truth. The mediaeval craftsman was not called a man of craft for nothing ! He had no more conscience than a plumber, and his knowledge of ways that are dark and tricks that are vain was extensive and peculiar. The subtle craft of the London bakers, who, while making up their customer's dough, stole a large portion of the dough under their customers' eyes by means of a little trap-door in the kneading-board and a boy sitting under the counter,[2] was exceptional only in its ingenuity. In 1472, nearly 450 years before the passing of ' the Rag Flock Bill ', complaints were made of frauds in the upholstery trade, in such articles as feather-beds, cushions, and quilts, where the buyer ' seeth withoute and knoweth not the stuf within ', down pillows being stuffed ' with thistill downe and cattes tailles ' (the vegetable variety, I imagine), and ' materas stuffed with here (hair) and flokkes and sold for flokkes '.[3] Cloth was stretched and strained to the utmost and cunningly folded to hide defects, a length of bad cloth would be joined on to a length of superior quality, or a whole cheap cloth

[1] Statutes, 3 Edw. IV.   [2] Riley, *Mems. of London*, 163.
[3] *London Letter Book L*, 121.

substituted for the good cloth which the customers had purchased ; inferior leather was faked up to look like the best, and sold at night to the unwary ; pots and kettles were made of bad metal which melted when put on the fire ; and everything that could be weighed or measured was sold by false measure.

Prior to the middle of the sixteenth century parliamentary attention was mainly concentrated on the cloth trade, and the preambles to the various statutes show that those in authority, including the more responsible manufacturers, realized that honesty is the best policy in the end. In 1390 it was pointed out that the frauds of the west-country clothiers had not only endangered the reputations, and even the lives, of merchants who bought them for export, but had brought dishonour on the English name abroad.[1] Two years later it was the reputation of Guildford cloths that had been damaged by sharp practices.[2] The worsteds of Norfolk had early come into favour on the Continent, but in 1410 the Flemish merchants became exasperated at their bad quality,[3] and thirty years later the foreign demand for worsteds had been almost killed,[4] while in 1464 English cloth in general was in grave disrepute, not only abroad, but even in its native land, foreign cloth being largely imported.[5] To give them their due, the gilds recognized the importance to their own interests of maintaining a high standard of workmanship, and co-operated loyally with the municipal authorities to that end.

Although we have classed the control of industries by

[1] Statutes, 13 Ric. II. [2] *Ibid.*, 15 Ric. II.
[3] *Parl. Rolls*, iii. 637. [4] Statutes, 20 Hen. VI.
[5] Statutes, 4 Edw. IV.

municipal by-laws as 'external', and control by gild regulations as 'internal', no hard and fast line can really be drawn between the two. In England, in contrast to the experience of many Continental states, the two authorities worked together with very little friction, the craft gilds recognizing the paramount position of the merchant gild or town council, and the latter, in turn, protecting the interest of the gilds and using their organization to control the various crafts. The question of the origin of gilds is interesting rather than important, and has given rise to much discussion. It is known that the Roman crafts were organized into *collegia*, but while it is quite possible that some of the trade gilds in Constantinople, and even in Italy and Spain, might be able to trace their pedigrees back to Roman times, it is more than improbable that there was any connexion between the Roman *collegia* and the English craft gilds of the twelfth century. The gilds of which we find mention in Anglo-Saxon records were clearly fraternities of purely social and religious import. These gilds, friendly societies for the support of religious observances benefiting the souls of all the members, and for the mutual relief of such members as had met with misfortune, survived the Conquest and increased greatly, till by the end of the fourteenth century there could have been hardly a village without at least one gild. It is natural to suppose that in towns, where the choice of gilds was considerable, there would be a tendency for members of the same trade to join the same gild. The strength gained by such union under the common bond of an oath to obey the same statutes and the same officers, and the advantage of the Church's protection, must soon have become obvious, and as in 1378 we find the weavers of London forming a fraternity whose ordinances are entirely of a religious nature, and contain no reference to the occupation of the members,[1] and the mercers of York doing the same in 1356,[2] so we may well believe that many of the early gilds, while apparently purely religious, were in fact trade societies.

Whatever may have been the methods in which craft gilds came into existence, we find them increasing in numbers and influence from the middle of the twelfth century onwards. Meanwhile, however, the capitalists and wealthy traders by means of 'merchant gilds' and similar bodies had so firmly established an oligarchic control over the towns and boroughs that they were able to keep the craft gilds in a subordinate position. This was so, in spite of the fact that in England the merchant gild in early times was largely composed of craftsmen, who were encouraged and even forced to receive its privileges, which virtually amounted to a monopoly of trading rights, in order that they might share its burdens, in the shape of rents due to the Crown or other lord. Although thus widespread and theoretically democratic, the gild was practically always controlled by the capitalist or trading classes ; as for instance at York, where the vast bulk of the commonalty hardly counted for anything, the 'forty-eight' (craftsmen-manufacturers) carried little weight, the 'twenty-four' (craftsmen-traders) had a good deal of influence, but the ' twelve ' aldermen (merchants) formed the real governing body.[3] Everywhere the town

[1] Unwin, *Gilds of London*, 139.
[2] *York Mercers and Merchant Adventurers*, 1–3.
[3] *York Memorandum Book*, i. vii.

authorities, whether they were mayor and council, or gild merchant, or governors, could impose regulations upon the crafts, while such rules as the crafts drew up for their own management were legal only if accepted by the town council. The case of Coventry was typical, where, in 1421, the mayor and councillors summoned the wardens of the crafts with their ordinances : ' And the poyntes that byn lawfull good and honest for the Cite be alowyd hem and all other thrown asid and had for none '.[1] In the same way at Norwich in 1449, the mayor drew up a complete set of ordinances for the crafts,[2] and in London ordinances that had not been enrolled in the books of the corporation and received the assent of the mayor and council could not be enforced.[3] But although keeping a firm hand on the gilds, and taking measures to protect the interests of the consumers and of the town in general, the civic authorities left the gilds in control of the internal affairs of their crafts. So that the crafts-man in his relations to another of the same trade was a gild brother, but in his relations to all other men he was a townsman.

From the consumer's point of view the regulation of prices was perhaps the most important problem. The price of raw material was too dependent upon supply and demand to admit of much regulation, though in 1355 Parliament interfered to bring down the price of iron,[4] forbidding its export, and ordering the Justices of

---

[1] *Coventry Leet Bk*. (E. E. T. S.), 32.

[2] *Norwich Recs*., ii. 278–310.

[3] e. g. *London Letter Book K*, 200.

[4] Statutes, 28 Edw. III. Is iron raw material ? Much labour has been expended on it before it reaches the market—but the same would apply to corn.

Labourers (i. e. those appointed to enforce the Statute of Labourers), to punish all who sold it too high. The local authorities, civic and manorial, took constant measures to prevent the artificial enhancement of what we may call raw food stuffs, corn, fish, and meat, the

ffor staller and regratter of markett and fevres and vittelars

Forestaller in the pillory
16th cent.

'regrater and forestaller', that is to say, the middleman, who intercepted supplies before they reached the market and forced prices up for his own sole benefit, being universally regarded as a miscreant.[1] The economists of that period had not grasped the fact that the cleverness shown in buying an article cheap and selling the same thing, without any further expenditure of labour, dear, if done on a sufficiently large scale, constitutes a claim to the honour of knighthood or a peerage. In the case of manufactured food stuffs, such as bread and ale, the price was automatically fixed by the price of the raw material, and in general prices of manufactures were regulated by the cost of the materials. Even in the case of such artistic work as the making of waxen images, it was considered scandalous that the makers should charge as much as 2s. the pound for images when wax was

[1] e. g. Riley, *Mems. of London,* 255.

only 6*d.* the pound, and in 1432 the wax-chandlers were ordered not to charge for workmanship more than 3*d.* the pound over the current price of wax.[1] The principle that the craftsman should be content with a reasonable profit, and not turn the casual needs of his neighbours to his own benefit, is constantly brought out in local regulations, as, for instance, in London in 1362, when in consequence of the damage wrought by a great storm tiles were in great demand, and the tilers were ordered to go on making tiles and selling them at the usual prices.[2]

The two principles of reasonable profit and service of the community are brought out in the case of the Chester bakers in 1557. Wheat having risen to 46*s.* the quarter, the mayor and council fixed the weight of the half-penny loaf at 6½ ounces : the bakers refused to bake at this rate, but the corporation, after careful consideration, decided that the charge was ' laufull necessary and suffycyent for the bayker to lyve upon '. On the bakers' refusal to accept this decision bread grew scarce, and the mayor issued a proclamation desiring everybody to provide for themselves as far as possible and authorizing anyone to bake good wholesome bread and bring it to the market, in which case they should ' not have onely redy monye for ther bred with hartye thankes ' but should be protected from prosecution for infringing the liberties of the bakers' gild. The bakers then appealed to the Council of the Marches, who upheld the action of the mayor ; considering that the bakers ' by ther doings manifestly declaring them selves rather the occasion of derthe than plentye agenest the comon

---

[1] Statutes, 11 Hen. VI.   [2] Riley, *Mems. of London*, 308.

welthe of this citye, yt was thought that they wer no
good citizenes nor worthie to enjoy that libertie ', the
mayor disfranchised twenty-seven of the bakers, who
then submitted and were restored on payment of fines.[1]
Just twenty years later the butchers of Chester,
annoyed at the recent admission of country butchers

KNIFE-GRINDER
16th cent.

to the city, refused to
kill any meat. The mayor
promptly committed the
whole company to prison,
only releasing them on
their complete submission,
' consideringe allsoe the
lamentable waylinge and
humble submission of the
said company, their great
charge of wives and
children, their imbesilitie
and wekeness, and danger
of the tyme, beinge very
fervent hott wether, the
company many in number,
and the straightness of
rome in the said gaole.' [2] Such extreme measures were
not usual in earlier times ; as a rule when a craft
attempted to exploit its monopoly, like the shear-
grinders in 1423, ' which for their singular proffit and
comon harme have taken fro day to day so excessiflieh
for their occupacion that it is shame and dole for to
here,' [3] it was sufficient to pass an ordinance regulating
their charges.

[1] Morris, *Chester*, 417–20.   [2] *Ibid.*, 440.
[3] *London Letter Book K*, 23.

The question of prices, which were thus so largely composed of a varying sum for material and a fixed sum for workmanship, is very intimately connected with the question of wages.[1] The mediaeval economist seems to have accepted the Ruskinian theory that all men engaged in a particular branch of trade should be paid equal wages—with the corollary that the better workman would obtain the more employment—as opposed to the modern practice of payment according to skill, which often results in the greater employment of the bad workman because he is cheap.[2] There were, of course, grades in each profession, as master or foreman, workman, and assistant or common labourer, but within each grade the rate of payment was fixed—at least within the jurisdiction of any gild or town authority[3] —unless the work was of quite exceptional nature, as, for instance, the making of carved stalls for the royal chapel at Westminster in 1357, where the rates of pay were almost double those of ordinary workmen.[4] Wages were at all times paid on the two systems of piece-work and time, and the hours, which varied in the different trades, and at different places and periods, were as a rule long. For the building trade at Beverley[5] in the fifteenth century work began in summer (from Easter to 15th August) at 4 a.m., and continued till

---

[1] For an exhaustive examination of all that concerns wages, see the works of Professor Thorold Rogers.

[2] From the end of the fifteenth century the gradation of payments to workmen becomes more pronounced, marking the institution of the modern system.

[3] In the case of carpenters, &c., employed in country districts there appear to have been considerable variations.

[4] Exch. K. R. Accts., 472, no. 4.

[5] *Beverley Town Docts.* (Selden Soc.), 56.

7 p.m. ; at 6 a.m. there was a quarter of an hour's interval for refreshment, at 8 half an hour for breakfast, at 11 an hour and a half to dine and sleep, and at 3 half an hour for further refreshment. During the winter months they worked from dawn till dusk, with half an hour for breakfast at 9 o'clock, an hour for dinner at noon, and a quarter of an hour's interval at 3. These hours agree fairly well with those laid down by Parlia-

Workmen at lunch
16th cent.

ment in 1496,[1] which were, from mid-March to mid-September, start at 5 and stop work between 7 and 8, with half an hour for breakfast and an hour and a half for dinner and sleep (the siesta was only to be taken from beginning of May to end of July, during the rest of the time there was to be an hour for dinner and half an hour for lunch—' nonemete '). The blacksmiths of London worked, at the end of the fourteenth century, from dawn till 9 p.m., except during November, December, and January, when their hours were from 6 a.m. to 8 p.m.[2] In the case of the cappers' gild at Coventry the journeymen's hours were in 1496 from 6 a.m. to 6 p.m. ;[3] but in 1520 they had been increased, being from 6 a.m. to 7 p.m. in winter, and from 5 a.m. to 7 p.m. in summer.[4] Wages, of course, when paid by the day, varied in winter and summer, if we may use

---

[1] Statutes, 11 Hen. VII.   [2] Riley, *Mems. of London*, 538.
[3] *Coventry Leet Bk.*, 574.   [4] *Ibid.*, 673.

these terms for the short and long days. In London the determining dates were Easter and Michaelmas,[1] at Bristol Ash Wednesday and St. Calixtus (14th October),[2] and in the case of the workmen at Westminster the Purification (2nd February) and All Saints (1st November), giving an exceptionally short winter period.[3]

Against the long hours we have to set the comparative frequency of holidays. On Sundays and all the greater festivals, as well as a variable number of local festivals, such as the dedication day of the church, no work was done, and on Saturdays and the days preceding festivals work as a rule ceased at four o'clock or earlier. This early closing was enforced at Norwich[4] in 1490, on the representation of the shoemakers that many of their journeymen were ' greatly disposed to riot and idelnes, whereby may succede grete poverte, so that dyuers days wekely when them luste to leve ther bodyly labour till a grete parte of the weke be almost so expended and wasted . . . also contrary to the lawe of god and good guydyng temporall they labour quikly toward the Sondaye and festyuall dayes on the Saterdayes and vigils fro iiij of the clock at after none to the depnes and derknes of the nyght foloweng. And not onely that synfull disposicion but moche warse so offendyng in the morownynges of such festes and omyttyng the heryng of the dyvyne servyce '. In the case of the founders in London,[5] while no ordinary metal work, such as turning, filing, or engraving, might be done after noon had rung, an exception had to be made in the case of a casting

---

[1] Riley, *Mems. of London,* 253.
[2] *Little Red Book of Bristol,* 15.
[3] Exch. K. R. Accts., 467, no. 7.   [4] *Norwich Recs.,* ii. 104.
[5] Riley, *Mems. of London,* 513.

which was actually in progress ; such work might be completed after time, as otherwise the metal would have to be remelted, even if it were not spoilt by the interruption. So far as Sundays and feasts were concerned no work was permitted except in the case of

SHOPS.　15th cent.

farriers, who were expected to shoe the horses of strangers passing through the town.[1] A good many shops were open on the Sunday morning until seven o'clock, especially shoemakers,[2] who in Bristol were allowed at any time of the day to serve ' eny knyght or Squyer or

[1] *Coventry Leet Bk.* (E. E. T. S.), 185.
[2] Riley, *Mems. of London*, 227; *York Memorandum Book*, i. 195.

eny other straunger goyng on her passage or journee,
merchant or maryner comyng fro the see ', or, during
the six Sundays of harvest, any one else who required
boots.[1] In the case of the London pastelers, or restaurant
keepers, only one shop in Bread Street and one in Bridge
Street might be open on Sundays, the others being closed
in order that their staff might ' serve Godde the better
on the Sonday as trew Cristen men shuld do '.[2] A less
pious reason for forbidding Sunday trading was advanced
in the case of the cutlers, it being alleged that the
journeymen and apprentices often purloined and wasted
their masters' property while they were in church.[3]
Markets during the early part of the thirteenth century
were often held on Sundays, but most of these were soon
shifted on to week days, though some continued right
into the sixteenth century in spite of continual denuncia-
tions by the clergy ; [4] and fairs were usually associated
with a saint's day, but a fair was an amusement at which
the ordinary craftsman was an interested spectator,
though the chapmen and merchants were kept busy
enough. The London rule that Saturdays and vigils
counted for wages as complete days, but that no payment
was to be made for the Sundays and feast days,[5] was
generally observed, but in the case of workmen engaged
in building operations at Westminster and the Tower
the custom was that wages should be paid for alternate
feast days, but not for any Sundays.[6]

Rules against working at night or after dark are

---

[1] *Little Red Book of Bristol*, ii. 168.
[2] *London Letter Book L*, 312.   [3] Welch, *Hist. of Cutlers' Co.*, 5.
[4] Lipson, *Economic Hist.*, 206.
[5] *Liber Cust.*, i. 99.   [6] Exch. K. R. Accts., 467, no. 7.

constantly found in all classes of industries, 'by reason
that no man can work so neatly by night as by day.'[1]
There was the additional reason that in many trades
night work was a source of annoyance to neighbours.
This was certainly the case with the blacksmiths,[2] and
was probably the cause of the enactment by the Council

BLACKSMITH.   16th cent.

in 1398, that no leather-
worker should work by
night with hammer and
shears, knife or file, at
making points or lanyers
(laces or thongs).[3] Worst
of all these offenders were
the spurriers,[4] for 'many
of the said trade are
wandering about all day
without working at all
at their trade ; and then
when they have become
drunk and frantic, they
take to their work, to the
annoyance of the sick

and all their neighbourhood. . . . And then they blow
up their fires so vigorously that their forges begin all at
once to blaze, to the great peril of themselves and of all
the neighbourhood round '. Nuisances of this nature
the authorities put down by stringent by-laws, in the
same way that they banished offensive occupations,

---

[1] Riley, *Mems. of London*, 226, 243. It is exceptional to find that
at Leicester in 1264 the weavers were allowed to work at night.—
Borough Recs. of Leicester, i. 105.

[2] Riley, *Mems. of London*, 538.   [3] *Ibid.*, 547.   [4] *Ibid.*, 226.

such as the flaying of carcases, the dressing of skins, and the burning of bricks, outside the walls.[1]

A third reason for the prohibition of night work was that candlelight not only made good work more difficult, but made bad work more easy. Not only was it easy to pass off faked leather and other deceitful goods by the uncertain, artificial light, which was one of the causes that moved the Council to try to put down ' eveche-pyngs ',[2] or evening markets, in London, but it also enabled fraudulent workmen to avoid the eye of the vigilant searcher or inspector.[3] All such evasion and secrecy was rightly regarded as suspicious, and at Bristol, to take a single instance, weavers had to work at looms visible from the public street, and not in cellars or upstair rooms,[4] the better class of furs had also to be worked in public,[5] and ale might not be sold in private.[6] The mediaeval system of search or inspection was very thorough, in theory and, so far as we can judge, in practice also. The search of weights and measures, provisions, cloth, and tanned leather usually belonged to the mayor or equivalent borough officer, or in country districts to the manorial lord; but usually with other manufacturers, and very often in the case of cloth and leather, the mayor deputed the duty of search to members of the craft gilds elected and sworn for that purpose. Where the articles made affected more than one craft it was usual to grant joint rights of search to

---

[1] *Little Red Book of Bristol*, 98; *Coventry Leet Bk.*, 302; *Beverley MSS.* (Hist. MSS. Com.), 47.

[2] Riley, *Mems. of London*, 532, 246.   [3] *Ibid.*, 226, 239.

[4] *Little Red Book of Bristol*, ii. 4.

[5] *Ibid.*, 97.   [6] *Ibid.*, 30.

the representatives of each craft. For instance, a silver-mounted knife would be put together and sold by a cutler, but it would be examined not only by the officials

TESTING MEASURES.   16th cent.

of the cutlers but also by those of the bladesmiths, sheathers, and goldsmiths, who would concern themselves solely with the blade, sheath, and mounting respectively.[1] So also, all leather brought into London

[1] Welch, *Hist. of Cutlers' Co.*, 109, 111.

for sale was inspected and stamped by a joint committee
of four cordwainers, two girdlers, and two curriers,[1]
though only the cordwainers had the right to use the
knife when it was necessary to test a hide by cutting it.[2]
The searchers could inspect the wares either in the workshops, or when exposed for sale, and seize any badly

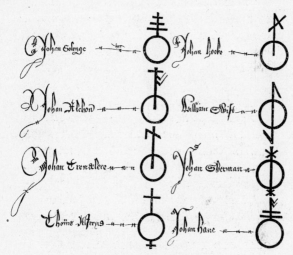

COOPERS' MARKS, 1420

made articles. The forfeited goods were either burnt
or given to the poor,[3] and the offending craftsman fined,
set in the pillory, or, if an old offender, banished from
the town.[4] To facilitate tracing the responsibility for
bad work, weavers, fullers, hatters, metal workers, tile-
makers, and other craftsmen, including bakers, were

[1] W. H. Black, *Hist. of Leather-sellers' Co.*, 25.
[2] *London Letter Book K*, 114.
[3] Riley, *Mems. of London*, 573.
[4] *Coventry Leet Bk.* (E. E. T. S.), 638.

ordered to put their private trademarks on their wares.[1]

The process of search must have been much simplified by the custom so prevalent in mediaeval towns of segregating or localizing the trades,[2] so that all the goldsmiths dwelt in one quarter, the shoemakers in

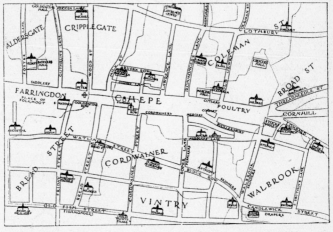

LOCALIZED TRADES IN MEDIAEVAL LONDON

another, the clothiers in a third, and so forth. How far this was compulsory and how far a mere matter of custom it is hard to say, but for those who in addition to or instead of shops sold by barrows or chapmen, definite districts were usually assigned. So the London shoemakers might only send out their goods to be hawked

---

[1] For reproductions of some of the marks used by worsted weavers, see *Norwich Recs.*, ii. 153.

[2] See the maps of mediaeval Bruges and Paris in Unwin's *Gilds of London*, 32–4.

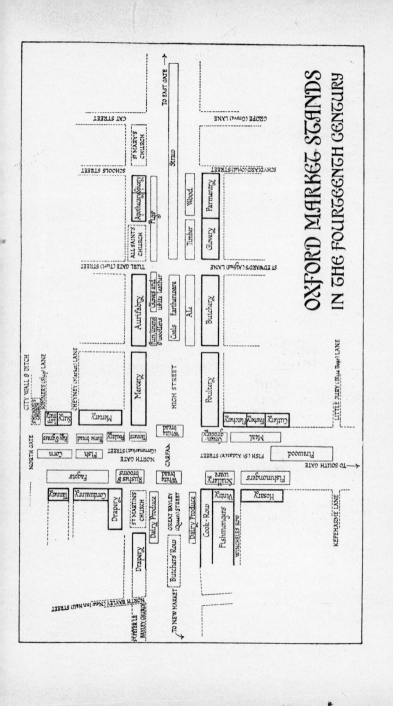

OXFORD MARKET STANDS
IN THE FOURTEENTH CENTURY

between Sopers Lane and the Conduit, and then only in the morning,[1] and at Bristol smiths were not to send ironware through the town for sale in secret places, but either to sell ' in here howse opynlych ' or else at their assigned place by the High Cross, where also all strangers coming with ' eny penyworthes yclepid smyth ware ' were to stand.[2] The principle of segregation was carried out still more strictly, as we might expect, in the markets. A list of the stalls in the provision market at Norwich in 1397[3] shows forty butchers' stalls together, followed by forty-five fishmongers and twenty-eight stalls in the poulterers' market, of which nine were used for fresh fish ; then there were fifteen shops belonging to the corporation in the wool-market, and the great building of the ' Worthsted Celd ', to which all worsteds sent in from the country had to be brought.[4] Other trades were localized in the same way, and the two divisions of leather-workers, the cordwainers and the workers of the inferior ' bazen ' or sheep's leather, were bidden each to keep to their own set of stalls to prevent confusion and fraud.[5]

As the trades were kept each to its own district, so was the craftsman restricted to his own trade. By a law issued in 1364 artificers were obliged to keep to one ' mystery ' or craft,[6] an exception being made in favour of women acting as brewers, bakers, carders, spinners, and workers of wool and linen and silk—the versatility

---

[1] Riley, *Mems. of London*, 392.

[2] *Little Red Book of Bristol*, ii. 182.

[3] *Norwich Recs.*, ii. 237.

[4] Cf. Blackwell Hall in London, the sole market for ' foreign ' cloth. Riley, *Mems. of London*, 550.

[5] *Liber Albus*, ii. 444. [6] Statutes, 37 Edw. III.

of woman, the ' eternal amateur ', being thus recognized some five centuries and a half before Mr. Chesterton rediscovered it. Later statutes forbade shoemakers, tanners, and curriers to infringe on each other's province. It is true that at Bristol [1] we find a puzzling regulation that if a man who had not been apprenticed to tanning practises the craft to which he was apprenticed and also uses the craft of tanning, he shall not pay anything to the tanner's craft but to his own craft, and his ' maistier servaunt de tanneres-crafte ' shall discharge the dues, &c., of a master of the craft. But probably this belongs to the later fifteenth century, after the rise of capitalist employers ; if not, it is certainly exceptional, the general tendency being to keep trades, and more especially the allied trades, separate, in order presumably to avoid the growth of ' combines ' and monopolies. For this reason fishmongers and fishermen were forbidden to enter into partnership in London, [2] because the dealers, knowing the needs of the city, would be able to manipulate supplies and keep up prices. The case against allowing all the branches of one trade to come under single control is vividly set out in the case of the Coventry iron-workers in 1435 : [3]

' Be hit known to you that but yif certen ordenaunses of Craftes withein this Cite, and in speciall the craft of wirdrawerz, be takon good hede to, hit is like myche of the kynges pepull and in speciall poor chapmen and Clothemakers in tyme comeng shallon be gretely hyndered ; and as hit may be supposed the principall cause is like to be amonges hem that han all the Craft in her

---

[1] *Little Red Book of Bristol*, ii. 117.
[2] *Liber Cust.*, i. 118.
[3] *Coventry Leet Bk.* (E. E. T. S.), 180–3.

own hondes, That is to say, smythiers, brakemen,[1]
gurdelmen and cardwirdrawers ; for he that hathe all
these Craftes may, offendyng his consience, do myche
harme.   First in the smethyng, yif he be necligent and
mysrule his Iron that he wirkithe be onkynd hetes or
elles in oder maner, the whiche when hit is so spilt is not
to make no maner chapmannes ware of, Neverthelater
for his own eese he will com to his Brakemon and sey
to hym :—" Here is a ston of rough-iron the whiche must
be tendurly cherysshet."   And then the Brakemon
most nedes do his maisters comaundement and dothe all
that is in hym ; and then when the Brakemon hathe
don his occupacion, that that the mayster supposithe
wilnot in no wyse be holpen atte gurdell, then hit shall
be solde for hoke wire.   And when hit is made in hokes
and shulde serve the Fisher to take fisshe, when comythe
hit to distresse, then for febulness hit all-to brekithe
and thus is the Fissher foule disseyved to hys grete
harme.   And then that wire that the mayster supposithe
will be cherisshed atte gurdell, he shall com to his
girdelmon and sey to him as he seid to the brakemon :—
" Lo, here is a stryng or ij that hathe ben mysgoverned
atte herthe ; my brakemon hathe don his dever, I prey
the do now thyne."   And so he dothe as his maister
biddethe hyme.   And then he gothe to his cardwirdrawer and seithe the same to hym, and he dothe as his
maister biddithe hym.   And then when the Cardmaker
hathe bought this wire thus dissayvabely wrought he
may not know hit tille hit com to the crokyng,[2] and then
hit crachithe and farithe foule ; so the cardmaker is
right hevy therof but neverthelater he sethe because
hit is cutte he must nedes helpe hymself in eschuing
his lòsse, he makithe cardes therof as well as he may.
And when the cardes ben solde to the clothemaker and
shuldon be occupied, anon the teeth brekon and fallon

[1] The ' brakeman ' reduced the bar iron to rods, ready to be
drawn into wire.

[2] i. e. bending.

out, so the clothemaker is foule disseyved. Wherfore,
sirs, atte reverens of God in fortheryng of the kynges
true lege peapull and in eschueng of all disseytes, weithe
this mater wysely and ther as ye see disseyte is like to
be, therto settithe remedy be your wyse discressions.
For ye may right welle know be experience that and
the smythier and the brakemen wern togider, and no mo,
and the cardwirdrawers and the middlemen [1] togider,
and no mo, then hit were to suppose that ther shuld not
so myche disseyvaball wire be wrought and sold as
ther is ; for and the craft were severed in the maner as
hit is seide above, then the cardwirdrawers and the
myddelmen most nedes bye the wire that they shull
wirche of the smythier, and yif the cardwirdrawer were
ones or thies disseyved with ontrewe wire he wolde be
warre and then wold he sey unto the smythier that he
bought that wire of :—" Sir, I hadde of you late badde
wire. Sir, amend your honde, or, in feith, I will no more
bye of you." And then the smythier, lest he lost his
custumers, wolde make true goode ; and then, withe
the grase of Godd, the Craft shulde amend and the
kynges peapull be not disseyved with ontrewe goode.'

Although it was a general principle that each craft and
each subdivision of a craft should keep itself strictly to
itself, we find that this often proved impracticable in the
case of the smaller crafts ; so that during the fifteenth
century there was a distinct tendency for these sub-
crafts, if we may so term them, to be absorbed into the
master-crafts. The standard of living was rising rapidly
at this time ; capitalism was becoming continually more
firmly established ; and the larger craft-gilds were becoming more oligarchic and more powerful—particularly
in London, where they were developing into the incorporated Livery Companies (so-called from their having a

[1] i. e. girdlers ; middle = waist.

special class who wore the livery of the company—the qualification for entry into that privileged class being the possession of a certain quantity of wealth). So we find the Leathersellers' Company, which was incorporated in 1444, absorbing the whitetawyers in 1479, the glovers and pursers (who had combined in 1498) in 1502, and the pouchmakers (who appear to have swallowed the bottlemakers and horners at some earlier date) in 1517.[1] In the same way the chapemakers (who made not only chapes or metal fittings of sword scabbards but also bread-graters, shoebuckles, tin spoons, and dripping-pans [2]) joined the wire-drawers in 1479 to form the wiremongers gild ;[3] and in 1497 the wire-mongers and pinners amalgamated under the title of wire-sellers.[4] So also the sheathers entered the Cutlers' Company about 1450, and the blade-smiths lost their independence and went partly into the cutlers and partly into the armourers in 1517.[5] In all these instances the compelling cause was poverty, the crafts having become too small or too poor to support the increasing burden of independence. An instance of

BLADESMITH.   16th cent.

---

[1] Black, *Hist. of Leather-sellers' Co.*, 38, 42, 47.
[2] *London Letter Book L*, 64.   [3] *Ibid.*, 185.   [4] *Ibid.*, 319
[5] Welch, *Hist. of Cutlers' Co.*, 21, 117.

the recovery of a separate existence can be found at
Lincoln, where the dyers had been allowed to practise
the trades of shearmen and fullers, but in 1563 were
forbidden to do so any longer, on the ground that they
were now a wealthy craft.[1]

The interests of the craftsmen, or producers, were as
a whole opposed to those of the consumers. It is true
that they co-operated, as we have seen, with the local
authorities in maintaining the standard of workmanship,
because the craft that did not do so would soon find
itself ' defamed and out of employ ',[2] but it was obviously
to their interest to keep up prices by the limitation of
competition and of output. Their success in restricting
competition varied very greatly in different trades and
places. In Lincoln, for instance, no tiler might come to
work in the town without joining the tilers' gild,[3] while
in Worcester, so far was this from being the case, that
the tilers were not even allowed to form a gild at all.[4]
As a whole the gilds had the townsmen behind them in
their opposition to outsiders. The traditional attitude
of the Englishman towards a stranger has always been
to ' heave half a brick at him ', and as far back as 1421
the authorities at Coventry had to order ' that no man
throw ne cast at noo straunge man, ne skorn hym '.[5]
The sense of civic, or even parochial, patriotism was
more developed in those times, and it was generally felt
that while artificers ought not to work for outsiders
unless there was no work to be had within the town,

---

[1] *Hist. MSS. Com. Rep.*, xiv (8), 55.
[2] *Little Red Book of Bristol*, ii. 85.
[3] Toulmin Smith, *English Gilds*, 184.   [4] *Ibid.*
[5] *Coventry Leet Bk.* (E. E. T. S.), 27.

on the other hand, employers ought to give the prefer-
ence to their fellow townsmen and not send work out
of the town.[1] As to encouraging strangers to settle
within their walls, sentiment varied in different places.
At Beverley in 1467 it was enacted that any person
might come and set up in his craft without any payment
for the first year—except a contribution towards the
church light and the yearly pageant maintained by his
craft—but after that he should pay yearly 12*d.* to the
town and 12*d.* to his craft until he became a burgess and
member of the gild.[2] But the attitude of Bristol, where
no one might weave unless he became a burgess (and
a gild brother) was more typical of the general feeling.[3]
There was, however, at Bristol a rule that a stranger
who had come to the town on a visit, or to wait for
a ship, might work at his trade for his support during
his stay.[4] This rule did not hold good, apparently, at
Hereford, as a London tailor, whose master had allowed
him during an outbreak of plague to go and stay with
relations in Hereford, was imprisoned by the wardens
of the local tailors' gild because he did some tailoring
for the cousin with whom he was staying, in order to pay
for his keep.[5] At Norwich, by the ordinances of 1449,
no ' foreign dweller ' might have any apprentices or even
a hired servant unless the latter was absolutely necessary
for his business, and in that case at the end of a year he
must either ' buy himself a freeman ', or, if too poor to
buy the franchise, ' live under tribute to the sheriffs.' [6]

[1] *Borough Recs. of Leicester,* i. 105; *Coventry Leet Bk.,* 95; *Little
Red Book of Bristol,* ii. 7, 8.
[2] *Beverley Town Docts.* (Selden Soc.), 53.
[3] *Little Red Book of Bristol,* 5.   [4] *Ibid.,* 98.
[5] Early Chanc. Proc., 61, no. 478.   [6] *Norwich Recs.,* ii. 289.

One advantage that the resident manufacturer had over the foreigner was that his wares entered the local

MARKET STALLS. 15th cent.

market without the handicap of paying customs or *octroi* dues. Long lists of these dues on every conceivable kind of merchandise, from bears and monkeys to peppercorns,

are to be found in the records of many towns,[1] more
especially seaports. It is true that the burgesses of many
towns and the tenants of many religious houses were
theoretically exempt from paying these dues, but it is
probable that the delay and worry of proving such exemption was often felt to be a greater loss than payment.
So far as the alien importer was concerned, although
there was no such thing as a protective duty (the import
of an article was either prohibited altogether or un-
restrained), he might find himself called upon to pay
a higher, even a double, import duty on all his merchandise.   This policy of discriminating against the
alien, combined with the continual harassing of the
unfortunate foreign merchants, induced many alien
settlers to take out letters of naturalization, and the
long lists of these in the fifteenth century [2] show how
numerous and widespread these aliens were. Coming
for the most part from Flanders and the Low Countries,
they settled not only in London and the other great
towns, but in the smaller market towns and villages
throughout the country, exercising their various trades
as goldsmiths, clothmakers, leather-workers, and so
forth.   In London in particular the foreign element was
very large from an early date, and, as a result of the
invitation issued by Edward III to foreign cloth-workers
and their exemption from the control of the native
clothiers' gild, we have the exceptional occurrence of
a gild of alien weavers.   This gild, itself divided by the
rivalries and quarrels of the Flemings and Brabanters,[3]

---

[1] e. g. *ibid.*, 199, 234 ; Woodruff, *Hist. of Fordwich*, 32–5.

[2] See, e. g., *Cal. of Pat. Rolls 1429–36*, 537–88.

[3] Riley, *Mems. of London*, 346.

was unpopular with the native weavers because, while competing with them for trade, they did not share in the farm or rent paid by the native gild to the king, and in general there was a strong feeling against the aliens in London, which was fanned by the craft. gilds and occasionally culminated in rioting, the murder of some of the foreigners and the plunder of their shops.

While the gilds were constantly coming into conflict with outside interests, there was also an internal conflict of interests between the masters, the hired servants, or journeymen, and the intermediate class of apprentices. This becomes more noticeable towards the end of our period. While there was occasional friction between employer and employed even before the second half of the fourteenth century, it was during the next two centuries that the rise of the capitalist, coupled with the descent of the small independent masters into the position of journeymen, brought about strained relations between the two classes. In the earlier period in most of the trades there was reasonable prospect for any craftsman that he would be able to set up as an independent master, but as time went on the difficulty of attaining independence increased. The growing attraction of town and craft life as compared with agriculture swelled the ranks of the craftsmen, and the gilds, whose management was in the hands of the masters, endeavoured to limit competition by raising their entrance fees and more especially by raising their ' upsets ', that is to say, the fees which had to be paid by a craftsman upon setting up as a master. One of the earliest instances of this restriction of competition occurred in connexion with the weavers' gild of London,

2586   z

concerning whom it was reported in 1321 that they had
during the last thirty years reduced the number of
looms in the city from 380 to 80.[1] In this case the
object was to benefit all the members of the gild at
the expense of the public, and not to protect existing
masters from rivals within the gild, and the method
employed was therefore the raising of the fee for
entrance to the gild. This same weavers' gild was so
far ahead of its times that it had instituted the modern
trade union's restriction of output, no member being
allowed to weave a cloth in less than four days, though
such a cloth could easily be woven in three if not in
two days.[2] But this was a most exceptional move, if
not absolutely unique.

How far the desire to restrict output was at the bottom
of regulations forbidding the employment of more than
a strictly limited number of apprentices and journeymen,
and how far such prohibitions were inspired by fear of
the monopolization of labour by capitalists, it is difficult
to say. Probably the dread of the capitalist was the
chief incentive for such regulations, which are very
numerous ; the cobblers of Bristol, for instance, being
restricted to a single ' covenaunt hynd ',[3] and the
cappers of Coventry allowed only two apprentices,
neither of whom might be replaced if he left with his
master's leave before the end of his term of seven years,[4]
while the London founders—many of whom had been
taking more apprentices than they could teach or keep,
' wherby good mens children of the contrey have be

---

[1] *Liber Cust.* i. 423.   [2] *Ibid.*
[3] A servant engaged by the year. *Little Red Book of Bristol*,
ii. 43.   [4] *Coventry Leet Bk* , 573.

gretely deeeyved,'—were in 1455 limited to two, except
that two years before an apprentice's term ended they
might take another so that he would not be quite new
to the work when the first apprentice left.[1] The same
principle of fair play between employers led to the
ordaining of heavy penalties for taking away another
man's servant, or employing any journeyman who had
not fulfilled his engagement with his previous master,
and to the strict prohibition of paying more than the
fixed maximum wages. As this last provision was sometimes got over by the master's wife giving his servants
extra gratuities and gifts, this practice was forbidden at
Bristol in 1408, except that the master might at the
end of a year give ' a courtesy ' of 20*d.* to his chief
servant.[2] As the unfair securing of labour by offering
high wages was forbidden, so the use of the cheap labour
of women was as a rule regarded with disfavour. The
fullers of Lincoln were forbidden to work with any
woman who was not the wife or maid of a master,[3] and
the ' braelers ', or makers of braces, of London, in 1355
laid down ' that no one shall be so daring as to set any
woman to work in his trade, other than his wedded wife
or his daughter '.[4] A century later the authorities at
Bristol went even farther, for finding that the weavers
were ' puttyn, occupien and hiren ther wyfes, doughtours
and maidens, some to weve in ther owne lombes and
some to hire them to wirche with othour persons of the
said crafte ', whereby many ' likkely men to do the
Kyng service in his warris, . . . and sufficiently lorned in

[1] *London Letter Book K*, 375.
[2] *Little Red Book of Bristol*, ii. 106.
[3] Toulmin Smith, *English Gilds*, 179.
[4] Riley, *Mems. of London*, 278.

the seid crafte . . . gothe vagraunt and unoccupied ',
absolutely forbad the practice in future, making an
exception only in the case of wives already so employed.[1]
Of child labour we hear very little, one of the few notices
being an order on their behalf made, suitably enough,
by Richard Whittington in 1398, that whereas some
' hurers ' (makers of fur caps) send their apprentices
and journeymen and children of tender age down to
the Thames and other exposed places, amid horrible
tempests, frosts, and snows, to scour caps, to the very
great scandal of the city, this practice is to cease at
once.[2]

Apprenticeship was from quite early times the chief,
and eventually became practically the only, path to
mastership. The ordinances of the London leather-
dressers,[3] made in 1347, and those of the pewterers,[4]
made the next year, give as alternative qualifications
for reception into the craft the completion of a period
of apprenticeship, or the production of good testimony
that the applicant is a competent workman. A similar
certificate of ability was required of the dyers at Bristol,[5]
in 1407, even if they were apprentices, but as a rule the
completion of a term of apprenticeship was a sufficient
qualification. That term might vary considerably, but
the custom of London, which held good in most English
boroughs, eventually fixed it at a minimum of seven
years. This would often be exceeded, and we find, for
instance, a boy of fourteen apprenticed to a haberdasher
in 1462 for the rather exceptional term of twelve years ;

---

[1] *Little Red Book of Bristol*, ii. 127.
[2] Riley, *Mems. of London*, 549. [3] *Ibid.*, 234.
[4] *Ibid.*, 244. [5] *Little Red Book of Bristol*, ii. 84.

but in this case the master had undertaken to provide
him with two years' schooling, the first year and a half
to learn ' grammer ', and the next half year to learn to
write.[1] In the same way a goldsmith's apprentice in
1494 agreed to serve ten years instead of nine provided
his master would keep him one year at a writing school.[2]
A certain amount of teaching, apart from technical
training, was usually stipulated for in indentures of
apprenticeship. A weaver at Taunton agreed to give
his apprentice ' instruction in the language of Britanny ',[3]
while conversely a London carpenter was allowed ' to
have home hys prentys tyll he can speke better engleys '.[4]
Amongst the goldsmiths fines were inflicted for failing
to have apprentices taught to read and write,[5] and by
the will of Maud, widow of John de Mymmes, image-
maker, who died, with her husband, at the time of the
Black Death, an apprentice, to whom she makes various
bequests, was to be handed over to the care and teaching
of Brother Thomas de Alsham of Bermondsey Priory
for three years.[6] In a list of apprentices who took the
oath of fealty to the king and the city at Coventry in
1494, the terms range from five to nine years, though
the majority were for seven years ; during the first
years of their terms, they were to receive nominal wages,
usually 12d. a year, and for their last year more substantial rewards, varying from 6s. 8d. to 25s.[7] The oath

---

[1] Early Chanc. Proc., 19, no. 491.
[2] Prideaux, *Mems. of Goldsmiths' Co.*, 31.
[3] Lipson, *Economic Hist.*, 280.
[4] Jupp, *Hist. of Carpenters' Co.*, 139.
[5] Prideaux, *op. cit.*, 27, 28, 36.
[6] Sharpe, *Cal. of Wills in Court of Hustings*, i. 576.
[7] *Coventry Leet Bk.* (E. E. T. S.), 560–1.

to obey the city laws serves as a reminder that the
apprentice, not being a full member of the gild, was
under the charge of the city authorities to some extent.
Indentures of apprenticeship had as a rule to be enrolled
by the town clerk,[1] and in London the transfer of an
apprentice from one employer to another was not legal
unless confirmed by the city chamberlain.[2]   Besides
having his indentures enrolled, and paying a fee to the
craft gild, the apprentice, or rather his friends, had to
give a bond for his good behaviour.   Masters had the
right of correcting their apprentices with the rod, within
reason, and the city authorities would have little mercy
on such young men as John Richard, who, when his
employer wished to chastise him ' as reson and comon
usage is ' for divers offences, ' of very malice and cursed-
nesse as an obstinat apprentis to his master ' picked up
an iron bar and threatened to kill him.[3]   The rights of
the apprentice, on the other hand, were probably always
guarded by a right of appeal to the wardens of his craft :
this was certainly the case at Coventry in 1520, the
masters of the cappers being obliged to go once a year
to all the shops of their craft and call the apprentices
before them, and if any apprentice complained three
times against his master for ' insufficient finding ', they
had power to take him away and put him with another
master.[4]   As a master's interest in his apprentice was
transferable to another master, so it was possible for an
apprentice to buy up the remainder of his term after

---

[1] e. g. *Norwich Recs.*, ii. 290 ; *Little Red Book of Bristol*, ii. 125.
[2] Early Chanc. Proc., 66, no. 244.
[3] Herbert, *Hist. of Livery Cos.*, ii. 168.
[4] *Coventry Leet Bk.* (E. E. T. S.), 672.

he had served a portion. He could not, however, be received into his gild as a master until the whole of his term had expired,[1] and although it would seem that he could set up in business by himself,[2] probably he might not employ workmen, and as a rule he no doubt spent the unexpired portion of his term as a journeyman.

The journeymen, working by the day (*journée*), either with their masters, or in their own houses, as opposed to the covenant servants, who were hired by the year,[3] and lived in their employer's house, constituted the fluid element in the industrial organization, and were composed partly of men who had served a full apprenticeship but lacked funds or enterprise to set up independently, and partly of others who had either served only a brief apprenticeship or had picked up their knowledge of the craft in other ways.[4] Although they were more or less free to work for what employers they would, practically all gild regulations contained a stringent order against the employment of any journeyman who had broken his contract or left his late master without good reason.[5] In the matter of homework, rules varied ; the journeymen of the wiredrawers and allied crafts at Coventry in 1435 were allowed to work

---

[1] Early Chanc. Proc., 66, no. 244.   [2] *Ibid.*, 38, no. 40.

[3] An ordinance of the fullers in 1418 forbade any master to take a stranger to serve him by covenant for more than fifteen days unless he engaged him for a whole year. *Little Red Book of Bristol*, ii. 142.

[4] In the case of the London founders an intending journeyman had to satisfy the masters of his skill ; if he could not, be must either become an apprentice or abandon the craft. Riley, *Mems. of London*, 514.

[5] They had to give, and were entitled to receive, eight days' notice. *Coventry Leet Bk.* (E. E. T. S.), 573.

at home and might not be compelled to come to their masters' houses,[1] but in London, in 1271, the shoe-makers were not allowed to give out work, as the journeymen were found to go off with the goods.[2] The vagaries of this class, indeed, caused much heart-searching to their masters. Instead of being content with their holidays and accepting their twelve hours' working day, they had a pernicious habit of going off on the spree for two or three days, and amusing them-selves by playing bowls, ' levyng ther besynes at home that they shuld lyve by ' ;[3] and the Coventry em-ployers, with that touching regard for widows and orphans (or in this case wives and children) which has always distinguished the English capitalists, forbade them to frequent inns on workdays, ' as it is daylye seen that they whiche be of the pooreste sorte doo sytte all daye in the alehouse drynkynge and playnge at the cardes and tables and spende all that they can gett prodigally upon themselfes to the highe displeasure of God and theyre owne ympovershynge, whereas if it were spente at home in theyre owne houses theyre wiffes and childerne shulde have parte therof.'[4] Not having any voice in the craft gilds, the journeymen were continually forming ' yeomen gilds ', ' bacheleries ', and other combinations, which the masters' gilds usually endeavoured to suppress. These yeomen gilds were the nearest mediaeval equivalent to the modern trade unions, as, unlike the full craft gild, they consisted

[1] *Coventry Leet Bk.* (E. E. T. S.), 185.

[2] *Liber Albus*, ii. 444.

[3] *Little Red Book of Bristol*, ii. 106 ; *Norwich Recs.*, ii. 104 ; *Coventry Leet Bk.* (E. E. T. S.), 656.

[4] *Coventry Leet Bk.* (E. E. T. S.), 786.

entirely of members of the employed or wage-earning
class and were entirely concerned in benefiting their
own particular section of society. Their weakness lay
in the fact that their most capable members usually
rose to the position of masters themselves. In 1387 the
London journeymen cordwainers formed a fraternity [1]
and endeavoured to secure it by obtaining papal protection ; nine years later the mayor and aldermen put
down a fraternity formed by the yeomen of the saddlers,
at the same time ordering the masters to treat their
men well in future ; [2] and in 1415 the wardens of the
tailors complained that their journeymen had combined, living together in companies in particular houses,
where they held assemblies, and adopting a livery,
whereupon the council, in view of the danger to the
peace of the city from such an uncontrolled and irre-
sponsible body, forbade the combination and ordered
the journeymen to live under the governance of the
wardens of the craft.[3] The fraternity of the yeomen
tailors, however, was not so easily suppressed, and is
found two years later petitioning for leave to hold their
yearly assembly at St. John's, Clerkenwell.[4] In the
same way at Coventry, when the journeymen tailors'
gild of St. Anne was suppressed in 1420, they simply
changed their patron and reappeared as the gild of
St. George, against which measures were taken in 1425.[5]
The charges against the yeomen saddlers in 1396 were,
that they had so forced wages up that whereas the
masters could formerly obtain a workman for from

---

[1] Riley, *Mems. of London*, 495.   [2] *Ibid.*, 542.
[3] *Ibid.*, 609-12.   [4] *Ibid.*, 653.
[5] *Hist. MSS. Com. Coventry*, 117-18.

40s. to 5 marks yearly and his board, they had now to pay 10 or 12 marks or even £10, and that also business was dislocated by the bedel coming round and summoning the journeymen to attend a service for the soul of a deceased brother. The clashing of religious observances with business led to an order at Coventry in 1528 that the journeymen dyers should make no assemblies at weddings, brotherhoods, or burials, nor make any ' caves ' (i. e. combinations), but use themselves as servants, and as no craft.[1] This was practically an enforcement of an order issued ten years earlier, that no journeymen should form ' caves ' without the licence of the mayor and the master of their craft.[2] Such a licence would not as a rule be granted, unless the masters were unusually broadminded, or the journeymen exceptionally strong. There was, however, at Coventry a recognized fraternity of journeymen weavers in 1424 ; their wardens paid 12d. to the chief master for every brother admitted ; each brother gave 4d. towards the cost of the craft pageant, and the chief master contributed towards the journeymen's altar lamp, while both masters and servants held their feasts together.[3] At Bristol also there was a gild of journeymen connected with the shoemakers' craft, sharing with the craft gild in the expenses of church lights and feasts.[4]

The success of the London saddlers in forcing wages up is a remarkable tribute to the power of union ; and we find that during the fourteenth century the strike was well known, and when a master would not agree with his workmen the other workmen of the craft would

---

[1] *Coventry Leet Bk.* (E. E. T. S.), 694.   [2] *Ibid.*, 656.
[3] *Ibid.*, 95.
[4] *Little Red Book of Bristol*, ii. 151.

come out and cease work until the dispute was settled.[1]
This practice was, of course, forbidden, but we may
doubt with what success. At the same time the masters
were pretty well unanimous in forbidding the employment of a craftsman whose dispute with his master had
not been settled. So far as the offence of detaining
wages due was concerned, penalties were often laid down
in gild ordinances,[2] while in the case of other disputes
the matter would be settled by the council or court of
the craft.[3] The existence of a craft gild practically
implied a court before which disputes between members
of the craft or between craftsmen and customers were
tried.[4] Such courts were at first directly under the
borough authorities, the mayor or his deputies presiding
over the weekly courts of the weavers in London in
1300,[5] and although they seem to have attained a greater
degree of independence, there seems usually to have been
a right of appeal to the borough court.[6] It was probably
to avoid this that some of the Coventry masters took to
impleading craftsmen in spiritual courts, on the ground
that they had broken their oaths in not keeping the
gild rules.[7]

Too much attention must not be given to the quarrel-

[1] Riley, *Mems. of London*, 248, 307 ; cf. *Acts of P. C., 1542-7*,
p. 367 ; *L. & P. Hen. VIII*, xiii (1), 1454, a strike of shoemakers
at Wisbeach for higher rates of payment.

[2] Riley, *Mems. of London*, 307, 514 ; Lambert, *Two Thousand
Years of Gild Life*, 216.

[3] e. g. *Little Red Book of Bristol*, ii. 13.

[4] See the proceedings of the court of the tailors at Exeter.
Toulmin Smith, *English Gilds*, 299-321 : cf. Jupp, *Hist. of Carpenters' Co.*, 348.

[5] *Liber Cust.*, i. 122 ; cf. *Borough Recs. of Leicester*, i. 89.

[6] *Little Red Book of Bristol*, ii. 14.

Coventry Leet Bk. (E. E. T. S.), 302.

some side of the gilds, for they were essentially friendly
societies for mutual assistance. One of the rules of the
London leather-dressers was that if a member should
have more work than he could complete, and the work
was in danger of being lost, the other members should
help him.[1] So also, if a mason wished to undertake a
contract he got four or six responsible members of the
craft to guarantee his ability, and if he did not do the
work well they had to complete it.[2] Again, if a farrier
undertook the cure of a horse and was afraid that it
would die, he might call in the advice of the warders of
his company, but if he was too proud to do so and the
horse died, he would be responsible to the owner.[3] The
rule of the weavers at Hull, that none should let his
apprentice work for another[4] was not an infringement
of the principle of mutual aid, but was designed to
prevent evasion of the order that none might have
more than two apprentices; the fact that a fine was
exacted only in the event of the apprentice so working
for more than thirteen days actually points to the loan
of temporary assistance being allowed. While help was
thus given to the craftsman when in full employ, a still
more essential feature of the gilds was their grant of
assistance to members who had fallen ill or become
impoverished through no fault of their own.[5] Nor did
their benevolence end with the poor craftsman's death,

---

[1] Riley, *Mems. of London*, 232.   [2] *Ibid.*, 281.

[3] *Ibid.*, 293.

[4] Lambert, *Two Thousand Years of Gild Life*, 205.

[5] Toulmin Smith, *English Gilds*, passim. The goldsmiths in 1393
established an endowment for those of their craft who had lost their
sight from the fire and the vapour of quicksilver. : Herbert, *Hist. of
Livery Cos.*, 290.

for they made an allowance to his widow and celebrated Masses for the repose of his soul. The religious element in the organization of gilds, though very strong, does not affect us very much in considering their industrial side, but there is one indirect effect which must be referred to. The custom of all the gilds and fraternities going in procession to the chief church of their town on certain feast days, carrying their banners and symbols, gradually developed during the fifteenth century until each gild endeavoured to outshine its rivals in pageantry. Payments towards the pageants, or religious plays, were exacted from all members of the trade even if they were not members of the gild, but in spite of this the expenses were so great that the smaller gilds were almost ruined; and consequently we find, during the latter half of the fifteenth century, schemes to amalgamate, or at any rate to unite for the support of a common pageant, many of the smaller misteries or crafts. An account of a pageant at Norwich [1] about 1450 is interesting as showing the numbers of these lesser crafts, and the way in which they were combined. Twelve pageants were presented : (1) The Creation of the World, by the mercers, drapers, and haberdashers. (2) Paradise, by the grocers and 'raffemen.' (3) 'Helle Carte,' by the glaziers, stainers, scriveners, parchemyners, the carpenters, gravers, coler-makers, and wheelwrights. (4) Abel and Cain, by the shearmen, fullers, 'thikwollenwevers,' and coverlet makers, the masons and limeburners. (5) 'Noyse shipp' (Noah's Ark), by the bakers, brewers, inn-keepers, cooks, millers, vintners, and coopers. (6) Abraham and Isaac, by the tailors, broderers, the reders, and tylers. (7)

---

[1] *Norwich Recs.*, ii. 230.

Moses and Aaron with the Children of Israel and Pharaoh and his knights, by the tanners, curriers, and cordwainers. (8) David and Goliath, by the smiths. (9) The Birth of Christ, by the dyers, calenders, the goldsmiths, goldbeaters, saddlers, pewterers, and braziers. (10) The Baptism of Christ, by the barbers, waxchandlers,

surgeons, physicians, the hardwaremen, the hatters, cappers, skinners, glovers, pinners, pointmakers, girdlers, pursers, bagmakers, 'sceppers,'[1] the wiredrawers and cardmakers. (11) The Resurrection, by the butchers, fishmongers, and watermen. (12) The Holy Ghost, by the worsted weavers.

In some cases the smaller crafts, as we have seen, were ab-

LOCKSMITH. 16th cent.

sorbed into the larger, but in the Norwich regulations of 1449,[2] when general orders were given for the annexation of the smaller crafts to the larger—the bladesmiths, locksmiths, and lorimers, for instance, being united to the smiths—it was laid down that such of the annexed misteries as had seven or more members should elect their own wardens, and that the mayor should appoint wardens for such as had fewer than seven members.

---

[1] Makers of 'skeps' or baskets.   [2] *Norwich Recs.*, ii. 280–2.

This, which is interesting as showing how small some of these misteries were, points to a retention of control, the amalgamation being mainly concerned, no doubt, with the expenses of the pageant and the gild feasts. These latter became so elaborate and costly that many of the unfortunate members chosen as ' feastmakers ' were ruined, and in 1495 orders were given at Norwich that the wardens alone should be feastmakers, and that they should provide one supper and one dinner, on the same day, and no more, and those should be at the common expense of the gild.[1] These orders had to be repeated in 1531, and it is rather interesting to read that in 1547 [2] the dishes which had to be provided by the cordwainers' feastmakers were ' frumenty, goos, vell, custard, pig, lamb, and tarte. At soper—colde sute,[3] hot sute, moten, douset,[4] and tarte.'

With the pleasant picture of our craftsman resting from his labours and regaling himself in true English fashion, we may take leave of him and his work.

[1] *Norwich Recs.*, ii. 111.   [2] *Ibid.*, 193.
[3] Sute, probably = course.
[4] Douset = a sweetmeat of cream, eggs, and sugar.

INDEX

Printed in England at the Oxford University Press